THE GARDEN ANSWERS

HERB GARDEN
(Missouri Botanical Garden)

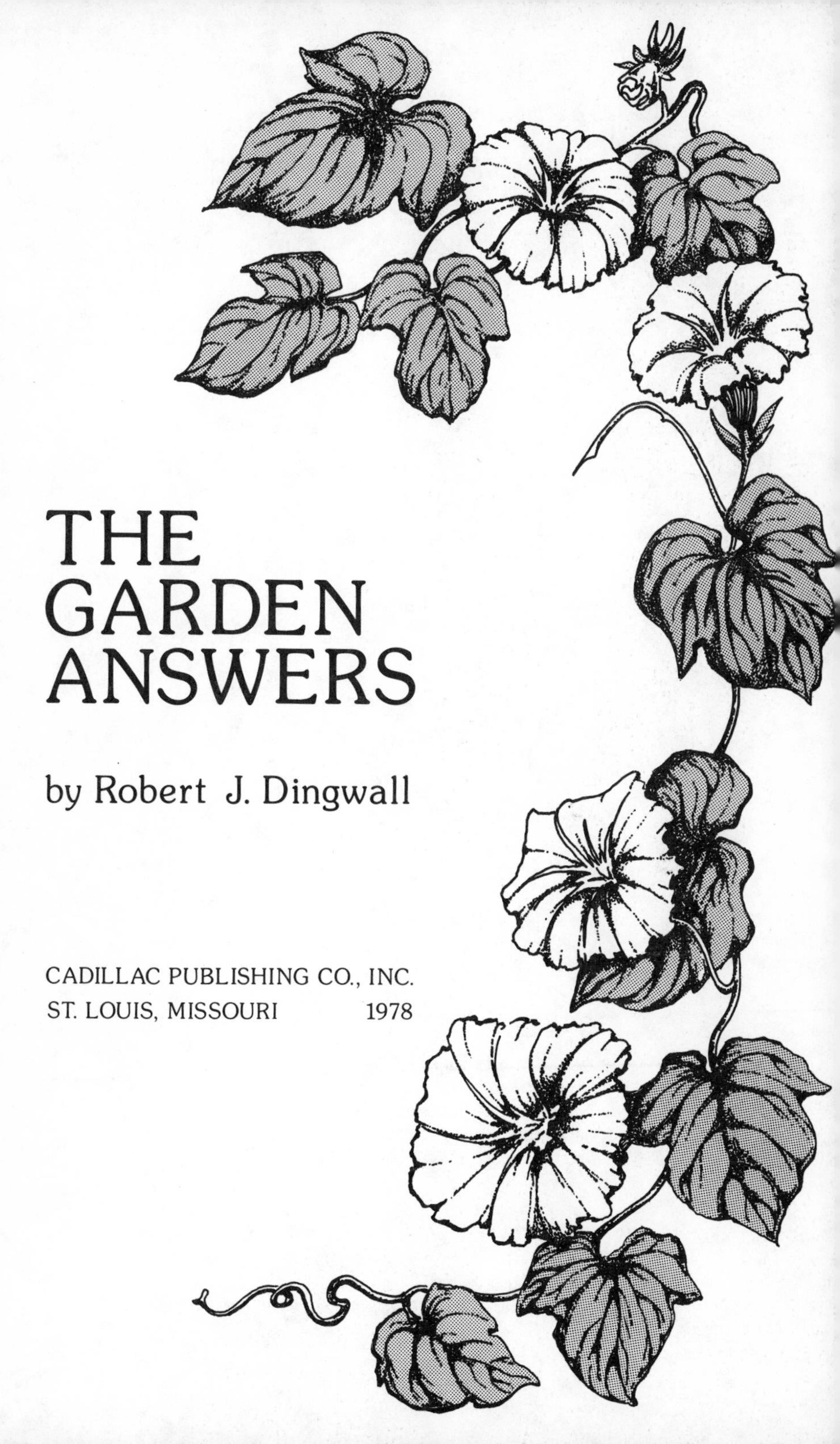

THE GARDEN ANSWERS

by Robert J. Dingwall

CADILLAC PUBLISHING CO., INC.
ST. LOUIS, MISSOURI 1978

Printed in the United States of America
Direct all inquiries to Cadillac Publishing Co. Inc.
6611 Clayton Road, St. Louis, Mo. 63117

Cover photograph of Climatron by Srenco Photography

ISBN: 0-87445-001-2
Library of Congress Catalog Card Number: 77-93696

INTRODUCTION

In 1972 the Missouri Botanical Garden, under the direction of Robert J. Dingwall, chief horticulturist at the Garden, initiated a service for the public interested in obtaining horticultural information. Trained volunteers at the Garden answer questions by telephone from the general public about all aspects of gardening, both indoor and outdoor. By 1977, these calls had reached a peak of over 1000 a month, indicating a strong curiosity about horticulture in the area.

Based on the success of this information service, Mr. Dingwall has organized this informative and interesting book. It covers a wide range of topics on gardening, including chapters on roses, lawns, indoor potted plants, vegetable gardening, herbs and pest control. The book contains over 1600 questions, the most frequently asked of the Answer Service at the Garden, along with up-to-date information on all areas of gardening.

Each chapter includes a general discussion followed by a series of questions most frequently asked. Although these questions developed locally, all of the information on indoor plants and most of that on general gardening is applicable throughout the temperate regions of the United States. For example, the chapter on indoor plants contains information on soil culture, propagation, potting methods, watering, fertilizing, insect and disease control with specific questions generating more material.

We at the Missouri Botanical Garden are delighted to contribute to the tremendous enthusiasm for gardening which has captured this country at the present time. With well over 35 million people actively growing vegetables in the United States and millions more cultivating plants both indoors and in their outside garden, the horticultural world offers an endless source of interest and enjoyment for nearly everyone. We hope you find the answers to your questions in this book. We welcome your suggestions about how to make subsequent editions even more useful.

Peter H. Raven, Director
Missouri Botanical Garden

PREFACE

The Missouri Botanical Garden, known as Shaw's Garden, is located in the center of the St. Louis metropolitan area. Through its many services it has spread a large amount of gardening information. It is one of the major botanical gardens in the world and boasts of increasing attendance each year. In 1972, the Garden started an important expansion program, bringing the full 77 acres under intensive cultivation. The Garden is noted for extensive research throughout the world, particularly in Panama and Africa. The Climatron in the Garden features over 1600 species of plants, many of which are considered rare and endangered species. The Japanese Garden, covering about 14 acres, is one of the largest in the United States as well as in the world. It was dedicated in May, 1977. The Garden also is constantly evaluating many of the new hybrids and cultivars as they become available.

THE GARDEN ANSWERS is the product of the successful Answer Service at the Garden. Besides the thorough introductions, questions and answers on the various types of gardening and plants, three glossaries have been added for the reader's convenience and understanding of horticultural language.

Most plants are lost through over-watering and an overuse of fertilizers. This book will help readers avoid these problems and successfully create an outdoor garden and propagate a variety of indoor plants.

This book would not have been possible without the aid of many people. I would like to give special thanks to Audrey Senturia for the painstaking task of sorting and categorizing the thousands of questions and selecting the 1600 that were used; to Grace Zimmermann for her excellent typing and research for the manuscript; to Mari Edlin for her extremely capable work in copy editing; to James Weldon for his generous help in preparing the many fine illustrations. And of course special thanks to Max Shapiro of the Cadillac Publishing Company for coordinating all my work and for making this book a reality.

Robert J. Dingwall, Chief Horticulturist
Missouri Botanical Garden

CACTUS GARDEN
(Missouri Botanical Garden)

CONTENTS

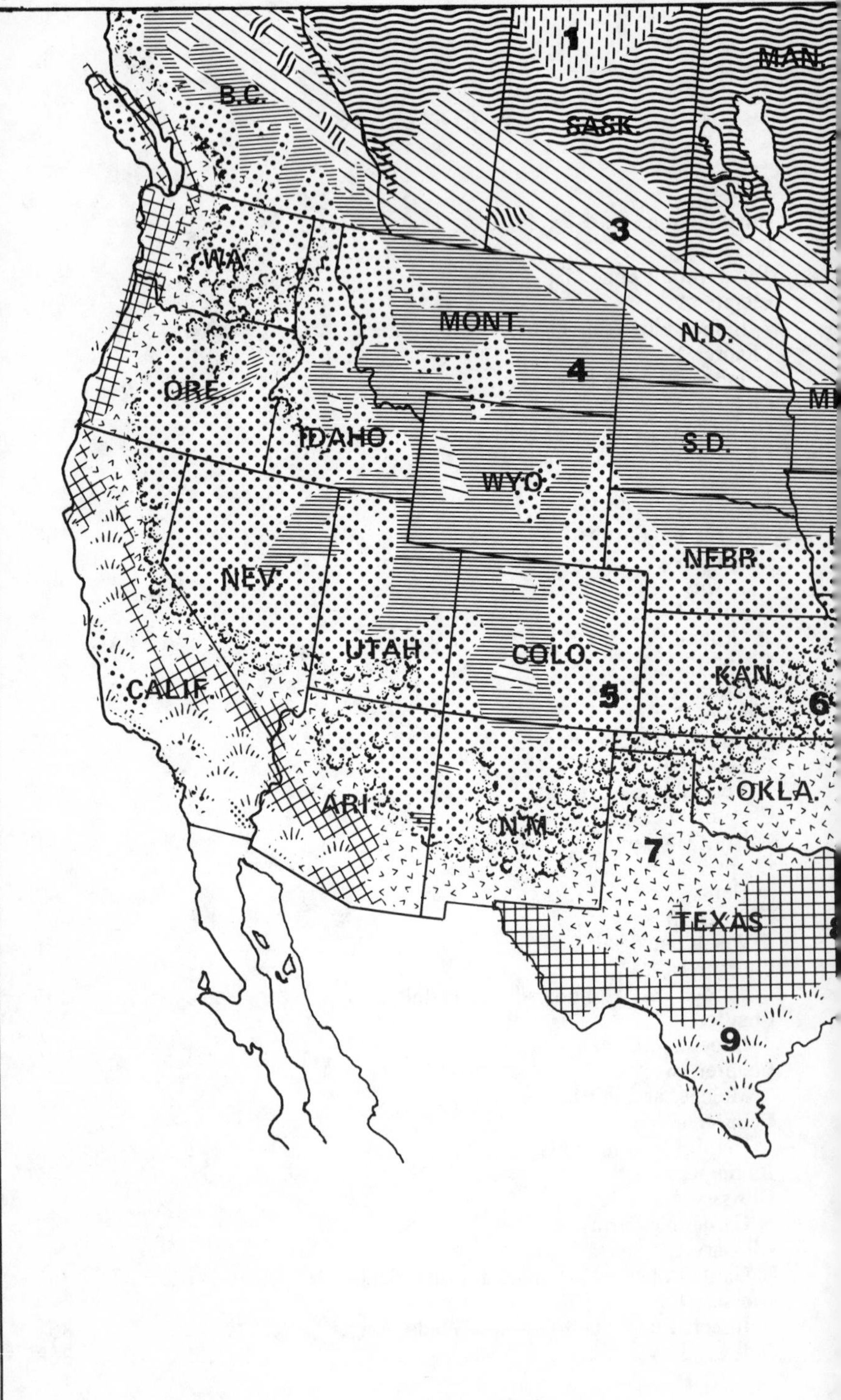

1
MAN.
B.C.
SASK.
3
WA
MONT.
N.D.
4
ORE
M
IDAHO
S.D.
WYO.
NEV.
NEBR.
UTAH
COLO.
CALIF.
5
KAN.
6
ARI.
OKLA.
N.M.
7
TEXAS
9

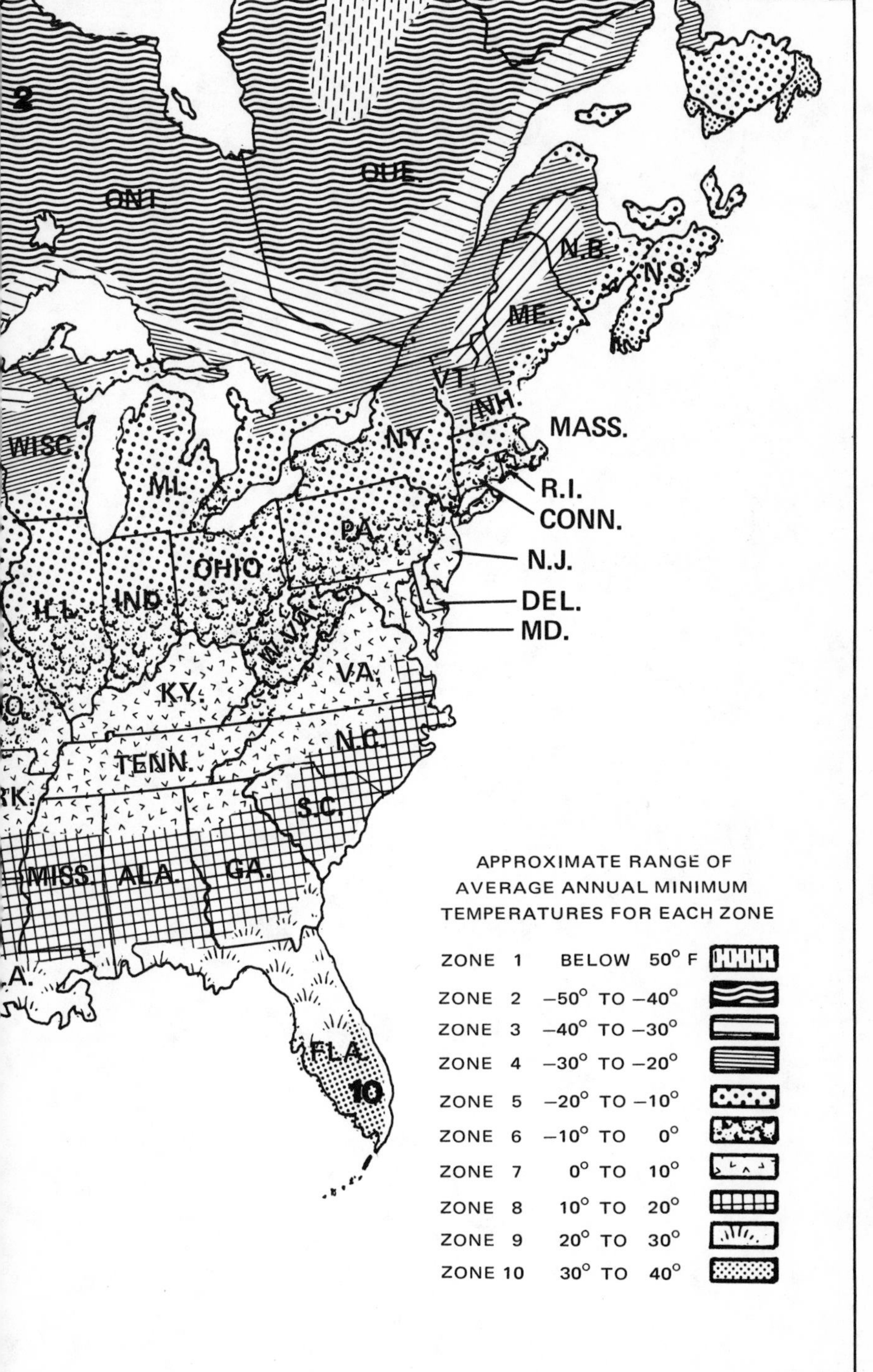

2
ONT.
QUE.
N.B.
N.S.
ME.
VT.
NH.
MASS.
WISC.
MI.
NY.
R.I.
CONN.
PA.
OHIO
N.J.
ILL.
IND.
W.VA.
DEL.
MD.
KY.
VA.
TENN.
N.C.
S.C.
MISS.
ALA.
GA.
FLA.
10
APPROXIMATE RANGE OF
AVERAGE ANNUAL MINIMUM
TEMPERATURES FOR EACH ZONE
ZONE 1 BELOW 50° F
ZONE 2 −50° TO −40°
ZONE 3 −40° TO −30°
ZONE 4 −30° TO −20°
ZONE 5 −20° TO −10°
ZONE 6 −10° TO 0°
ZONE 7 0° TO 10°
ZONE 8 10° TO 20°
ZONE 9 20° TO 30°
ZONE 10 30° TO 40°

Chapter One
Indoor Flowering Plants

General Information

In selecting indoor flowering plants, consider their exposure and select plants from reliable sources. It is important to select plants which are healthy; avoid plants with damaged leaves, insects, blotchy leaves or plants that are leggy unless that is the particular nature of the plant. When at home, isolate the plant for several days to make sure that no insects appear. If it is insect and disease-free, it is then ready to place in its permanent position.

It is important to remember that plants coming from a florist shop or greenhouse are used to high humidity so try and duplicate the natural environment when growing in the home. Plants grouped together give off more moisture and do much better in groups than they do individually; however, they can be gradually adjusted to an environment where the plant sits by itself. To increase the humidity for the individual plants that need it, use the tray method. Select glass or aluminum trays with one-half inch to one inch of pebbles in the bottom of the tray and place a block in the center on which the plant can sit so that it is suspended above the pebbles. Then add water so that pebbles are just covered. As the water evaporates, it will create higher humidity around the plant enabling it to grow much better.

Most flowering plants require good light and for some, sunlight for a part of the day is necessary. Many flowering plants can be grown under artificial light in the basement or another part of the home, but in all locations, they need a minimum of 12 to 14 hours of light per day. Plants fail to flower when light is reduced. In some cases, such as African violets, if they are getting too much light they will not flower and once the plant starts to bloom, leave it in the environment it is in to grow successfully.

When starting small plants, it may be necessary to pinch the tips to cause them to bush out and remain compact. Plants become long and spindly usually through improper growing practices, such as over-watering or insufficient light. If it is a compact grower and the plant becomes spindly, increase the light.

Soil Culture

Proper soil for indoor plants is well drained and contains plenty of organic matter. This can vary according to the type of plant being grown. Orchids, for instance, require a media that almost totally consists of fir bark, which is chopped up to a fairly fine to medium consistency, depending on the type of orchids being grown. General potting soils are available, and in some cases may need more peat moss or some source of organic matter to lighten them in addition to perlite, an inert material which keeps the soil from becoming compact. Sterilize soil before using. This can be done at home by placing soil in a metal tray, keeping it uniformly moist and placing it in the oven along with a dish of water in the lower level of the oven. Set the oven at 200 degrees, allow it to warm up and leave the soil for approximately half an hour to thoroughly sterilize. Remove the soil from the oven and allow to sit for 24 to 48 hours to thoroughly cool before using. In preparing your own soil mixes consider equal amounts of good top soil with equal amounts of organic matter and sand or perlite to provide the needed drainage. Along with this add superphosphate at the rate of a five-inch pot to each wheelbarrow load of soil. Mix in thoroughly and proceed to sterilize the soil as outlined above.

Propagation

Most flowering plants can be propagated from seed. Select seed from a reliable source and sow it immediately in a sterile media. Jiffy Mix is one of many preparations which is a sterile media and ideal for sowing seeds. Another good method is to take milled sphagnum, thoroughly moisten it, place in a tray and sprinkle seeds lightly over this. In either case, fill the container where the seedlings are going to be planted to within about one-half inch from the top. Level off and scatter the seed uniformly over the top. The normal rule is to cover the seed twice the depth of the diameter of the seed itself with the medium in which it is being grown. Place the pot in a tray of water so that the water is thoroughly absorbed. Remove as soon as the moisture begins to show at the top of the container, let it drain well and then place a piece of glass or plastic over the top of the pot to hold moisture in.

Light is not essential for sowing seeds until the seedlings start to sprout. Proper temperatures are 75 to 80 degrees. Observe the seed tray daily. As soon as germination begins, place the seedlings where they receive good light, either in a south or southwest window or under grow-lights. Gradually remove the glass or plastic from the tray until the seedlings are completely exposed to air. The closer the seedlings are to the source of light, the more compact and uniform they will be. When the seedlings grow the second or third set of true leaves, they are then ready for transplanting into the permanent growing media.

Another method of propagation is to use cuttings. Select cuttings from healthy plants. If using stem cuttings, use those with four to six nodes. Select cuttings from plants which flower heavily; this characteristic will be carried over in the new cuttings. Plants which fail to flower regularly are poor ones from which to propagate. Let cuttings sit from one to three hours so that the ends seal up and then place them in a good media. A good media for propagation consists of perlite with about one-third the amount of peat moss added to it. Thoroughly mix and moisten, place in a rooting tray and insert cuttings. In many cases, cuttings are benefited by using a rooting hormone. Dip the cuttings in as directed on the container and keep them in an area where temperatures are as uniform as possible in a range of 60 to 65 degrees. They may be covered with a plastic bag or placed in a glass container to keep the humidity high. The cuttings need good light but no direct sun until they are well rooted.

Another method of propagating is to take leaf cuttings, for example, from African violets or gloxinias. Healthy leaves with a petiole of about an inch long are used. Allow leaves to sit for about three hours and then insert in the propagating media as outlined. In four to six weeks, roots and small plants will develop.

Potting Methods

Many pots are available for growing plants today and are equally good. It is a matter of personal preference. Many prefer the normal clay pot which has the drainage holes in the bottom and allows air to pass freely throughout the sides as well as on the top. The watering pattern in plastic pots is different. Plastic pots usually have drainage holes in the bottom or near the base on the sides. The plastic does not let air or water pass out through the sides or the bottom except through the holes; therefore, they do not dry out as rapidly and less watering is required. They are excellent pots and are easy to keep clean by using a damp cloth and wiping them off. Ceramic containers are often used and are excellent; however, they do not have any drainage in them. In using these, be careful not to over-water because there is no place for excess water to drain. A good idea is to place one to one and one-half inches of coarse pebbles in the bottom of the container. Cover these with a layer of sphagnum moss, place the potting media and plant into this and moisten the soil. Regardless of the type of container you grow a plant in, select one which is pleasing to you and fits in with the other decor in the room.

Many plants, when they become pot-bound, need to be repotted into larger containers. The general rule is to go two sizes larger. For instance, if you are growing in a four-inch pot, transplant the plant into a six-inch pot. In transplanting, remove about one-third of the base of the old root system and taking a sharp knife, cut this off and score "V" cuts down two sides of the remaining soil ball, cutting in one-half to one inch. Then place the plant in the new container, as outlined above, and proceed to fill in around it with the recommended soil media. This allows the new roots to form and readily pass into the new soil. Avoid using too large a pot as this tends to keep the soil more moist and makes it more difficult to get the plant established. Also, many plants will flower better when they are on the root-bound side.

In repotting, many plants may be set somewhat deeper than they were in the original container. One should use a light media and be careful not to over-water until the plant has the chance to establish new roots above the old soil ball. This is particularly true of African violets. As the stems grow up they can be repotted as outlined, placing them in so that the leaves are just above the soil. With careful watering, plants will grow successfully and continue flowering.

Watering

Watering is very critical as far as growing any type of plant is concerned. More plants are destroyed through over-watering than through any other method of growing. Plants, in most cases, need to be kept just moderately moist. They should never be allowed to sit in water. It is important to moisten the soil down to the bottom and every third or fourth watering, a bit of excess water can drain through into the saucer below. Fifteen minutes after watering, drain off water and do not allow it to be re-absorbed up through the plant itself. Letting excess water drain through helps to eliminate accumulated salts, which are detrimental to the plant.

To find out if a plant needs watering, take your finger and dig down into the soil one to two inches, depending on the size of the container. Always use water at room temperature and avoid getting the water on the leaves of the plants. Sun on wet leaves may cause a burn. Ordinary tap water is ideal, rain water is also excellent. Plants may be watered from the top or from the bottom; however, if watering from the bottom of the plants, do not let them sit in water too long. During every third or fourth watering put more than enough in the top of the container and let excess water drain out.

Fertilizing

Nearly all plants require fertilizing at some time. Many fertilizers recommended for house plants are available on the market today. When using good potting soil, it is not necessary to use fertilizer at first; however, once the plant is growing actively and starts flowering, more nourishment is required. Establish a routine feeding program. Most flowering plants will benefit from a routine feeding of liquid fertilizer once every 12 to 14 days, according to the directions on the container. In applying fertilizer, have the soil moderately moist or apply about half of the normal amount of water to moisten the soil one day and then use the recommended feeding the following day. Avoid fertilizing soil that is too dry because this will burn the roots.

Plants which are pot-bound will require heavier feeding than those which have more room for root growth. Learn to observe by the growth of the plant and its characteristics when feeding is required. In some cases, a balanced fertilizer along with iron chelate is advised to keep the plants in good green condition. One suggestion is epsom salts at the rate of one tablespoon per gallon of water along with an equal amount of iron chelate on some plants, such as gardenias, azaleas and other acid loving plants although it is beneficial on nearly all flowering plants. It is applied in April and again in October. The iron and epsom salts help the plants retain healthy green leaves and retain the buds to flower better.

Insect and Disease Control

A healthy plant has little chance of insects and diseases attacking it. Examine plants that have been brought into the home. Isolate them for several days before placing with the rest of the plants. Check all house plants on a regular basis to see that no insects or diseases are prevalent. It is important to examine underneath the leaves and in the crowns of the plants. As soon as insects are noticed, isolate the plant and take the necessary steps to eradicate the insects. If the plant becomes diseased, it is much better to discard the plant then to try to cure it. However, if it is an important specimen find out what the disease is and follow the necessary directions in bringing the disease under control. Do not leave the diseased plant with your healthy plants.

A number of insecticides and fungicides are available for plants. It is a matter of knowing what particular insect or disease the plant has and following the necessary control measures. The more common insects that attack house plants are aphids and these are easy to control by the use of an aerosol pesticide underneath and on top of the leaves.

Cyclamen mites are insects which are common, particularly on cyclamens and on African violets. These usually attack the center of the crown of the plant, causing the leaves to curl and become brittle and hard. These are difficult to control so resort to a strong insecticide, such as Malathion, and use a spray to force it into the base of the plant.

Gnats are gray to near-black insects about one-eighth of an inch in length. The adults, while harmless to plants, are a nuisance. These are usually noticed around the base of the plant and they can be controlled by applying a soil drench, such as Synthetic Pyrethrin or Pyrethrin and Diazinon to the soil.

Mealy bugs are soft insects covered with a waxy white powder. They look like little specks of cotton and feed by sucking on the juice of the plants. These can be eradicated by washing them off with a forceful stream of water or by using cotton swabs dipped in alcohol and touching the insect. Another good method is using a forceful sprayer with the recommended insecticide to break through the hairs of the insect.

Pill bugs or sow bugs are grayish insects which, when touched, roll up into a small ball and feed on the roots of the plants. They can be eradicated by using a soil drench on the plant, such as that recommended for gnats.

Red spider mite is a prevalent insect in house plants and is difficult to see because it is very tiny. The mites usually start underneath the leaves and suck the juices or are found in infestations at the tops of the plants where they form small webs over the plants. Use a good pair of eyeglasses or a magnifying glass to see these insects. To bring mites under control, it is important to use an insecticide such as Kelthane, applying it at three-day intervals for at least four applications. Cover underneath the leaves as well as on top.

Scale is another common problem with house plants and is a hard covering; brown, black or tan in color. Usually this hard covering has numerous small insects underneath which feed by sucking the juices out of the plants. To be thoroughly controlled, use an oil-based spray, such as Malathion or Volck. They can also be removed by scraping them off and then by washing the plant with soap and water. Slugs can also be a problem and are noticed by a slimy line that is left behind. These can be hand picked, if not too heavily infested, and eradicated; otherwise, apply insecticide around the plants themselves.

Springtails are nearly microscopic insects which scurry busily on the surface of the moist potting soil when watering. They can damage tender seedlings and again are controlled the same as for gnats.

Thrips are small sucking insects that feed on the juices of the foliage and flowers. They rasp away the plant tissue leaving papery scars. These are controlled by using a general insecticide, applying both underneath and on top of the leaves.

Whiteflies are small insects which start on the underside of the leaves and when touched become small white-winged flying insects. They are more difficult to control than other insects and most often attack fuchsias and members of the tomato family although they do attack nearly all plants. They are controlled very effectively by using the new synthetic Pyrethrin, applying this underneath and on top of the leaves and repeating in three or four days for good control.

Some of the best fast-flowering plants are the following: begonias, flowering maple (*Abutilon*), African violets (*Saintpaulia*), impatiens, hibiscus and geraniums. Many others are available depending on the whim of the individual selecting them.

QUESTIONS

1. What kind of spray do I use on a flowering maple that seems to have some insects?

The flowering maple, *Abutilon*, is subject to whitefly and this is controlled by using the synthetic Pyrethrin. Other insects that may attack it are the white aphids. These are easily controlled with a forceful stream of water or a mild insecticide applied as needed. Occasionally, scale may be a problem and use Malathion or Volck on this.

2. How do you cultivate aeschynanthus?

The aeschynanthus is a member of the Gesneriaceae family which includes the African violets and gloxinias. They all require a soil high in organic matter, uniform temperatures of 70 to 75 degrees and good light, but not necessarily direct sunlight. Keep the plant moderately moist for best growing conditions. Once the plant is growing actively, it will benefit from a regular feeding of a liquid fertilizer. Avoid over-potting the plants; they have a shallow root system.

3. How do I care for a blue African lily in the winter?

The blue African lily is grown in large pots due to a heavy root system and they flower better when they are pot-bound during the winter months. Keep the plant in an area where temperatures are 60 to 65 degrees with good light and keep it moderately moist. An occasional feeding is beneficial if the plant is pot-bound. It will flower near early spring.

4. Is there a way to dry the flowers of the blue African lily?

A silica gel dries the flowers.

5. How do I best care for an amaryllis plant?

The amaryllis is a common plant grown from a bulb. These usually are secured from September to December. Put in container which is about one inch larger than the bulb itself. Use soil which is well drained and has plenty of organic matter. Place the bulb so that about one-third of the base is covered. Keep moderately moist until growth begins. Once the plant starts growing actively, increase the watering gradually but avoid over-watering. The plant needs good light and preferably some sun, if possible, or put under artificial light for 12 to 14 hours. The plant starts to flower in four to six weeks after potting and is followed by leaf growth. It is important to keep the plant moderately moist with good light. It needs occasional feedings of liquid fertilizer while the leaves are in full growth. In spring, about mid May, the plant can be placed outdoors by plunging pot and all to the rim, or by removing the plant from the pot, putting it in the ground and leaving it there for the summer months. It needs normal watering during drought periods. In early fall, the plant can be taken up and leaves cut back to about one inch from the top of the bulb. Allow the plant to dry out and store for six to eight weeks before starting to grow it again.

6. How do I force an amaryllis to bloom?

An amaryllis can be brought into bloom if it has had good culture (see Question 5). It is important to let the plant rest for a period of six to eight weeks before allowing it to grow. Keep a uniform temperature of 65 to 70 degrees and allow plenty of light.

7. How do I care for my amaryllis plants and can they be placed outdoors?

Amaryllises are grown under cultural conditions as given above and can be placed outdoors during the summer months. They are not hardy during winter; therefore, they need to be brought inside in the fall before temperatures get too low.

8. When I bring my amaryllis indoors, how do I care for it?

Allow the plant to dry off and place in an area where the temperature is 40 to 45 degrees (light is not important) and allow to remain for six to eight weeks to thoroughly rest before letting it grow.

9. How is a zebra plant best watered?

The zebra plant (*Aphelandra squarrosa* 'Louisae') likes a soil extremely high in organic matter and needs to be moderately moist. Allow the soil to dry out between waterings; then water it to barely moisten the soil again.

10. When do you separate an air-layered zebra plant from the mother plant?

As soon as roots begin to appear on the outside of the air-layering, the plant is ready to be severed. Take a sharp knife and cut just below the place where air-layering has occurred and then pot it.

11. How do you care for a zebra plant?

The zebra plant requires a very humid atmosphere, and when first placed in the home, put it in a terrarium or glass bowl where humidity is high or in a tray containing pebbles. Suspend the plant above the pebbles with water over the top of the pebbles so that the water evaporates around the plant. The plant needs good light, such as in an east or west window. Keep out of the direct sun during the hot part of the day. When growing actively and flowering, it needs an occasional feeding of liquid fertilizer. Once flowering has stopped, continue normal watering and occasionally pinch the plant to keep it bushy.

12. What causes the leaves of the zebra plant to fall?

This leaf drop is usually caused by lack of humidity in the room or through over-watering. Increase the humidity (see Question 11) or avoid over-watering.

13. What do you do for a wilting zebra plant?

Wilting will occur if the plant is kept too dry and can be corrected by simply watering it. On the other hand, if the plant is wet and is wilting, this indicates that the leaves have been lost through over-watering. Withholding water, watching the plant carefully or repotting into fresh media corrects the situation.

14. How do you air-layer a zebra plant?

Air-layering is done when the plant has become tall and spindly. Tie a sturdy stake below the area to be air-layered. The air-layering is done six to eight inches below the top of the plant. Take a sharp knife, cut in just below a node (about one-third of the way) and then bring the cut up at a slant. Place a toothpick in the cut to keep the stems from coming together. Take a sheet of plastic, place on this some milled sphagnum moss which has been thoroughly moistened and which has a small amount of moist perlite in the center and very carefully work the moss with the perlite around the cut part of the plant. Tie the plastic securely at the base to keep the material from falling away. Then wrap the plastic carefully around the stem, being careful not to break it off. Tie the top with a twistum and tie the top part of the plant to the stake itself. Keep the media moderately moist until rooting occurs.

15. What causes browning on the leaves of a zebra plant?

Browning of the leaves is usually an indication of low humidity. This is corrected by increasing the humidity by using the tray method or by keeping the plant in a glass container. See Question 11.

16. Our zebra plant is getting tall and spindly. Why?

This occurs for two reasons. The plant is not getting sufficient light, causing it to stretch to the light and/or the plant is getting older and needs to be pinched back. Pinching, as the plant develops, causes it to branch out and keeps it more compact.

17. What is the best culture for growing zebra plants?

Zebra plants like a soil high in organic matter and a media which has plenty of aeration. Do not over-water the media at any time but keep it moderately moist. Allow the plants to dry out between waterings but not to the point of wilting. When the plants are growing actively, they benefit from an occasional feeding of a liquid fertilizer. The plants like good light but do not need direct sunlight. If grown under artificial light, 10 to 12 inches away from the source of light is usually sufficient. As the plant develops, pinch the center to cause the plant to branch out and remain bushy. Watch for insects.

18. Which is the best window in which to set an azalea – north, south, east or west?

Flowering azaleas grown in the home are best in an area where it is as cool as possible and where they receive good light, such as in a south, east or west window during the winter months. During the summer months, keep out of the direct sun and grow the plant in a north window or shaded area outdoors.

19. Will an indoor azalea plant bloom a second time and how do I do this?

An indoor azalea plant is usually forced into bloom some time between Christmas and May. The plant needs adequate watering to keep it from wilting and needs good light at all times. It prefers a temperature of 55 to 60 degrees so place it where it is as cool as possible and yet receives enough light. The plant will need an occasional feeding of iron chelate to avoid the yellowing of leaves, and it will need regular feedings of liquid fertilizer when growing actively. The plant can be placed outdoors in the spring when all danger of frost is passed. It can receive filtered sun. It needs to be kept moderately moist throughout the summer months and pinched occasionally to keep the plant bushy. Buds set in late summer, usually during the month of August. Keep the plant outside until quite cool in the fall, such as mid October, at which time move it into a frame or protected spot where it is held for forcing at the proper time.

20. The azalea we received for Easter wilted very quickly. How do I prevent this? And may I put it outdoors?

An azalea from a florist shop is grown in a media of almost pure peat moss and if allowed to dry out too much, will tend to wilt very rapidly. When receiving a plant like this, place it in a container of water so that the complete soil ball is below the water level and hold it there until bubbles stop rising, at which time place the plant on the drain board and allow excess water to drain away. Then place it back in its normal position. Once the plant is through flowering, remove the soil ball from the pot. Remove one-third to one-half of the growing media and replace this with a good potting soil, as outlined in the General Information Section at the beginning of this chapter. Keep the plant in an area where it is as cool as possible with good light until new growth begins and then increase to a normal watering pattern and feeding program. The plant can be placed outdoors.

21. How do you get second growth from a florist's azalea?

The azalea will make new growth once flowering stops. Pinch the new growth to keep it compact and the plant will produce good growth and flower buds. See Questions 18 through 20.

22. How do you care for a Rex begonia when brought into the house?

Rex begonias make beautiful house plants and require fairly high humidity until they become established. I advise using the tray method with the plant suspended above water. Avoid over-watering the plant as you can lose the root system very quickly. By creating a high humidity, the plant does well. Occasional misting the first week is beneficial. See that it gets good light but not direct sun.

23. How do you grow and care for Rex begonias?

Rex begonias like a soil high in organic matter and pots which have good drainage. Watering is very critical. They like a temperature of 55 to 70 degrees and humidity of 40 to 50 percent, which is somewhat high for most houses during winter. Therefore, by using the tray method, humidity can be increased to this level. Avoid over-fertilizing if the plant is growing well. Feedings once every five to six weeks is all that is necessary.

24. My Rex begonia is wilting. What should I do?

Check the plant thoroughly to see if wilting has been caused by over-watering. If the soil is moderately moist, I suspect the loss of roots; therefore, let the soil dry out. Increase the humidity around the plant by enclosing it in a plastic bag or container until a new root system begins and then gradually expose it to normal house conditions. It may be necessary to remove the plant from the pot and repot it into fresh growing medium being extremely careful not to over-water until the root system is established.

25. What is the best cultural medium for Rex begonias?

The best cultural medium is the following: one-third part good top soil, one-third part leaf mold or peat moss and one-third part perlite. Mix these together thoroughly with a small amount of superphosphate. Water the plant lightly, keep it barely moist until steadily growing and then increase your watering until you reach a normal stage where the plant is growing actively.

26. What do you do for leaves dropping from an angelwing begonia?

Check the plant thoroughly to see that the plant is not root-bound. If so, repotting is necessary. Leaf drop may be occurring due to over-watering or to a lack of fertility. If the plant seems to be growing actively and is not pot-bound or over-watered, then an occasional feeding of liquid fertilizer every two or three weeks is advised.

27. How do you root tuberous begonias?

Tuberous begonias are usually propagated by dividing the tubers themselves. If the plants are growing actively, take cuttings as you do for any other plant. Select healthy ends that are four to six inches long and cut just below a node where the leaf comes out. Remove the lower one or two leaves and let the cuttings sit for several hours to thoroughly dry. Then place the cuttings in a good rooting medium where the humidity is quite high.

28. How do you root the fibrous begonias?

These *Begonia semperflorens* are rooted in the same way as for the tuberous begonias. See Question 27.

29. How do I control a powdery mildew on tuberous begonias?

Place plants where they get more air circulation. Use a good fungicide, such as Captan or Benlate, to bring it under control. Increasing air circulation with the use of a small fan will sometimes be all that is necessary to bring this under complete control. Also, avoid over-watering.

30. How do I best root a Rieger begonia?

The Rieger begonia is a hybrid. To root one, wait until flowering has stopped, cut the plant back and then when new growth begins, select healthy ends that are in good condition and are compact. Take cuttings four to six inches long and allow the cuttings to sit for several hours before placing them in the rooting medium. See Question 27.

31. Our begonia plant rotted off at the stem level. What do we do?

The rotting usually occurs from over-watering and is caused by a bacterial disease. As soon as this is noticed, treat the soil with a good fungicide, such as Phaltan or Captan. Also, keep the soil on the dry side.

32. Our begonia leaves are turning red. What is happening?

This may be due to the variety of begonia. Red leaves grow on some varieties as they develop. If it is an older plant turning red, it is usually an indication of a change in light or a lack of nutrients. If it is on young plants, do not be concerned. On an older plant, it may be necessary to increase the use of fertilizers, introducing more potassium into the soil.

33. Is it Okay to put begonias outdoors in April?

April is usually too early in Zone 6 to place begonias outdoors. It is much better to wait until about the third week of May after all danger of cold weather is passed before planting them outdoors.

34. What do I do about begonia seedlings that are damping-off?

With a spoon, carefully move the portion of seedlings which are damping-off. Immediately following this, dust the surrounding area with dry sand, if possible, or a good fungicide, such as Captan. Avoid over-watering and give the plants as much air circulation as possible. Cooler temperatures also are helpful in preventing this.

35. The leaves on our begonias are curled. What is causing this?

It is important to check the underside of the leaves for insects which can often cause the curling. If no insects are apparent, then curling is caused by cultural conditions and needs to be corrected by changing the watering or feeding pattern of the plant.

36. How do you repot a begonia when the roots are on top of the pot?

Carefully remove the complete plant from the pot. Remove one-third of the base of the old soil ball. Then carefully cut a "V" insert an inch deep in the sides in about three areas and remove this soil. Repot into new potting medium in a pot one to two sizes larger and place it deeper than it was originally. Avoid over-watering until a new root system is established.

37. What is the best way to grow begonias?

It depends on the types of begonias. Either use seeds or cuttings. Grow them in a good potting medium that is high in organic matter. Use good light but avoid direct sun if the plants are not flowering types. If flowering ones, give them good light but avoid direct sunlight during the hot part of the day.

38. How do you get begonias to rebloom?

Many of the fibrous begonias bloom almost continuously if given proper cultural conditions and regular feeding to keep them in good condition. Others, like the hybrid Rieger begonias, flower over a period of several months and then need a resting period. At this time, cut back the plants and cut down watering until new growth begins. Then increase watering and feeding once they get back into more normal growth. They can be brought back into bloom in three to four months following this procedure.

39. Our begonias are getting very lanky. How is this avoided?

Pinch the plants when small to cause bushiness. Also, see that they are getting sufficient light to avoid stretching of the plants.

40. What causes the flowers on my begonia plant to be a pale color?

This is usually a change in the light factor or the plant not getting sufficient nourishment. This causes the flowers to decrease in size and become paler in color.

41. What do I do for leaves dropping from begonias?

Check the cultural conditions. If a plant is pot-bound, it may be necessary to repot into a larger container or to increase the feeding of the plant at more regular intervals. Also, avoid over-watering, which can cause a loss of roots and leaves to drop.

42. Why did the leaves on my begonia turn white on a recently transplanted plant?

This usually occurs when plants are repotted and placed in stronger light. The light is too strong and bleaches the color out of the plants. This is avoided by gradually increasing the intensity of light.

43. How do I propagate begonias?

Begonias can be propagated from seeds. Select fresh seeds, sow them in a sterile media and then transplant when large enough. The second method is to take cuttings and root them in a combination of peat and perlite. Another method is dividing the plants. In many cases, plants are divided by carefully removing the soil and dividing them into sections that are already rooted. Begonias, such as the Rex and other types, are started from leaf cuttings. This is done by selecting a leaf, removing it from the parent plant, slitting the veins and then fastening the leaf down with a toothpick so that the cut edge is in contact with the rooting media. Jiffy Mix is ideal to use. Keep the leaves moderately moist and place in high humidity until the new plants are formed.

44. How long does it take to root begonias?

Cuttings are rooted thoroughly in four to six weeks at which time they are ready to pot into individual containers.

45. What is the best media for growing a shrimp plant?

The shrimp plant (*Beloperone guttata*) is best grown in an area where it gets good light and in a potting soil that is high in organic matter.

46. May I place a shrimp plant outdoors?

Place the shrimp plant outdoors once all danger of frost is past. It makes an excellent outdoor specimen grown this way. It needs an area where it is exposed to sun during the morning or afternoon rather than all day. The plant is not hardy in winter and needs to be brought indoors in the fall by bringing in the whole plant or taking new cuttings.

47. What is the best care for a shrimp plant?

The shrimp plant is best cared for by giving it the soil mentioned in Question 45, growing the plant indoors in a southern exposure, in another area where it receives sufficient light or under artificial light 10 to 12 hours per day. Pinch the plant occasionally to keep it low and bushy. When actively growing, feed at regular intervals with a liquid fertilizer. The plant requires average house conditions as far as moisture and temperature are concerned. Check periodically to make sure that it is insect free.

48. Why did the leaves on my bougainvillea turn black when I moved it outside?

The discoloring of the leaves when moved outdoors was possibly due to an increase in light or sudden change in temperature. Move plants from the indoors to outdoors by gradually exposing them to stronger light and higher temperatures. Sudden shocks cause discoloration of the foliage.

49. Why does my bougainvillea fail to flower?

A bougainvillea likes an area where it gets plenty of sun, which is in a southern exposure. Allow the plant to grow actively and to become somewhat pot-bound. Use liquid fertilizer high in phosphorus to help encourage flowering.

50. What is the best planting medium for cuttings from bromeliads?

Bromeliads have a very fine root system and are ideally grown in a combination of fir bark and sphagnum moss. Pack this thoroughly around the base of the plants.

51. How do I take care of bromeliads?

Bromeliads like fairly high humidity. Place water in the cup or center of the plants to keep the plants moist at all times. In watering, fill the centers up, allowing it to spill over to moisten the media around the base of the plants. The plants need good light but do not need direct sun. Occasionally dip the plants in water and spray them thoroughly. Very little fertilizer is required, but a weak solution applied around the base of the plants at intervals of six to eight weeks is ideal.

52. What do I do with pups on bromeliads?

Pups are the small off-shoots around the base of the plants which usually occur after flowering. When these are large enough, you will notice on close examination that they have begun to produce side roots. When the root system is active, cut them away from the parent plant with a sharp knife and pot individually.

53. The leaves on our bromeliads are turning brown? What do we do?

This is usually due to too dry an atmosphere. Remove the brown leaves and increase the humidity of the plants by grouping them together or by placing trays of water near the plants.

54. How many offshoots can I expect from one bromeliad?

It depends on the particular plant you are growing. Some will produce one or two; others may produce up to a half dozen shoots.

55. Please furnish information on growing an aechmea plant.

The aechmea, which is one of the many members of the Bromeliadaceae family, likes sunny to semi-sunny conditions, temperature 60° and a humidity level of around 30 percent or more. Use soil of sphagnum moss with shredded bark in coarse leaf mold into which it will lightly root. Water the roots sparingly but keep the center filled with water. Propagate by removing the offsets from the parent plant when they are large enough to handle.

56. What is the best way to get an aechmea fasciata to flower?

See Question 55 for growing an aechmea. Have patience. Your plant will send up its own magnificent spike of long-lasting, highly colored blossoms. When the plant is mature but is not flowering, place the plant in a plastic bag with a cut apple in the bag. Close the top and leave it for a period of several weeks at which time remove the apple. The apple, as it is enclosed in the bag, gives off ethylene gas, which, if the plant is ready to flower, will trigger the plant into producing the flower spike. At the end of the six-week period, remove the plant from the bag. In six to eight weeks, if it is ready to flower, the flower bud will be noticeable in the base of the plant.

57. What do I do about bud rot on my bromeliad guzmania?

Avoid letting the water sit too long in the center. Drain this out and flush out with fresh water. Do this once every week to 10 days. Avoid keeping the base of the plant too wet at anytime. If rot does occur, carefully remove this with a sharp knife.

58. What is the best way to cultivate a pineapple plant?

The pineapple plant (*Ananas comosus*) is readily started from taking the top of a store-bought pineapple. Remove the top with about an inch of the top of the pineapple itself attached. Let this sit for 24 hours to thoroughly dry out. Then select a good medium, such as Jiffy Mix or potting mix, and place the top of the pineapple on this, pushing it in so that about an inch is covered with the medium. Keep it moderately moist and put the plant in a fairly humid spot with good light. In six to eight weeks new roots will emerge from the side. Once the plant is rooted and is trying to grow, keep it moderately moist and place water over the crown to flow down into the soil around it. Avoid over-watering and do not fertilize it until the plant is well established. This makes an attractive potted plant for indoor use.

59. How do I force a pineapple plant to bloom?

The pineapple plant will start to flower when it has matured and if given proper cultural conditions, is no problem. See Question 56.

60. How do we encourage a pineapple plant to flourish?

Keep the plant in good light and avoid over-watering and too much fertilizer.

61. What is the best care for a bromeliad tillandsia?

Tillandsia usneoides is a native Spanish moss and has no roots attached. It usually is fastened to a tree trunk or tree branches and needs high humidity to survive. These conditions are difficult in an ordinary house unless grown in a terrarium case where humidity is high and where the plant receives sufficient light either from artificial light or from a window. In a small greenhouse, the plant can flourish where orchids and other plants are growing.

62. How do I care for a tillandsia to make it bloom?

The plant grown under regular conditions and of a mature size will flower if getting sufficient light and moisture. Again, enclose the plant in a plastic bag with an apple for six weeks and then expose it to normal growing conditions.

63. My pocketbook plant is dying. What do I do?

The pocketbook plant (*Calceolaria*) is an old-fashioned pot plant that is grown under cool conditions. It is usually available during the late winter and spring months. The plant, an annual, flowers once and only can be grown by taking seed and starting it again. It thrives best under temperature conditions of 45 to 55 degrees at night with about a 15-degree rise during the day. Some of the varieties can be grown from cuttings but need to be grown under cool conditions to survive in the home.

64. How do I grow camellias?

Camellias make nice house plants. Select healthy, well-grown plants; average soil conditions for them are suitable. They need good light, preferably some sun in south window or sunroom. Place the plant outdoors when all danger of frost has passed in the spring and leave out until late fall. Buds will form during the summer months and once temperatures drop down to 45 to 50 degrees at night, bring inside and grow in as cool a spot as possible. Keep the plants moderately moist and when actively growing, give occasional feedings of liquid fertilizer. The use of iron chelate and epsom salts twice a year is recommended. Remove some of the side buds to produce larger blooms on each plant.

65. Our Christmas pepper plant blooms but does not set fruit. Why?

The Christmas pepper plant (*Capsicum annum*) makes an attractive house plant but to set fruit, it needs to be grown outdoors during the summer months where it can be pollinated by insects. They will rarely set fruit when grown indoors unless hand pollinated with a small brush. Take pollen from one flower and place it on the pistil of the other flower.

66. How do I raise a Jerusalem cherry as a house plant?

The Jerusalem cherry (*Solanum pseudo-capsicum*) is another plant commonly grown outdoors during the summer months. Remove from the garden in late fall before the weather gets too cold. Pot it and keep it in an area where it is relatively cool and moist for several days before bringing it indoors. The plant needs plenty of light, such as a south window or sunroom, and the berries will start to ripen and be in good condition by Christmas time. Many of the berries will last until early spring. The plant is subject to whitefly and needs to be constantly checked and sprayed. Keep the plant moderately moist. When heavily set with fruit, feed with a liquid fertilizer once every 12 to 14 days.

67. What do I do with my chrysanthemum plant after it stops flowering?

Most flowering chrysanthemums purchased from florists are not suitable for growing indoors as these are usually light response groups and are usually grown under black cloth to bring them into bloom. When grown in the home, they usually fail to bloom because they are getting insufficient light to establish good growth. When placed outdoors they tend to flower late in the fall and are very tall, even with adequate pinching.

68. I have a non-hardy chrysanthemum. May I plant it outdoors in October?

If the chrysanthemum is not hardy, do not plant it outdoors in October or it will freeze. Non-hardy chrysanthemums need to be put indoors during the winter months, placed in an area where it is relatively cool and kept somewhat on the dry side to encourage little growth. As the weather warms up or days start to lengthen in February, repot and make fresh cuttings when it is actively growing during the spring and summer months.

69. What do we do with a pot of chrysanthemums that have stopped flowering?

Cut back the plant when it stops flowering and keep it barely moist. As new growth begins, increase the watering until you are back to a normal watering schedule. The plant, if grown with good light 12 to 14 hours, will grow. As the days shorten, put the plant in the dark from 6 p.m. until 8 a.m. and flowers will set again.

70. How do I get a cultivated chrysanthemum plant to re-bloom?

The best way to get the plant to re-bloom is to let it rest after flowering indoors. When all danger of frost has passed in the spring, remove it from the pot, divide the plants and place them in an area in the garden where they are in well prepared soil and where they get full sun. Keep the plants pinched until mid July to encourage short, compact growth. Plants start to flower in mid to late October depending on the variety being grown.

71. How do I care for a cineraria?

This is an attractive potted plant that can be grown in the home and is usually purchased in full bloom from the florist shop. It is a plant that likes to be kept moderately moist and grown in low temperatures. It prefers night temperatures of 45 to 55 degrees with a rise in temperature of about 15 degrees during the day. The plant needs as much sun as possible. Watch for aphids, a common problem. These usually attack the underside of the leaves and growing buds and need to be sprayed with a good insecticide when first noticed. In spraying the plant, remove it from the sun and allow the spray to dry thoroughly before placing the plant back in the sun. When the plant is growing actively, it needs a liquid fertilizer once every seven to 10 days. The plant only flowers once. New plants are started from seeds. Sow the seeds during the month of August and grow indoors during the winter for flowering in March and April.

72. How do I encourage a cineraria plant to flower?

The cineraria plant, if given good light and grown under cool conditions, will normally flower successfully in the home. High temperatures, 70 to 75 degrees, prevent the plant from flowering under normal conditions. See that the plant receives as much sun as possible.

73. How do I best care for a clivia and is it a recommended house plant?

The *Clivia miniata* is an attractive bulbous plant that can be grown as a suitable house plant. Give the plant good potting soil and plant it so that the bulbs are about halfway into the soil itself. The plant needs as much sun as possible during its growing stage and needs occasional feedings of liquid fertilizer. The plant flowers once it becomes pot-bound. It usually blooms anytime from October through early spring. When flowering has ended, remove the flower stalks and gradually withhold watering to allow the plant to rest for six to eight weeks. At this time, increase the watering gradually back to a normal watering period, and the plant will bloom again the following year.

74. Our cyclamen is wilting. What do we do?

The cyclamen is a bulbous plant grown from seed. It is one which likes very cool growing conditions, temperatures of 45 to

55 degrees at night with a 15 degree rise during the day. Plants grown where it is too warm tend to flag or wilt. Give the plant as much light as possible and grow it in temperatures as low as possible. Keep the plant moderately moist and avoid over-watering which can cause the loss of roots.

75. How do I best care for a cyclamen plant in order for it to bloom again?

The cyclamen is grown from seed and usually takes anywhere from 9 to 12 months to bring it into bloom. As soon as flowering is finished, the plant is seldom worth keeping; however, if you wish to keep it, give the plant plenty of light and keep it fertilized regularly for a period of up to two months. At this time, stop feeding and gradually withhold watering until the leaves start to yellow. Once the leaves begin to turn yellow, take the plant and store it in an area such as a basement or other area where temperatures are anywhere from 45 to 65 degrees. Let the plant remain there for a period of about three months. At that time, remove the corm from the soil. Select a clean pot and new potting soil high in organic matter. Clean the corm thoroughly, remove old roots and place the bulb about one-third of the way into the soil. Place the pot in an area where it receives as much sun as possible and in as cool condition as possible. Keep it moderately moist until growth begins at which time you will gradually increase watering until you return to a normal watering schedule. Once the plant is actively growing, feed it with a liquid fertilizer once every two weeks until buds begin to form. At that time, an increase in feeding may be necessary to keep the plant in good condition. Remove any leaves at the base of the corm which turn yellow or start to rot to prevent damage to the corm. Place bulbs outside in a semi-shaded area and grow that way for the summer.

76. How do I care for an ailing dipladenia?

The *Dipladenia splendens* is sometimes referred to as a mandevilla and is an attractive vining plant when grown in the home. The plant needs plenty of light, preferably some sun and a good potting soil well enriched with organic matter. Keep the soil moderately moist but avoid over-watering. When the plant is growing actively, occasional feedings of liquid fertilizer are needed to keep it in good condition. Over-watering causes yellowing of the leaves and damage to the plant.

77. How frequently does a night-blooming cactus flower?

The night-blooming cactus is *Epiphyllum oxypetalum* and usually flowers about once during the year. The amount of flowering depends on the size of the plant. Often small plants started from cuttings will bloom within a year after taking cuttings. Others may take several years and depending on the size of the plant may have anywhere from two or three to as many as 30 or more flowers at irregular intervals over a period of six to eight weeks.

78. How do we start cuttings of Crown of Thorns?

The Crown of Thorns (*Euphorbia splendens*) may be started from selecting cuttings from actively growing material that are four to six inches long. Remove the cuttings with a sharp knife and sear the ends with a hot match to stop the bleeding or rub with a bit of sand over the base to seal it. Leave cuttings for a period of 24 hours to dry out completely. Then place in a good rooting medium and keep moderately moist in a uniform temperature of 70 to 75 degrees until rooted. Once the cuttings are rooted, pot in the normal manner.

79. How do I propagate a Crown of Thorns plant?

The Crown of Thorns is propagated almost entirely from cuttings. See Question 78. Occasionally, seed will form from the flowering and the plant can be started from a seed by sowing it in the regular manner.

80. How do we best take care of a tiger plant?

The tiger plant is often referred to as *Faucaria tigrina* and is in the cactus family. Grow the plant in a soil that has a high content of sand and give it plenty of light, preferably some direct sun. Keep fairly close to the source of light if grown under artificial light. The plant needs just enough water to moisten the soil. Let it dry out between waterings. During the winter months, plants can go for three to four weeks with little or no water, enough to keep them from shriveling. Towards the spring increase the watering to a shorter period and plants will flower during the summer months.

81. What do I do with my wilting fuchsia plant?

Wilting of a fuchsia is usually caused by growing it in too high a temperature or by over-watering, which destroys the root system. Move the plant out of direct sun and avoid over-watering.

82. Why are my fuchsia buds dropping and not flowering?

Dropping of flower buds usually is due to too high temperatures and to over-watering. Keep the plant out of the direct sun and keep the soil just moist. Avoid over-fertilizing at this time.

83. My fuchsia plant is doing poorly and has white insects around it. Why?

The white insects are whiteflies and need to be controlled by using a good spray, such as synthetic Pyrethrin. The plant likes soil which is high in organic matter and needs good light but not necessarily direct sun. Temperatures of 65 to 75 degrees bring the best results. Pinching the plant occasionally to cause bushiness is also helpful. When the plant is growing actively, feed with a liquid fertilizer at regular intervals. When the weather gets hot, plants tend to stop flowering and start to lose their leaves. At this time dry the plant out by reducing the watering but do not let it wilt completely. Cut back the plant severely, allowing it to go through a period of several months rest. Then start again in early fall at which time it can be grown indoors. If it receives adequate light, it will bloom when growth is back in full stage again.

84. Can a fuchsia be forced so that it blooms all year?

Fuchsia, if grown under cooler conditions, will flower most of the year; however, when heavy blooming stops, it is best to cut down watering and feeding and cut back the plant. When growth becomes active again, increase both the watering and the feeding until buds begin to form again.

85. A flowering stem is dying on my fuchsia hanging basket. What do I do?

If one branch is dying, cut this back to the base stem from which it is emerging. Be careful how much water the plant receives and feed as needed.

86. The leaves are yellowing on my fuchsia. What do I do?

Yellowing leaves are possibly due to insufficient feeding. If watering has stayed the same, try increasing the amount of liquid fertilizer. If yellowing continues, replant to prevent the roots from becoming too restricted.

87. What causes fuchsia flowers to drop?

Over-watering or irregular watering causes the flowers to drop; keep the plant uniformly moist. Feed with liquid fertilizer at regular intervals. High temperatures also cause flower buds to drop.

88. The buds on our fuchsia are dropping before flowering. What do we do?

Feed the plant more regularly; it may be a lack of nutrients. Also, try giving the plant an application of epsom salts about once every three months when growing actively. This helps the flowers mature.

89. How do we transplant fuchsia seedlings?

Transplant fuchsia seedlings as soon as they get their second or third set of leaves. The first pair are the seed leaves. Wait until at least two or three sets grow above this. At that time, carefully remove the seedlings with a sharp pencil or other small stake and transplant them to potting soil high in organic matter. Keep the seedlings moderately moist until they are actively growing. See that they get good light but avoid direct sunlight during the hot part of the day.

90. What is the best culture for our gardenia plant?

Gardenias are plants which like an acid-type soil. Soil mixtures high in peat moss or partially decomposed oak-leaf mold is ideal. Adding a small amount of sulfur also helps to keep the acidity down. The plants make heavy root systems. Grow them where they get good light and preferably some sun with temperatures of 65 to 75 degrees being ideal. Keep plants moderately moist. When actively growing, they need occasional feedings of liquid fertilizer. About twice a year use a feeding of iron chelate and epsom salts combined at the rate of one tablespoon of each per gallon of water. Use this in place of regular watering in April and again in October. This will keep the plant from becoming yellow and will prevent the buds from dropping off. Occasionally mist the plant to keep it dust-free. Gardenias are subject to mealy bugs so check regularly for these. When mealy bugs are first noticed, bring them under control by using a good stream of forceful water or insecticide applied under pressure. Scale insects also are a problem so use an oil-base spray. Apply it thoroughly underneath the leaves as well as on top.

91. Our gardenia is budding but the buds are not opening. What do we do?

Use iron chelate and epsom salts, applying about twice a year to help prevent this. See Question 90. Keep the plant moderately moist when buds begin to form.

92. Do gardenias need pruning after blooming?

Pruning at regular intervals is ideal to keep the plant in compact uniform growth. Remove the tips of new growth as they develop or elongate. Avoid pruning once growth slows down as flower buds form then.

93. Our gardenia has yellow leaves. How is this avoided?

Yellowing of leaves is usually an indication that the plant is not getting sufficient iron. Use iron chelate and water regularly to prevent this.

94. Gardenia leaves are dropping without discoloring. What is the cause?

A change in watering patterns or over-watering can cause leaves to drop very rapidly. Keep the plant uniformly moist at all times.

95. What is the best fertilizer for gardenias?

An acid-type fertilizer is ideal; however, almost any liquid fertilizer for house plants is suitable. Avoid feeding when plants are not growing actively.

96. Is it okay to put gardenias outdoors in April?

In most areas April is too early if there is still any chance of frost or severe cool nights. It is much better to wait until all danger of frost is passed and more uniform temperatures exist before placing outdoors.

97. How do I start geraniums from seeds?

Select fresh seeds. Sow seeds at 70 to 75 degrees and keep moderately moist. Germination is usually erratic, occurring over a period of four to 15 days. Avoid over-watering and see that the seedlings receive plenty of light to prevent legginess.

98. How do I propagate geraniums?

Geraniums are propagated from seeds (see Question 97) or from cuttings. Select cuttings from healthy flowering plants, usually four to six inches long. Take cuttings just below the node or where the leaf stem comes out. Remove the lower one-third of the leaves and allow the cuttings to sit for approximately 24 hours before placing in the rooting medium. Once placed in the rooting medium, keep moderately moist and allow good light but no direct sun. Rooting usually occurs in four to six weeks. At that time pot the plant.

99. What is the best culture for geraniums?

Geraniums propagated from seeds or cuttings are best grown in regular potting soil in temperatures anywhere from 55 to 75 degrees. They like as much sun as possible and most of the newer strains need to be kept moderately moist at all times. Also they are heavy feeders. When actively growing, the plants need liquid fertilizer at one to two-week intervals. Pinch the growth occasionally to keep the plants low and bushy. When flowering begins, it will continue as long as the plants are receiving plenty of food and water.

100. New geraniums are being placed outdoors and are dropping leaves. What do we do?

A sudden shock to plants can cause this. Harden-off geraniums for a week to 10 days by gradually exposing them to outdoor conditions for an hour or two the first day and increasing this until they are out all day. At the time of transplanting, carefully remove them from the container to avoid root damage. Place the plants into the soil at the same level and water with a weak feeding of liquid fertilizer. Avoid setting them out when temperatures are too low. Do not put geraniums outside until all danger of frost has passed and average temperatures are 55 to 60 degrees. Setting them out too early causes discoloration and loss of foliage.

101. Why do the buds on my geraniums keep falling off?

This is usually due to insufficient nutrients or to poor light. Give the plants as much sun as possible and when buds form, increase the feeding to 12 to 14-day intervals.

102. When geraniums are moved indoors, how do we care for them?

First lift them from the soil when the ground is moderately moist or after watering thoroughly. Pot the plant and place in a protected spot where they keep as cool as possible and are out of direct sun for several days to give them a chance to develop new roots. Then gradually move them indoors. In many cases it is better to start with cuttings taken in August for winter flowering. When the plants are growing actively, they need plenty of light, preferably some direct sun and fertilizer every two weeks.

103. Our geraniums are very leggy. How do we make them bushier?

Pinch the centers out, causing them to branch out, and give them plenty of light.

104. May I set geraniums outdoors in February?

February in most areas is much too early. Do not set them out

ORCHID
Cattleya bowringiana
(Missouri Botanical Garden)

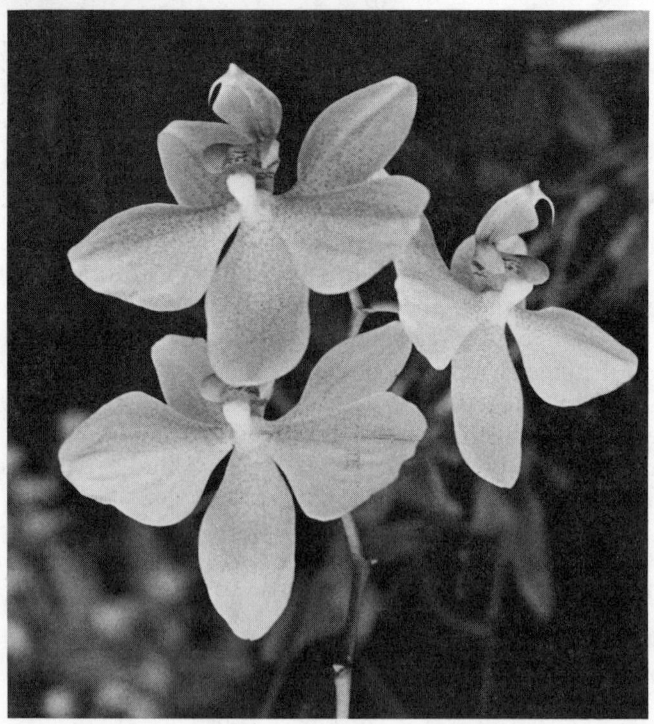

ORCHID
Phalaenopsis White Falcon x Manii
(Missouri Botanical Garden)

CHRYSANTHEMUM
Large Flowered Commercial Type
(Missouri Botanical Garden)

GLAMOUR PICOTEE
A delicate pink and white begonia for shade and sun
(Pan-American Seed Co.)

until all danger of frost is past and night temperatures are fairly uniform.

105. How do I eliminate brown stem fungus on geraniums?

This usually occurs when plants have been grown where it is too wet or where there is a lack of air or when grown from cuttings which have been kept too wet or are selected from plants which are diseased. Avoid over-watering. Also, when taking cuttings allow them to dry for 24 hours before placing them in the rooting medium. If any disease is noticed, take the cuttings out and destroy them.

106. What do yellow leaves on my geranium plants mean?

In many cases, if the plants are growing actively, yellow leaves are usually an indication of not enough nourishment. Increase the use of liquid fertilizer to more regular intervals.

107. Geranium plants were placed outdoors and temperatures dropped to 40 degrees, causing the buds to turn brown. What do I do?

Avoid putting geraniums outside too early. If sudden drops in temperature do occur, it is important to cover the plants or move them back indoors until more uniform temperatures exist.

108. How do we prepare geraniums for the winter?

Take cuttings in August, root them, potting them into suitable containers and then grow them in an area where they get as much light as possible. Keep them moderately moist and feed as needed. Dig up older plants, pot and store in the basement or somewhere where they get little light. Keep moist enough to prevent them from drying out. In late February cut them back, repot into fresh containers and move where they get excellent light conditions. Keep moderately moist until growth begins. Then water until they are back to a regular pattern and then start feeding again.

109. Malathion does not seem to eradicate scale on geraniums. What kind of spray will?

Scale usually is not much of a problem on geraniums, but if it does exist use an oil-base spray such as Volck but not more than two or three applications during the year. Keep the plants healthy and in good condition to avoid scale.

110. May I take ivy geraniums indoors after a summer outdoors? What is the best method for doing this?

Ivy geraniums are usually grown in hanging baskets or pots. In late fall when you are ready to bring them indoors, cut them back considerably and cut down watering and feeding until they start new growth. Plants can be overwintered where they are kept in low temperatures with average light conditions. Avoid watering to increase growth. In early spring, move the plants into fresh containers with fresh potting soil. As new growth begins, increase the watering until back to a normal watering period. Another method is to take cuttings. See Question 98. Ivy geraniums, if placed in a sunny south exposure and fed and watered properly, continue flowering indoors during the winter months.

111. May I take ivy geranium cuttings in September for indoor planting?

Yes. Select cuttings from healthy plants rooted in the regular manner.

112. Do ivy geraniums flourish or even survive in full shade?

Ivy geraniums will grow in semi-shade although flowering will not be as good as it is in full sun. Full shade often prevents any flowering and causes little growth.

113. The leaves on my ivy geranium turned yellow when brought indoors. What do I do?

Avoid sudden changes when bringing plants indoors or taking them outside. Gradually adjust them from one exposure to another. When moving from one exposure to another, it is much better to withhold watering. Keep the plant on the dryer side for a week to 10 days to help harden them off. When placed in their new location, move them back into a normal watering and feeding schedule for best results.

114. How do I best propagate an ivy geranium?

Select cuttings from healthy, heavy flowering plants – cuttings usually taken from wood which is not flowering too heavily. Remove the flowers and any large buds. Cut just below a node and root in the regular manner. Geraniums will root sometimes in water, but are best propagated by rooting the cuttings in a mixture of perlite and peat moss.

115. The buds are falling off our ivy geraniums. What do we do?

Avoid over-watering at this period and see that the plants are getting plenty of nourishment through regular feedings of liquid fertilizer.

116. May I put hanging baskets of geraniums outside in March?

March, in any area, is much too early. Wait until all danger of frost has passed and until night temperatures are fairly uniform.

117. How do we plant and train a climbing geranium?

Climbing geraniums require the same cultural conditions as regular geraniums. Place in pots of sufficient size to allow them to develop. Staking or trellises are needed and as the plant grows, carefully tie it with a soft tie to the container. Pinching is recommended to cause the plants to bush out and keep uniform growth.

118. Can bulbs be forced indoors and if so, how?

Many bulbs can be forced indoors. Select healthy, grown bulbs of top size in early fall while supplies are good. Tulips, daffodils, hyacinths and crocuses may all be forced successfully. Bulbs are usually available in early September. For best results they should be potted up by mid October. In potting, place several bulbs in a pot or pan and cover them up about halfway. Lightly water and then place in a cool area. Cover them with a layer of sand and as temperatures get lower, cover this with a layer of straw or hay to protect them from freezing. Use leaves as a good mulch on top. Then when the weather gets really cold, place a top on the frame. Bulbs need a period of temperatures around 40 to 45 degrees for a good root system to form. When potting in mid October, do not bring indoors for forcing until the beginning of January. Early forcing does not allow sufficient time for plants to form a good root system.

Bulbs may also be placed in a refrigerator where temperatures are around 40 to 45 degrees. Leave in the refrigerator for the same period of time. Do not freeze the soil because this prevents the bulbs from forming roots.

In early January bring the bulbs indoors and place in an area where it is dark with temperatures of 45 to 55 degrees. Keep moderately moist. Examine them every few days and when growth is fairly active and the first node is above the soil or the new growth is three to four inches long, move into areas where they get good light such as from an east, south or west window or in a sun-room. Keep temperatures around 65 to 70 degrees and place as close to the source of light as possible. Keep them moderately moist and when growth becomes active, occasionally feed liquid fertilizer. The plants need to go through the dark period indoors to allow the flower bud to be drawn out of the bulb itself. Being placed in too high a temperature and in light too early usually causes the flowers to blast, which means that the flower bud does not come out of the leaves and usually has little or no color to it. Once the bulbs are in bloom, move back to a lower temperature.

Lily-of-the-valley is another one that can be forced. Buy the prepared pips from garden centers or seed houses. Grow in moss and keep the corms or pips barely covered. Keep moderately moist in a cool area for several weeks to allow good rooting. Then bring into warmer temperatures with plenty of light.

119. What do I do with paper-white narcissus bulbs after flowering?

Paper-whites are forced by placing the bulbs in trays containing water and pebbles to hold the bulbs upright or by placing them in soil. They do not need the cooling period that tulips, daffodils and hyacinths need. Place in a growing medium and then in the dark for a period of three to four weeks to allow a good root system to form. Temperatures are around 45 to 65 degrees. Once a good root system is established, move the plants into a location where they get plenty of light and they will flower in four to six weeks. Once the bulbs are forced, they are no longer of any value and are best discarded.

120. What is the best fertilizer for paper-white narcissuses?

Paper-white narcissuses need very little feeding since flower buds are already formed and if properly forced, will bud. However, add a weak feeding of liquid fertilizer once growth becomes active and again just before flower buds begin to open.

121. How do I force lily-of-the-valley pips to bloom indoors?

Select healthy grown pips by digging them out of your own garden in late fall or by purchasing bulbs that have been grown for this purpose. Plant immediately so that they are not allowed to dry out and place in an area where it is relatively cool, 40 to 45 degrees, for a period of several weeks to allow a good root system to form. At this time bring indoors into a temperature of 45 to 55 degrees and keep moderately moist. When growth becomes active, move to a place where they get excellent light during the day and an increase in temperature of 10 to 15 degrees.

122. What is the proper way to plant a bulb in a pot?

It depends on the type of bulb being planted. Tulips are usually placed with four to five in a pot so that the flat side of the bulb is against the outside edge or near the outside. Cover about half of the bulb. For hyacinths, put one bulb to a pan, fill the pot up to the desired height and press the bulb so that it is covered about halfway. The same applies for daffodils and crocuses. It is not necessary to completely cover the bulb with soil since the roots are formed from the base. The more room for rooting, the better the plant will do.

123. We have a pot of flowering tulips and now that the blooms are dying and leaves yellowing, what do we do to have them flower again?

Tulips cannot be forced the second time. Once they start yellowing, stop watering. Place the pot in the basement or somewhere to dry off and remain for several weeks. About April examine the pot, remove the bulbs from the soil, clean them off and separate the new bulbs. Store them in an area that is well ventilated; light is not a factor. Leave them there for the summer months and in the fall, place the bulbs in nursery rows in the back of a shrub border or flower bed where they can grow. By preparing the soil adequately with plenty of superphosphate, bulbs will begin to flower again in a year or two when they reach sufficient size.

124. How do I grow and care for a gloxinia?

Gloxinias are members of the same family as the African violets and require a soil high in organic matter. Purchase tubers during the fall and winter months. Place tubers so that they are just barely covered in the rooting medium. Carefully moisten the medium and then place the plant in a temperature of 65 to 70 degrees. Avoid over-watering at this time until growth becomes active. As soon as the plant starts to grow, place the pot where it receives good light, preferably some sun. As growth begins, increase the watering as needed. Once the plant is in active growth, start using liquid fertilizer at 10 to 14 day intervals. Avoid poor light; this causes the plant to stretch upwards. In a period of two to three months, the plant will be very full and compact and buds will begin to show. At this stage avoid getting any water on the foliage. Increase the feeding as needed and plant will start to flower in six to eight weeks following the formation of the buds.

125. How do you propagate gloxinias?

Gloxinias are propagated from bulbs and from leaf cuttings by selecting a healthy leaf with about an inch of the leaf petiole. Let this dry for several hours and place in a good rooting medium. About six to eight weeks later small bulblets form on the end of the leaves at which time new leaves will emerge from the rooting medium. At this time, give the plants plenty of light and avoid over-watering. Once growth is active, remove the leaves from the medium, carefully separate small plants and pot in individual pots. See Question 124.

126. What is the best fertilizer for gloxinias?

Any of the liquid fertilizers applied according to the directions on the containers are ideal for gloxinias. Keep soil moderately moist before applying fertilizer; otherwise, it will burn.

127. How do I care for a gloxinia after it stops flowering?

Once the gloxinia stops flowering, place in a resting position. Gradually withhold watering and foliage will yellow. Place the pot in an area where the temperature is 45 to 65 degrees and leave for a period of up to two to three months. At that time carefully remove the bulb and pot into fresh soil or fresh growing medium, according to the size of the bulb. Keep the bulb moderately moist until growth begins and increase watering as needed.

128. What happens when a gloxinia is over-watered?

Usually over-watering causes the loss of roots and the plant will become soft or will decay at the soil line. Avoid over-watering at all times. If over-watering has occurred, move the plant out of direct light and let it dry out somewhat until growth begins again. In many cases, it may be necessary to dry the bulb off completely and then after a period of six or eight weeks, start it back into growth.

129. What causes bud blast on gloxinias?

This is usually caused by insufficient light or by too high a humidity. Keep the buds as dry as possible; avoid getting water on them. Keep the plants properly fertilized. Carefully remove deformed buds by removing the stems at the base so that they do not have a chance to rot.

130. How do you get rid of thrips on gloxinias?

Spray thrips with a forceful spray of insecticide, getting underneath and on top of the leaves. Spray the plant when it is out of the sun and leave it out of the sun until it is thoroughly dry.

131. What causes leaf curl on gloxinias?

Thrips (see Question 130) or improper growing conditions cause leaf curl.

132. May I move gloxinias outdoors?

This is not recommended unless they can be grown in a

semi-shaded spot where protected. Do not expose to heavy rains at any time which can cause the loss of foliage. Bring in before danger of frost occurs in the fall.

133. How do I carry a gloxinia through the dormant stage?

A gloxinia, once it goes dormant, is easy to carry over. Place it in a cupboard or other similar area and where temperatures are from 45 to 65 degrees. It needs a resting period of anywhere from six weeks to three months.

134. How do I let a gloxinia go dormant and re-bloom?

Gradually withhold watering and as leaves begin to yellow, stop watering entirely. Place it in storage (see Question 133). Then after a sufficient resting period, repot and allow to flower again.

135. How do I care for my gloxinia plant?

Isolate gloxinia plant when first brought into the home to make sure it is free of insects or diseases. Put it where it receives good light but not necessarily direct sun. Keep the plant moderately moist. While the plant is in bloom, feed at regular intervals with a liquid fertilizer.

136. How do I get a Rose of China plant to re-bloom?

The Rose of China is *Hibiscus rosa-sinensis* and is grown in many homes as a popular flowering plant. Pot in good soil and in a pot large enough to allow for plenty of growth. The plant grows well under normal house conditions and needs an area where it receives some sun or very strong light during the day. The plant needs occasional pinching to keep it low and bushy. Once flower buds begin to form, occasional feedings of liquid fertilizer are needed to keep it in good growth. Watch for aphids which can be a problem and as soon as noticed, spray to bring them under control. Mealy bugs can also be a problem and needs to be controlled when first noticed. Cut back the plant when it stops flowering and withhold watering somewhat until it is growing again. The plant is a heavy feeder and if given plenty of light and food, will bloom almost continuously.

137. How do you care for a Chinese hibiscus during the summer and winter?

A hibiscus can be left indoors if getting sufficient light; otherwise, place outdoors during the summer months. Gradually move outdoors to adjust it to both light and temperature; keep it well watered and well fertilized during the summer months. Pinch occasionally during the summer to keep the plant low and compact to ensure full growth when it is time to bring inside in the fall. Bring indoors before it gets too cold. Gradually allow it to adjust to the indoor conditions and then give it plenty of light for best results.

138. What is the best cultural method to use in putting a hibiscus outdoors?

Put the plant outdoors as soon as all dangers of frost are past and night temperatures are uniform. Place the plant in a semi-sunny position. Plunge the pot in the ground or place it on top of the ground and keep it moderately moist. Pinch and feed occasionally.

139. May I plant a potted hydrangea in soil outdoors?

The potted hydrangea is *Hydrangea macrophylla.* It may be placed outdoors during the summer months and treated as any other house plant. Take them out of the pots in spring and plant them in an area where they receive sufficient sun and are in a soil which is well enriched with organic matter and plenty of superphosphate. They continue to grow and then harden-off in the fall. In some cases, they may freeze back to ground level; however, they will send up new growth in the spring which will flower in mid summer. Bring most of the potted hydrangeas indoors in the fall. Keep outdoors until just before heavy frost, at which time practically all leaves drop. Then place in a cool area where they are just above freezing for two to three months. Then bring indoors, repot into fresh soil and place where they receive full sun with a temperature of 55 to 65 degrees. Plants grown this way will flower towards the spring. If the pots are treated with sulfur or aluminum sulphate, the flowers will tend to be blue in color rather than the normal pink.

140. How do I treat potted hydrangeas after they flower.

Cut the blooms off the plant. If necessary, repot into larger pots, growing the plants until temperatures are high enough to place them outdoors in a frame or protected spot during the summer months. Leave outside with adequate feeding and watering and bring back indoors when cool temperatures begin.

141. What is the best culture for an Indian Rope plant?

An Indian Rope plant is a hoya and is grown as a hanging plant, usually indoors. The plant likes a soil which is high in organic matter, a temperature range of 65 to 75 degrees and good light, but not necessarily direct sun. No feeding is needed unless the plant is growing actively. Lack of light can cause loss of color, particularly in the variegated forms; however, too much light can also cause the color to fade out. Keep moderately moist but avoid over-watering or the plant will lose roots quickly.

142. Our hoyas do not bloom. Why?

The hoyas or wax plants as they are commonly called, will vary as far as flowering is concerned. Select cuttings from plants which are heavy flowerers and they usually will flower at an early stage. Cuttings taken from plants which rarely flower will seldom bloom. In some cases, plants will bloom the first year and in other cases may take two to three years. One of the best methods is to keep the plants under good light conditions. In late fall or early spring, keep the hoya on the dryer side by watering less for a period of six to eight weeks. Do not let it dry out completely during this period or the plant will shrivel. At the end of the five-week period, start watering normally again. This dry period often will trigger the plant into flowering. Once flowers form, it is important not to remove the spurs in which the flowers are formed because even though the flowers drop off, new buds are produced from the same spur. During the first year one or two clusters may be formed and then as the plant develops and gets older, more flowers will fall.

143. What kind of temperature does the hoya tolerate?

The *Hoya carnosa* does best in temperatures of 65 to 75 degrees. It can also be grown under much cooler conditions, temperatures as low as 45 to 50 degrees; however, avoid too low a temperature which can cause leaves to drop. During the lower temperature, cut back watering as plant will not dry out as rapidly.

144. May I grow impatiens indoors?

Yes. They like a fairly sunny to semi-shady area and temperatures of the average house, 60 to 65 degrees, but preferably not over 70 degrees in winter. They like a fairly high humidity, 40 to 50 percent and a soil of equal parts of loam, sand and peat moss kept evenly moist. To propagate use cuttings inserted in moist sand or perlite at any time. Keep moderately moist and occasionally feed them liquid fertilizer to keep them in good condition.

145. What is the best cultural medium for impatiens?

See Question 144. Use any potting soil high in organic matter.

146. How do I propagate my indoor impatiens?

Grow impatiens from seeds or from cuttings selected from healthy, flowering plants. Root cuttings in perlite.

147. How do I make my hanging basket of impatiens continue to bloom indoors?

See that the plant is getting good light and some sun during winter months. Pinch the plant to keep it bushy and keep it moderately moist with regular feedings of liquid fertilizer.

148. May I winter-over sultanas?

Sultanas is another common name for impatiens. They may be over-wintered. See Question 147.

149. Do I pinch back impatiens?

Yes. Impatiens need pinching periodically to cause them to remain bushy and compact.

150. What is an improved method for bringing impatiens (sultanas) indoors after summering?

Bring the plants inside the house from a semi-shaded position outdoors. Do this over several days, gradually withholding water for several days before bringing them indoors. Reduce light gradually, moving them from the outside to the garage for a couple of days and then from the garage into the house where they are going to grow. Once indoors, increase the watering back to normal and keep the plants well fertilized. It may be necessary to cut them back severely to cause them to bush out and be more compact. During this period, cut back watering until they return to normal growth.

151. How do you care for impatiens when they are in a hanging basket?

Keep moist at all times and give regular feedings of liquid fertilizer. Pinch occasionally to keep the plants uniform.

152. What is a good rooting medium for California jasmine?

Root the jasmine, known as *Jasminum*, in a mixture of perlite and peat moss, using one-third peat moss to two-thirds perlite. Cuttings root in four to six weeks, at which time move into a potting soil high in organic matter.

153. How do I propagate kalanchoes?

Kalanchoes usually are propagated from seeds. Also, grow from cuttings taken from a healthy plant or from individual leaves from the parent plant. Allow the leaves to sit for several hours to dry off and then place so that about one-third of the base of the leaf is in the rooting medium.

154. How far do I pinch back a kalanchoe?

Remove the center growing tip when it has three or four inches of growth. This causes the side shoots to break out. When they grow three or four inches, pinch back and they will tend to branch out the same way. Once the plant has reached the desired shape and form, no further pinching is required.

155. How do we make a kalanchoe bloom?

A Kalanchoe normally blooms during the winter. Buds usually set in late fall and flower around Christmas or February. If growing indoors, try to remove the plant from the source of light by 6 p.m. with no additional light under 8 a.m. If grown under artificial light, turn the light off after 10 hours. Temperature is also a factor. Try and reduce temperature five to 10 degrees to 55 to 60 degrees.

156. What do I do with a kalanchoe when it has finished blooming?

When the plant has finished blooming, cut it back, removing about two-thirds of the growth. Reduce water and repot, if necessary, into a larger pot. Gradually increase watering as growth begins until you are back to a normal watering procedure. Pinch the plant at regular intervals to keep it compact. This gradually brings it back into bloom at a later date.

157. The leaves are turning brown on our peacock plant. What do we do?

The peacock plant is usually referred to as the *Kaempferia roscoeana.* It is a member of the ginger family and likes to be grown in fairly high humidity. Use a tray method with pebbles with the plant suspended over the pebbles for extra humidity. Keep the soil uniformly moist except during late fall and winter months. Then keep it on the dryer side.

158. Is there some way I may encourage an Easter lily to flower again?

The Easter lily (*Lilium longiflorum*) is forced into bloom. When flowering is finished, cut the flower stalks off, leaving as many leaves as possible. Give the plant plenty of light and regular feedings. At the end of two or three months remove the plant from the pot and after all danger of frost is past, place outdoors in the garden. To do this remove it from the pot and plant it three or four inches deeper than it was in the pot. The old stalk will gradually die and in many cases, a new stalk will come up shortly afterwards. The flower will produce blooms in late summer or early fall. This is a hardy species and can be left outdoors. It will remain over winter and flower the following year, usually early in June. It is not recommended for forcing a second time because the bulb is usually too weak and needs a growing period to build up the bulb again.

159. Is there any way to get a second blooming from an Easter lily plant?

Yes. See Question 158. After flowering a normal year in the garden, lift it up in the fall and grow under very cool conditions to establish a solid root system. Keep in a cold frame or refrigerator where the temperature is around 40 to 45 degrees. Then bring into a temperature of 55 to 65 degrees, starting in early January. If given plenty of light and kept moderately moist, the plant blooms again around Easter time.

160. How do I best care for a firecracker plant?

The firecracker plant is often referred to as the *Manettia, bicolor* or *inflata*. The plant likes average house conditions, fibrous potting soil and a sunny window. Keep it moderately moist and avoid over-watering.

161. How do I grow oleanders from seeds?

Take seeds when ripe from the existing plants or use from a packet. Seedlings germinate in a temperature of 70 to 75 degrees in 10 to 12 days. At this time allow to grow until ready for transplanting. Then put in pots of three or four inches. Repot as needed.

162. How do we stop our oleander from losing leaves?

Leaves dropping from the oleander is usually due to the plant being pot-bound or to insufficient nutrients. Check the plant to see if it needs repotting into a larger container. If so, do this; otherwise, supplement the nutrients by using liquid fertilizer when the plant is growing actively. Occasional feedings during the winter help to keep the plant in good condition. Avoid over-watering but keep it uniformly moist. Give the plant plenty of light, preferably some sun.

163. Will an oleander harm children if grown in the same room?

The oleander is one of the poisonous plants. If one is growing it in the home, see that small children cannot reach the plant. Chewing the leaves is dangerous. Also, do not use the wood of the plant near food because this is another way of contacting the poison.

164. What is the best culture and mix for orchids?

Grow orchids in the home where they receive good light and normal house temperatures, 60 to 70 degrees. The best bark mix is redwood bark which is especially sold for orchids. The type of bark, as to fine or coarse grade, depends on the type of orchid being grown. Clean clay pots are desirable. Place the bark in the pot with the plant. Often staking is required to hold the plant upright until a new root system is formed. Give orchids strong light but not direct sunlight. Keep the medium moderately moist and when growing actively, feed with liquid fertilizer at regular intervals. Occasional misting of the plant keeps it in good condition.

Temperatures vary for the orchids, depending on the different types. They make excellent specimens for growing under artificial lights in basements where temperatures are cooler. They grow successfully in a south, east or west window.

Avoid letting the plant sit in water and drain off the excess immediately after watering. Repotting is needed only when the plant becomes root-bound. This is usually indicated by a heavy mass of roots produced outside the pot. Most orchids flower once a year. Once flowering is finished, remove the flower and keep the plant moderately moist until new growth begins, at which time an increase in watering may be needed. Start feeding the orchid again. Fertilizing during the summer months at two or three-week intervals is recommended. Use a balanced liquid fertilizer.

165. Why did the buds fall off our orchid plants before they flowered?

This is usually due to dry conditions. It is important to mist the plants more often when the flower buds are formed or grow them in groups so that there is higher humidity. Also, grow by the tray method where plants are placed in trays with pebbles and the pots are suspended above the pebbles. Keep the water in the tray to create a higher humidity around the plants. Take the plants to the sink and spray with water.

166. Our orchid plant is turning black from the roots up. How do we care for this?

Carefully remove the decayed part, take the plant out of the pot and cut away all infected parts. Repot healthy ends back into the orchid fiber. Keep it moderately moist until it starts to actively grow and at this time, increase the watering. Avoid over-watering and do not allow it to sit in the water.

167. How do I get rid of mildew on orchids?

Increase the air circulation around the plants, if possible, by using a small fan or by using a good fungicide. Apply this thoroughly around the leaves and the base of the plants.

168. How do we eliminate insects on orchids?

Scale is often a problem with orchids and is difficult to see. It usually starts along the base of the stem. Keep the plants in healthy condition. Periodic inspection is advised. Once insects are noticed, use a recommended spray to bring them under control. Several applications may be needed.

169. The leaves on my orchid plant are becoming crinkly. What do I do?

This is usually due to dry conditions. Try and increase the humidity around the plant by using the tray method. See Question 164.

170. How do I care for a peacock orchid?

See Question 164. Give it good light but not necessarily direct sun. It also needs a temperature of around 60 to 65 degrees and occasional misting.

171. My shamrock plant is dying. What do I do?

The shamrock plant is *Oxalis*. There are a number of species that are grown as house plants. All of these require good light and will tolerate some sun. It likes an average potting soil and when actively growing, keep moderately moist and give regular feedings of liquid fertilizer. When the plant's leaves start to yellow, withhold water and feed less. It is necessary to let the plant go through a resting period of six to eight weeks, at which time completely withhold watering. Then repot and redivide, if needed, and start over.

172. Is the food edible from a passion plant?

The passion plant, *Passiflora*, is commonly grown in the home. It depends on the type being grown as to whether fruit is edible. Some of them produce fruit which makes excellent eating, but primarily seed only.

173. May I grow the passion plant from seed?

The passion plant is easily grown from seed. Sow the seed and transplant when quite young. It makes an attractive flowering plant.

174. May I plant pittosporum outdoors?

The *Pittosporum tobira* is a small shrub often grown as a foliage plant. The plant is not hardy outdoors; therefore, only grow it during the summer months. It will need to be brought in before heavy frosts in the fall. Do not place outdoors until all danger of frost is past.

175. How do I care for a poinsettia plant?

The poinsettia is an attractive flowering plant and is usually secured when in full bloom. Grow it where it receives good light and a uniform temperature of 60 to 75 degrees. The plant needs adequate watering to keep it moderately moist at all times but avoid over-watering, which quickly causes a loss of roots. Occasional feedings of liquid fertilizer at two or three-week intervals when in full bloom is advised. When the plant stops flowering, gradually withhold water and place the plant in a basement or some area where it can rest for a period of two to three months. At that time, cut back the plant to within about one-third of the total height and repot into fresh soil. Place it where it receives full light and, preferably, some sun. Keep barely moist until growth begins, at which time increase watering as growth increases.

Once the plant has reached a steady growing stage, pinch it occasionally to keep it bushy and uniform. Remove small weak growth at the main stem. Once the temperatures have risen and all danger of frost has passed, place the plant outdoors where it gets the sun during morning or afternoon. Put where it receives adequate watering during the summer months.

Early in the fall before the nights get too cool, move the plant where there is less light and it is partially shaded for a couple of days. Then move into the garage and finally into the house where it is going to grow. When indoors it needs some sun. In late September, place the plant in the dark at 6 p.m. in a closet or similar area where there is no artificial light. Then take it out of the dark again at 8 a.m. and place in full light, preferably with some sun. This needs to be done every night until the plant is showing color, which is usually late October. By that time, leave it in the growing area and it will bloom normally for Christmas. If you do not put in the dark every night, it will not bloom.

176. My poinsettia rested until September. Now what do I do?

Do not allow the poinsettia to rest this long. The plant needs to rest for a period of three to six weeks early in the spring and to grow actively during the summer. A plant started in September will not flower for the following Christmas. It first needs a considerable period of steady growing. This means that little flowering will occur until the following spring. At that time when the days get longer, there is little chance of the plant forming any flower buds. It normally flowers during the shorter days. It is much better to discard the plant and purchase a new one.

177. How do I take a cutting from a poinsettia plant?

Cuttings are taken from healthy growth, usually four to six inches long just below the node. Allow the cuttings to sit for about 24 hours to thoroughly seal the ends. Then root in a mixture of peat and perlite in a temperature of 70 to 75 degrees under high humidity. Once the cuttings are rooted in four to six weeks, pot into a soil high in organic matter and grow under the normal procedure.

178. How do I establish a new poinsettia plant?

A new poinsettia plant which is rooted is grown in a soil mix high in organic matter with good drainage. Be careful not to over-water it or the roots will rot very quickly. Give it plenty of sun or grow the plant under artificial lights for 12 to 14 hours per day. Keep it as close to the light as possible. When the plant has reached sufficient height in late September, revert to placing the plant in the dark. See Question 175.

179. I want to carry my poinsettia over and flower it again next year. What is the procedure?

When flowering is finished, cut the plant back partway and place it in a storage area, basement or some other area where temperature is around 45 to 50 degrees. Leave it there for several months and in late April, grow it again. See Question 178.

180. My poinsettia has been growing well but now appears to have tiny white flies. What are they and how do you control them?

The flies you mention are called whiteflies, which are particularly prone to poinsettias. The adult lays its eggs underneath the leaves, which in turn hatch. Control these by using the synthetic Pyrethrin. Spray it thoroughly under the leaves and then on top, repeating in four to five days, if needed. Do not use the spray in enclosed areas; move the plant to a garage or open area and out of direct sun until it has had a chance to dry off.

181. How do I care for my African violets?

African violets are popular plants grown in the home, either under artificial light or near a window. The plants require 12 to 14 hours of strong light daily. They like a soil medium that is high in organic matter. They are shallow-rooted; therefore, they do not need deep pots.

Grow in either clay or plastic pots, but watch the amount of water. Keep moderately moist; avoid over-watering. Water just enough to moisten the soil and then let it dry out somewhat between waterings. Water from the bottom of the pot, but about every third or fourth watering, sufficiently water from the top and allow the excess to run into the container below. Remove the excess water about 15 minutes after watering so it is not reabsorbed into the plant medium.

The plants need good light and yet, not too much sun. If leaves are very flat on the plants, this is usually an indication that the light is too strong. On the other hand, if the leaves are upright and stretching, they are not getting enough light. Plants, once they start to bloom, will remain in constant bloom if given a proper watering and feeding program. Fertilize at regular intervals of every 12 to 14 days.

Many people prefer to grow them by the wick method. Pot them with a wick, extending it through the bottom of the pot into a reservoir below. This is ideal and an excellent way to carry plants for several weeks without having to resupply the nutrients. Periodically, however, clean the reservoir thoroughly to avoid the buildup of algae.

Plants which stop flowering when brought in the home is usually an indication that they are getting too much light or not enough light. Plants which stop flowering towards the spring usually indicates that the light is too strong. Moving them to an area where they get less light will bring them back into bloom. On the other hand, if they flower well during the summer and stop flowering towards the fall, they are not getting sufficient light. Violets do well in an east, west or north window.

Plants flower best in relatively small containers and only need repotting when the plants appear to be much too large for the pot itself. In repotting, carefully remove the plants from the pots. Then cut off about one-third of the base of the old soil ball. Loosen the sides and place them back in a good growing medium in containers somewhat larger than the original ones. Keep them barely moist until the plants are making new growth. Then go back to a normal watering period.

182. My African violets appear very dusty. How do I clean them?

The ideal way to clean the plants is to take them to a sink that has a spray nozzle and adjust the water to lukewarm. Then wash the foliage carefully, being sure you do not get excess water into the pot itself. Place the plants on a drainboard or somewhere out of direct light until they are thoroughly dry before moving them back into their permanent location. Misting and syringing plants occasionally is also helpful but avoid spreading diseases.

183. How often do African violets need fertilizer?

When African violets are growing actively, feed at regular intervals using a liquid fertilizer every two or three weeks. Any of the balanced liquid fertilizers are ideal.

184. What type of soil is best for African violets?

African violets are best grown in what is known as a soilless medium. This is a medium which contains no soil, such as one with equal amounts of fine fir bark, peat moss and perlite or other similar materials. There are several commercial African violet mixes on the market. All are ideal, although most are better with some extra organic matter, such as peat moss along with some perlite to lighten them.

185. Do I need a male and female African violet in order for them to bloom?

No. African violets do not need separate male and female plants for flowering. Flowering occurs when plants are well grown and are receiving adequate light and moisture levels. Too much light or lack of it retards flowering.

186. My African violet bloomed well until recently. Now there are no new buds. What do I do to have it bloom again?

Check back to see what has happened as far as the moisture and feeding habits are concerned. If these have remained constant, then check for a change in the light pattern. Either an increase or decrease in day length has caused this. Otherwise, if the plant has been blooming well and has stopped, increase the feeding program to allow the plant to form new buds.

187. What is and how do we treat a gray mold on the flower petals of African violets?

This is a fungus disease and is usually caused from lack of aeration. Increase the air circulation around the plants and/or apply a good fungicide to the top of the plant as needed.

188. What causes African violets to die in the center and how do we prevent this?

Plants dying in the center is often due to what is known as crown rot, a bacterial disease. It is usually caused by over-watering. If plants are kept too wet, the roots are lost and the plant starts to decay. This works up into the center of the plant. Also, mites may attack the center of the leaves. These start on the center leaves, appearing to be grayer or hairier. Leaves become very brittle and can cause the loss of the plant. In cases like this, they are difficult to control so it is better to get rid of the plant. In the case of bacterial crown rot, if it is a good variety and you want to keep it, propagate the leaf cuttings by removing a leaf and all portions of the stem except one-half inch below the leaf.

189. How do I propagate African violets?

African violets are propagated from seed, from leaf cuttings or from division. Take leaf cuttings from the healthy plants and remove all but one-half inch of the stem below the leaf. Allow leaves to sit for several hours. Then place in a rooting medium so that the stem is in the medium and the leaf is just touching. Space leaves one or two inches apart. Keep the medium at a uniform temperature of around 70 to 75 degrees and keep moderately moist. Rooting occurs in several weeks; repot four to six weeks later.

In division a plant has several crowns. Remove the plant from the potting medium, divide with a sharp knife and allow to sit for several hours to dry and dust with sulphur to prevent a fungus from getting into the stem. Place back in the rooting medium and keep barely moist until new roots are formed.

190. May I put African violets outdoors in May?

It depends on the area in which you are living. If violets are placed outdoors, put them where they are getting the same light conditions as indoors and in an area where they are protected from heavy rains to avoid over-watering. They do well in a protected spot.

191. African violets have mealy bugs. How do I control these?

Mealy bugs are a problem in African violets and with heavy infestations are rather difficult to control. Use alcohol with a cotton swab on the insects. In severe cases, apply insecticide with a pressure sprayer, getting into the base of the plant where the bugs start. Several applications are needed to bring them under control.

192. How do I care for plants in the African violet family?

The African violet family includes a broad range, such as *Gloxinia, Aeschynanthus, Columnea* and *Episcia*. This family all require a growing medium high in organic matter with good aeration. They like temperatures of 65 to 75 degrees. They need good light but no direct sun and a humidity of 30 to 40 percent. All members make excellent house plants. Check each individual species for the proper requirements.

193. How do you care for Christmas cactus?

The Christmas cactus (*Schlumbergia bridgesii*) is now available in several colors and is becoming more popular for growing in the house. The plant likes a soil that is well drained with fairly high sand content and temperatures of 65 to 75 degrees. It will grow where it receives good light and preferably some sun for two or three hours daily. Keep moderately moist when growing actively with an occasional feeding of liquid fertilizer. Avoid feeding when the plant is not growing actively. In early September, keep the plant on the drier side for a period of six to eight weeks to prevent the plant from shriveling or wilting. It needs just enough water to moisten the soil. At the end of six to eight weeks, gradually return to the normal watering period. Within the normal period, plants will set buds by Christmas.

Once the plant has flowered, it will soon start to form new growth. At this stage, increase the feeding to once every three weeks with a liquid fertilizer until growth begins to slow down. Keep moderately moist and give plenty of light. Pinch off the ends on the longer parts to ensure uniform growth. This causes the other section to branch out. Place Christmas cactus outdoors in the summer in a protected area where it receives good light and leave outdoors until early fall. At this time put it through the dry period to cause flowering again.

194. When do I dry out my Christmas cactus?

Dry out the cactus anytime from early September to the end of October or early November.

195. My Christmas cactus flowers every year around Thanksgiving and not at Christmas. How do I delay this?

This is the Thanksgiving cactus and is known as *Zygocactus truncatus*. The leaf pattern or stem pattern varies somewhat from that of the Christmas cactus. The culture, however, is the same for both with the only difference being in stem formation, the Thanksgiving cactus flowers earlier. There is also another cactus, known as the Lenten cactus, that flowers in spring. All three are very closely related.

196. Tell me how to care for a Japanese skimmia plant?

This is a small shrub that is not hardy in Zone 6 north where it is sometimes grown as a potted specimen. It likes very cool growing conditions during the winter months with temperatures around 40 to 50 degrees. The plant likes a medium light soil. Keep moderately moist and give plenty of light. Some sun is beneficial. It will flower early in the spring followed by small clusters of berries. The fragrant, yellowish flowers appear in pyramidal-shaped clusters, two or three inches long. The bright red fall fruits are a third of an inch across. The plant is grown more as a foliage decorative plant than it is as a flowering pot plant.

197. How do I care for a Bird-of-Paradise plant?

The *Strelitzia reginae* is the common Bird of Paradise plant grown as a house plant. This plant grows three to four feet high and is one that requires normal house temperatures of 65 to 75 degrees. It likes good light, preferably a south or east window where it gets some sun and an average potting soil. Check the plant periodically for scale which can be a problem and spray if needed. The plant needs to be pot-bound for best flowering. Also keep the plant somewhat on the acid side by using vinegar water or sulphur to increase the flowering.

Once the flowers have ended, remove the flower stalks. It sends up new stalks at the base of each leaf. Flowering usually occurs from early spring to late fall. Place the plant outdoors during the summer months where it recieves good light and bring indoors again before cold weather sets in in the late fall.

198. What is the best potting mix for tubers like anemones?

A good potting soil high in organic matter with superphosphate added is ideal.

199. What houseplants especially need iron?

Houseplants such as gardenias or azaleas which are acid loving can become deficient in iron, usually indicated by a chlorosis or yellowing of the leaves.

200. What is the best houseplant for a sunny location?

A wide variety of plants will grow in a sunny location and many of the flowering plants are excellent. Foliage plants, if not exposed too rapidly to strong sunlight, will also do well.

Chapter Two
Indoor Foliage Plants

General Information

There is a wide range of plant material which grows well indoors. In this particular section we will be talking about plants which produce little or no bloom but the plants are worth growing for the foliage.

In selecting foliage plants for indoors, consider the location where you want to grow them and the amount of light that is available or can be made available. Plants grow under different light conditions so consider plants which grow best under the light conditions available. The amount of direct light, as well as sufficient water and food are factors in whether the plant is successful. Most indoor foliage plants are purchased as small plants and allowed to grow; others are purchased at a desirable size and growth is maintained.

When selecting a plant, make sure that it is insect and disease-free by carefully examining the plant and the growing medium in which it is potted. When bringing the plant home, isolate it for several days to see whether any sign of insects or diseases appear. After that period if the plant appears in good condition move it to its permanent location. When moving a plant from a plant shop or other area into the home, humidity changes so accustom the plant gradually. If plants are grown under strong light, they grow under less light if the transition period is gradual. Avoid shocks.

When first bringing the plant inside, mist the plant once or twice for the first few days. Gradually decrease this to the point where misting is not necessary. Allow the plant to adjust to the humidity conditions in the area in which it is going to grow.

For the first few days, give the plant approximately the same amount of light that it had where it was purchased. Then gradually move it back to where it is getting less and less light until it is in its regular position. This transition period takes seven to 10 days. During this period keep the plant on the dry side and very few leaves will drop or change color. Sudden change in color and loss of leaves indicates shock from moving it too rapidly or from overwatering.

Give foliage plants an occasional bath by placing them in a shower or similar area and washing the foliage off thoroughly with lukewarm water. Avoid extremely cold water; this can shock the plant. When washing it off, make sure that the soil is not saturated. Wash a plant with broad leaves by hand, using a solution of warm soapy water or warm milk. Warm milk, which will not clog up the plant's pores, removes the dust and acts as a wax, giving the plant a gloss which repels dust. Avoid using commercial plant shine which plugs up the leaves and burns the foliage if used where the light is very bright.

Soil Culture

Most foliage plants are grown in a soilless media which is one that has no soil at all or, in some cases, soil is only part of the media in which they are grown. Foliage plants like a well drained media which does not allow water to sit in the media and yet allows excess water to drain through readily. Use a media which contains plenty of space for air to move freely through the root system. Lack of air in the roots causes the plant to suffocate and die. A good growing medium that is open and has good drainage is peat moss with perlite which anchors the plants. A number of commercial mixtures are available which are disease and insect-free.

Propagation

Many foliage plants are propagated from cuttings which are insect and disease-free and in good growing condition. Avoid cuttings which are long and spindly or cuttings which are taken from plants which are not a healthy color. Take cuttings six to eight inches long and cut just below the node, removing about one-third of the lower leaves. In most cases dip the cutting in a rooting hormone and then place it in a rooting media of two-thirds part perlite to one-third part peat moss. Keep moderately moist. Put cuttings in a medium and place in an area where humidity is high and temperatures are 70 to 75 degrees until the cuttings are rooted.

Many of the foliage plants are propagated from seed. Purchase fresh seed and sow it in the regular manner. Give the seedlings plenty of light until they are well established and keep the temperature 70 to 80 degrees. Many plants are also propagated by division (see Glossary), e.g. ferns. Carefully divide the plants when they become too large, keeping as much of the root system as possible. Place them back in suitable containers, keeping them moderately moist until growth becomes active.

Another method is air-layering. This is particularly effective with many members of the ficus or rubber tree family. When plants become too tall or you want to start a new plant, select a healthy stalk and then stake the plant so that it will not break off. The end to be air-layered must have good growth. Put a stake below the first cut. With a sharp knife, make a cut just below the node, about one-half inch, going in about one-third of the way on the stem and then very carefully work the knife up through the node itself. Allow the upward cut to barely penetrate the node. Be careful not to cut too far and sever the whole thing. Remove the knife and place a toothpick or other small splinter of wood at the top of the cut to keep the node apart. Take a small piece of plastic which contains a layer of wet spagnum moss with moist perlite in the center. Carefully lift the plastic with moss and perlite around the plant, making sure that the perlite comes in direct contact with the cut on the stem. Carefully work the moss around the base so that the perlite is completely around the cut end. Tie the plastic firmly below the cut then work the rest of the material in a firm ball around the cut part of the plant. It may be necessary to remove some of the leaves if they are in the way. Cut these away from the parent stalk before trying to work the plastic and moss around the plant's base. When it is thoroughly placed around the cut, add a bit of extra water to thoroughly moisten the media and then seal the top. Tie the top of the plant carefully to the stake so that it does not break off. Examine the media at regular intervals to see if extra moisture is needed. Do not allow it to dry out at any time.

Rooting starts fairly quickly. When roots show through the moss to the plastic, then the cutting is ready to remove from the parent plant. With a sharp pair of pruners, remove the cutting below where the plastic has been attached. Carefully remove the ties and the plastic from the moss, leaving the moss and perlite attached to the cutting. Pot this in a normal soil medium in a pot of sufficient size for growing. Many plants are started from air-layering in this way.

Another method of propagation is done by cutting the plant stems into sections containing at least two or three nodes. Lay the sections on their sides and cover up about halfway with soil. Keep moderately moist and place in an area where temperatures are 70 to 75 degrees. In a short period these send out new roots and make new leaf growth from a node. Once these are of sufficient size, pot individually. This works well with dracaena, the long-stem Ti plant and dieffenbachia.

Potting Methods

A number of containers are available for growing foliage plants. If the containers have drainage, no problem exists as far as watering. Containers that do not have drainage are more difficult in which to establish a good watering pattern. Put drainage material, such as coarse rock, about one to two inches in the bottom of the pots. On this place some moss or other suitable material to prevent the soil from getting down into the rocks itself. Then add the soil medium to the desired height so that the plants are no deeper in the containers than they were in the original pots. Carefully work the media firmly around the plants and moisten the soil.

Another method for containers that do not have drainage is to put a plastic tube about one inch in diameter down the side of the pot when first placing the stones in the bottom. Allow the tube to sit about halfway into the stones. Fill the containers up with soil and cut the plastic pipe to the level of the top of the container. Find out if you are over-watering by using this as you do to test oil in a car. When the plant is watered, take a stick and insert it down the plastic tube to see if water has reached the bottom; if water has, siphon the excess out. Too much water is difficult to remove without the tube.

In repotting most plants, remove one-third of the bottom of the soil ball from the old container. It contains many of the old roots which have rotted. Then on the remaining soil ball make a couple of "V" cuts on each side, removing about one inch of soil. Then add the new soil medium. This allows the new roots to penetrate into the new growing medium and quickly become established. Repotting is only needed when the container has a heavy root system which is growing above the soil or growing out through holes in the container. Avoid over-potting; this tends to spoil the appearance of the plant if the container is too dominant. In addition, a pot too large keeps the soil too wet so plants do not do as well.

Watering

Watering is extremely critical as far as foliage plants are concerned. More plants are killed through over-watering than under-watering. Keep the soil moderately moist at all times. Some plants such as cacti prefer to have soil dry out between waterings. Learn the requirements for the individual plant.

Water from either the base of the plant or from the top. Wick watering (see Glossary), is workable in many cases. The plant draws the water up from the base of the container or from a nearby container to avoid over-watering. While watering from the bottom, also water periodically from the top so that excess water is allowed to wash out through the base of the container to wash away any excess salts which build up in the soil and cause burning. In containers that do not have drainage, make sure not to over-water or the water builds up and shuts off the air of the plant, causing roots as well as the plant to die.

There are no set instructions for watering plants. It depends on the individual plant, its rate of growth and under what conditions it is growing. If it gets a lot of light and is in an area that is quite warm, the plant needs more water than the plant does under cooler conditions. Examine the growing medium at regular intervals, checking with your finger or by using a soil meter. If using your finger, water when the plant is dry two inches into the medium. Thoroughly moisten the medium and then let it dry out between waterings. Always use water at room temperature. Excessively cold water is a shock to the plants and can cause loss of part of the root system. Hot water also kills the roots rapidly.

Fertilizing

All plants need nutrients to grow. A plant which has just been repotted usually has sufficient nutrients to supply the plant for three to four months. Plants in established pots need feeding occasionally to keep them in good condition. Only fertilize when plants are growing actively. This usually is from early spring through early fall. Avoid feeding plants during winter when the plants are resting. Over-feeding causes burning of the roots and loss of the plants.

In most cases, a balanced fertilizer is recommended such as 20-20-20. Feeding most foliage plants two to three times during the growing season is sufficient. If a plant is in a container where it is extremely pot-bound and you do not plan to repot it, extra feeding is needed. Avoid feeding a plant if it is doing poorly. If a plant is dropping leaves, find out if it is from over-watering; feeding only compounds the problem. If there has been a loss of roots, excess feeding burns the roots even more. In applying fertilizer to foliage plants, keep the soil moderately moist and if necessary, apply half the recommended amount of water one day followed by the proper application of fertilizer the next day. Applying fertilizer to very dry soil burns the root system of the plants.

Insect and Disease Control

Even though you try to grow an insect and disease-free plant, the plant may still become infected. In selecting new plants, examine them carefully and make sure that they are free of all insects and diseases. When first bringing them into the home, isolate them for seven to 10 days before placing them with the rest of your plants.

Insects which attack indoor foliage plants are listed below.

Aphids are common problems easily controlled by either a forceful stream of water, use of a mild insecticide, or by dipping parts of the plant in soapy water.

Mealy bugs appear as small bits of cotton usually at the base of the stem or underneath the leaves and feed by sucking the juices out of the plant. They are easily controlled by washing with a strong force of water or by using an insecticide with a pressure sprayer which penetrates through the hairs of the insects.

Scales are more difficult to control. They usually appear as sticky substances on the leaves of the plants. Brown scales often appear on the main stems of the plants or on the undersides of the leaves. Numerous small insects lie underneath the hard scales and feed by sucking the juices out of the plants. To control scales effectively, use an oil-base spray and apply it two or three times. In applying insecticides, move the plants outside or to a well ventilated area, keeping them away from areas where food is being stored or served.

Spider mites are a common problem with houseplants, particularly during the winter months, during dry conditions, or in high temperatures during the summer. Use an insecticide just for spider mite control and apply at regular intervals every three days until brought under full control. Kelthane is an excellent insecticide for spider mites.

Whiteflies are tiny white flies usually found underneath the leaves. Eggs hatch out when the temperature is fairly warm. They fly onto other parts of the plant when the plant is moved. Control the flies by using synthetic Pyrethrin. Plants grown in cool areas have less problems as far as insects and diseases are concerned than those in warm temperatures.

Bacterial and fungus diseases are fairly prominent on some plants and are usually noticed by a change in the color or by spotting or dying leaves. Examine the plants at regular intervals and at the first sign of any problem, have it diagnosed and follow the methods for control. If plants are infected with an insect or a disease, avoid washing them. This spreads the disease more quickly. Isolate infected plants until the insect or disease is brought under control before placing them back with your other plants.

QUESTIONS

1. If a houseplant has yellowing leaves, does feeding help?

Feeding may help if other conditions are correct. Check to make sure the plant has not been over-watered. If the plant is pot-bound, yellowing leaves is usually an indication that the plant is under-nourished. If the plant is growing actively, feed at regular intervals. If the plant is pot-bound, even if it is not actively growing, continue feeding it. Feeding foliage plants three to four times during the growing season and an occasional feeding when it is not actively growing is sufficient.

2. What are the signals that plants are over-watered?

One indication is a sudden dropping of leaves with no discoloration or leaves yellowing rapidly and then falling. If the plant is being over-watered and leaves are dropping, allow the soil to dry out between waterings and then only use enough water to moisten the soil. Under-watering also causes the same symptoms.

3. I have over-watered a succulent plant. Is there any way to salvage it?

The succulent is salvaged by removing it from the container it is in and replacing with fresh soil. Repot as soon as the condition is first noticed. When repotted, apply just enough water to moisten the media and then allow to dry out somewhat until the plant is healthy again. Now use a normal watering pattern.

4. Our houseplants under artificial light are dropping their leaves. What do we do?

Plants under artificial light need at least 12 hours of light during the day. Place the lights as close to the plants as possible. If they are receiving sufficient light, check that the plants are not being over-watered or under-watered. If light conditions and water are satisfactory, the plants may need extra feeding to correct the situation.

5. After air-layering, the plant has rooted. Do I remove or leave the moss on a new shoot?

I prefer to leave the moss. In removing the moss be extremely careful that you do not break the root system.

6. What is the best care for aloes?

Aloes make excellent houseplants and are a member of the lily family. They like a potting soil high in organic matter and enriched with superphosphate. Small plants are readily obtained from garden centers or by dividing a large plant which has produced a number of offshoots. Remove the plants from the parent plant, keeping small roots attached and place so that the crown of the plant is just below the level of the medium. Plants like as much light as possible. Keep the soil moderately moist and avoid over-watering. They will take more moisture than cacti since they are not a real cactus. Once the plants are well established in the pots, an occasional feeding of liquid fertilizer may be necessary. Apply this when the soil is moderately moist.

7. The leaves are dropping off our aloe plant. What do we do?

Avoid over-watering the plant which causes the leaves to rot at the base. Remove any leaves which are in poor condition and withhold the water until the soil is allowed to dry out considerably. Avoid over-feeding the plants.

8. How do I best care for an aluminum plant?

The aluminum plant (*Pilea*) is best started by new cuttings each year from the parent plant. It likes a light, semi-sunny, semi-shaded area, temperature of 70 degrees and a soil which is well drained with plenty of organic matter. Keep it evenly moist with an occasional feeding of liquid fertilizer once the plant is well established. Pinch the tip to make the plant compact and prevent legginess.

9. Our asparagus fern is growing out of the pot. What do we do?

Asparagus fern is a member of the lily family and not a true fern. It grows by producing a lot of thick, fleshy roots and when these become extremely heavy, they tend to push the soil out of the pot. The plant needs repotting. Carefully remove from the pot and put into a larger container. You can also divide it by cutting the parent plant in sections retaining some of the thick, fleshy roots with some of the prongs attached for potting in appropriately sized containers.

10. Our asparagus fern tips are browning. What do we do?

This is due to low humidity. Increase the humidity in the room or place the plant on a tray of pebbles with water so that the pot itself is not sitting in water. As the water evaporates, this increases the humidity around the plant.

11. Branches on our asparagus fern are starting to spread and they are dropping leaves quickly. What do we do?

This can be caused by the plant not getting enough nourishment. If it is pot-bound, extra feeding of a liquid fertilizer is necessary. Also, give the plant as much light as possible. Some sun is beneficial.

12. How do we divide an asparagus fern?

Remove plant from the pot and cut the growth into sections, retaining some of the thick, fleshy roots with new fronds attached. Pot these up in new containers and cover the fleshy roots. Keep them moderately moist until growth becomes more active.

13. Why are the leaves turning yellow and dropping off our asparagus fern?

This is usually an indication the plant is not getting enough nourishment. If you are using a liquid fertilizer, apply more regularly.

14. How do I propagate an asparagus fern from its tuberous roots?

Carefully remove the parent plant from the pot, wash off all the excess soil and carefully separate the roots. Cut off each root which has a frond attached and place in a container with soil. Keep moderately moist until growth becomes more active. Another method is to cut the plant into several sections and pot.

15. What do I do to get rid of the brown needles on my asparagus fern?

Remove by hand. The brown needles are avoided by increasing the feeding of the plant or by giving it more light if the plant is getting sufficient nourishment.

16. When is the best time to divide an asparagus fern?

This is done almost anytime during the year once the plant becomes pot-bound; otherwise, divide it in early spring or late fall.

17. We have a beautiful old aralia, a parsley type, that is dying. What do we do to salvage it?

The parsley aralia (*Aralia fruticosa* 'Elegans') is probably dying due to over-watering. Aralias like to receive sufficient light and moisture and then be allowed to dry out considerably before more water is applied. Over-watering quickly causes the leaves to drop. Repot your plant into a smaller container with fresh growing media that is high in organic matter and has plenty of drainage. Barely moisten the soil and keep it just moist until the plant begins to show new growth. Then return to a normal watering pattern. Give the plant sufficient light but not direct sunlight until it is back to normal conditions.

18. I have a false aralia plant. Do I cut it back?

Cut back the false aralia (*Dizygotheca elegantissima*) if it has become tall and spindly. When cutting back, withhold water considerably until new growth begins.

19. How do I propagate an aralia?

Aralias are best started from fresh seeds. Cuttings also work if rooted under high humidity conditions, 50 to 60 percent, and temperatures of 75 to 80 degrees.

20. How do we eliminate scale on a false aralia?

Control scale by using an oil-based spray under and on top of the leaves. Move the plant to a well ventilated area when doing this and keep it out of direct sun until the plant has dried. Repeat in two to three weeks, if necessary.

21. What is the best way to take care of a balfour aralia?

The balfour aralia (*Polyscias balfouriana*) likes a barely sunny to semi-shaded area with a temperature of around 70 degrees and fairly high humidity, 40 to 50 percent. The appropriate growing media is high in organic matter with good drainage. When watering, moderately moisten the soil and let it dry out somewhat before watering again. Avoid over-watering which causes leaves to drop. When the plant is well established, occasionally use liquid fertilizer.

22. My ming aralia has little brown spots on it. How do I eliminate them?

The ming aralia (*Polyscias fruticosa*) has scale. These are usually found along the main stem and on the leaf stems, and sometimes both underneath and on top of the leaves. This is best controlled by using an oil-base spray, applying it in a well ventilated area to the underside and top of the leaves and along the main stem. Allow the plant to dry thoroughly and keep away from direct sun until the plant is thoroughly dry. Repeat in two to three weeks as needed.

23. My six-foot aralia is dropping leaves. What do I do?

Avoid over-watering. Allow plant to dry out between waterings and give plenty of light.

24. How do I care for an areca palm?

The areca palm (*Chrysalidocarpus lutescens*) is a plant which likes a warm, partially sunny location with a sandy soil kept constantly moist. Avoid over-watering. The best soil media is well drained, which allows excess water to pass through and yet does not dry out too rapidly. Avoid over-feeding the plant and apply liquid fertilizer only when the plant is making new growth.

25. The leaves on our areca palm are turning yellow. What do I do?

Keep the plant moderately moist. If the plant is actively growing, occasionally feed it liquid fertilizer.

26. Our areca palm is turning brown. What do we do?

Browning occurs on the tips due to low humidity. If more rampant, have the plant checked to see if there is another leaf problem. Use the appropriate sprays to bring it under control. If necessary, remove the frond. If disease is in the center of the plant, take it out of the present container, remove all infected parts and repot with fresh soil.

27. Our palm tree is losing leaves. What do I do?

As new fronds appear, the older ones die periodically. Keep the plant moderately moist with good light conditions and occasional feeding. Avoid over-watering.

28. The leaves on our areca palm are splitting. What do we do about it?

Splitting of the leaves is caused from damage to the plant. Avoid brushing against the plant. Move it to a protected spot.

29. How do I know when to water an areca palm?

If the palm is in a container with good drainage, keep it moderately moist at all times. Avoid over-watering. If the plant has no drainage, let it dry out two to three inches into the soil before reapplying water. Then add just enough to moisten the media.

30. What are the light requirements for an areca palm?

The areca palm stands strong light or semi-shaded conditions. If grown in poor light, do not water as often and avoid over-feeding.

31. How do I divide an areca palm?

Divide the plant in early spring by removing it from the present container and separating the base into several parts that separate freely.

32. What kind of soil mixture is best for growing an arrowhead vine?

The arrowhead vine (*Syngonium albolineatum*) likes a growing media with plenty of organic matter and good drainage.

33. What is the best care for an arrowhead plant?

Keep the arrowhead plant in an area with a moderate amount of light. Remove the growing tip from the plant at intervals to make the plant bush out and prevent it from becoming too long and leggy. Once the plant is heavily rooted, occasionally feed it liquid fertilizer.

34. How do I best propagate an arrowhead vine?

Remove the growing tip back to three to four leaves, cut just below the first leaf and then remove the two lower leaves. Place it in a rooting media of three parts perlite to one part peat moss. Keep it moderately moist and quite humid and it will root in two to three weeks.

35. How do I repot an aspidistra?

The *Aspidistra elatior* is best repotted in early spring before new growth begins. Divide the plant up into sections with good growing eyes. Repot into ordinary potting soil and keep just barely moist until new growth begins.

36. Do aspidistra plants grow in poor light?

Aspidistras grow well under poor light conditions. Adjust them gradually to this and water occasionally.

37. What are the requirements for growing avocado seedlings?

Use a soil that is well drained with plenty of organic matter. Transplant seedlings as soon as growth is two to three inches long. Keep them moderately moist and give them as much light as possible, preferably some sunlight.

38. I have black spots on the leaves of my avocado plant. What do I do?

Black spots on leaves indicate improper nutrition or disease. Spray underneath and on top of the leaves with a fungicide at 10-day intervals.

39. Do I pinch back an avocado plant to make it grow more fully?

Pinch avocado seedlings when growth is small by removing the growing center. This causes the plant to send out new ends. As these start to elongate, pinch back which keeps them branching out. Occasionally when removing the growing tip only one side branch emerges; however, pinch this back when of sufficient length and it in turn will rebranch.

40. How do I start a plant from an avocado pit?

Select a ripe pit and place three toothpicks in the center of the pit. Place the larger half of the base in water. It takes several weeks to a couple of months before growth from the pit begins. When the growth sends out roots, pot it. See Question 37.

41. May I plant an avocado plant grown from seed outdoors?

Place the plant outdoors in Zone 6 when all danger of frost is past and bring inside before heavy frost occurs in the fall.

42. Do I cut back an avocado plant to make it sprout branches?

Cut back avocado plant anytime. If it is quite tall, do not cut back too severely; otherwise, it is difficult to get side branches to emerge. Pinch back three to four inches of the top growth only.

43. May I grow baby's-tears in a hanging basket?

Baby's-tears (*Helxine soleirolii*) likes high humidity and does not adapt too well to hanging baskets except in greenhouses or areas where humidity is very high. It is better to suspend the pot over a tray of moist sand or water. As the water evaporates, it creates a higher humidity and the plant trails down over the sides of the pot.

44. Baby's-tears continue to brown on the edges. What causes this and how do I prevent it?

The browning is caused by too low humidity. Place the plant on a tray of moist sand or pebbles to prevent this from reoccurring.

45. Some of the fronds on our bamboo palm are dying but new shoots are appearing. What do we do?

This often happens with a bamboo palm. Avoid this by giving the plant plenty of rooting room. Keep moderately moist at all times and give it sufficient light. Cut off old fronds as close to the main trunk as possible once they start to brown heavily.

46. May I cut off the top of my bamboo palm?

Avoid removing the top unless new shoots are coming from the base. Remove the top only to control the height of the plant.

47. I have some root cuttings of a bamboo plant I got in Washington, D.C. How do I propagate them?

Place them in an area where the soil is well prepared with plenty of organic matter. Keep moderately moist, not allowing the soil to dry out at anytime. Apply a light mulch to keep the soil more moist. As the weather conditions stay around 55 to 65 degrees, the cuttings begin to root and send up new shoots very quickly.

48. When and how do I cut back a bamboo?

Cut back a bamboo in early spring to control the height of the plant. Remove a lot of the top growth and keep moist at all times. As new growth begins, start feeding the plant with a regular fertilizer. Bamboo is a heavy feeder.

49. When is the best time to transplant bamboo?

Transplant in early spring by digging up the clumps as growth first starts to show above ground. When bamboo is grown as a potted plant indoors, early spring is also the time to take it out of the pot. Redivide it and repot into fresh containers.

50. How do I best grow a banana plant?

The banana plant (*Musa* sp.) adapts well to pot culture. Grow indoors where plenty of light is available. It likes a light, sunny to semi-shaded area, temperatures of 60 to 70 degrees and normal humidity of 30 to 40 percent. The soil should be high in organic matter and well drained. Keep young plants evenly moist and feed biweekly in spring and summer with a liquid fertilizer. Propagate new shoots in March by removing the suckers which form at the base of the parent plant. Also, some species are available from seed. Start them in late winter or early spring. Place plants outdoors in protected positions during the summer months but bring inside before cold weather comes in the fall.

51. What kind of fertilizer do I use on banana plants?

Any of the fertilizers recommended for houseplants of a balanced nature such as a 20-20-20 would be ideal to use on the plant as needed.

52. How do I grow banana cavendish?

Banana cavendish is *Musa nana* and is commonly called the dwarf or lady-finger banana. It is from southern China and bears edible fruit over 13 inches long. See Question 50. for proper growing conditions.

53. How long does it take to root begonias?

Root begonias from leaf cuttings by separating the leaf from the parent plant, leaving about one inch of the petiole attached to the leaf. Use a seed mix such as Jiffy Mix. Lay the leaf on the mix with the petiole buried. The plant will send up new shoots around the base of the leaf where the stems are attached in four to six weeks. Keep at temperatures 70 to 75 degrees.

54. My rex begonias are growing well but outer leaves keep turning brown. How do I prevent this?

Rex begonias like high humidity of 50 to 60 percent. Place over trays containing pebbles with water to create a higher humidity around the plants. Avoid too high of a humidity which causes fungus disease.

55. What is the best culture for a bird's-nest fern?

The bird's-nest fern (*Asplenium nidus*) is an excellent plant for growing in the home. It likes medium light to semi-shaded conditions. Keep temperatures on the cooler side and not over 70 to 75 degrees. Humidity is best at 30 percent or more except during the winter when high humidity can cause browning of the fronds. It likes soil media that is well drained and high in leaf mold. Keep it evenly moist and avoid applying fertilizers which burn. Use fertilizer once or twice at half strength when new fronds are forming on an established plant.

56. I have spots on a bird's-nest fern. What is the cause and how do I get rid of them?

If the spots are on the underside of the fronds near the middle section, these are spores, the plant's way of producing new plants. On the other hand, if these are irregular spots and up to one-fourth inch in length, it may be scale. Carefully remove the scale by scrapping it off with a toothpick or other similar object, making sure that you do not injure the fronds, or by using a light oil-based insecticide. Move the plant to a well ventilated area, out of the direct sun and spray the fronds.

57. What caused the leaves of my bird's-nest fern to turn brown and what do I do about it?

Browning of the fronds is caused by too high humidity. If plant is in a very humid condition move it to a drier area. Make sure the plant is disease-free.

58. How do I best repot a bloodleaf plant?

Remove the plant from the old pot. Then remove one-third of the growing media at the base of the plant. With a sharp knife, make two slits on the opposite sides of the remaining soil ball. Remove about one inch of soil out of this, repot into a general potting soil and keep moderately moist until well established.

59. Our bonsai tree is turning brown. What do I do?

Keep the bonsai plant where humidity is quite high. Spray or mist occasionally. If growing actively, the plant needs sufficient nourishment, but do not overfeed. Over-fertilization causes browning of the tips.

60. When do I prune my bonsai plants?

Prune bonsai plants as soon as the new growth begins to harden-off. Remove most of the growth with a sharp pair of pruners or scissors. At least once a year, remove the plant from the container it is growing in and prune the root system.

61. My bonsai plant has done well all summer but in the fall started turning brown. How do I prevent this?

It is normal for the bonsai to lose leaves. On the other hand, if the plant is an evergreen, browning is caused by too high of a temperature. Move the plant to a cool area where there is good air circulation. Keep it out of direct sunlight and keep moderately moist, allowing it to harden-off for the winter.

62. How do I best care for a Boston fern?

The Boston fern (*Nephrolepis*) likes a growing medium high in organic matter with good drainage. It grows best in a semi-sunny to semi-shady area with temperatures not over 75 degrees in winter with high humidity. For best results grow on a pebble tray of water with the plant suspended above the water. As the water evaporates, it increases the humidity around the plant. When the plant is growing actively, give it regular feedings of fertilizer. When plant is over-grown and producing a lot of roots outside of the pot, repot it. Remove from the old container along with one-third to one-half of the old soil from the bottom of the pot and divide the plant up into several sections. Repot it back into suitable container. Keep barely moist until new growth begins; then gradually return to a normal watering pattern.

63. How do I propagate a Boston fern?

The Boston fern is propagated by dividing the plant as described in Question 62 or by taking the spores which are produced on the under side of many of the fronds. Dust these spores, which look like tiny brown dots onto a soil seedling medium. Moisten the medium thoroughly and then place a pane of glass over the top, keeping the pot in an area where it receives little light and a temperature of 60 to 70 degrees. In six to eight weeks, the tops appear green and shortly after, miniature fronds appear. When large enough, separate into individual containers.

64. What is the best food for fertilizing a Boston fern?

Any of the fertilizers for houseplants are ideal. Follow the directions on the container and apply when the growing medium is moderately moist.

65. Our Boston ferns are turning brown at the tips. What do we do?

Browning of the tips is caused by very low humidity. Increase the humidity and remove the brown tips with a sharp pair of scissors.

66. How do I repot a spindly Boston fern?

Remove plant from the old pot and cut the growth back to within two to three inches of the top of the growing medium. See Question 62.

67. What is causing my Boston fern to die?

Boston ferns die for several reasons – not high enough humidity or because the plants have outgrown the pots and are not getting sufficient nourishment.

68. We have scale on our Boston fern. What do we do?

Cut the plant back heavily, removing most of the growth. Then use Diazinon at about half strength and repeat again in about 10 days. During this period keep the plant on the dry side. Repotting may be necessary. Make sure the spray does not burn the plant.

69. When is a good time to transplant a large Boston fern?

The Boston fern is best transplanted in early spring just before it makes new growth or in late fall.

70. How do I eliminate bugs on the underside of the fronds of the Boston fern?

Make sure the bugs are not the tiny spores the plant uses to reproduce itself. Spores are produced in two lines on each side of the small fronds. If the spots are irregular, they are scale. See Question 68.

71. How do I best care for a fluffy-ruffle fern?

The fluffy-ruffle fern is a variety of Boston fern and requires the same treatment but a higher humidity than the Boston fern.

72. We have cotton-like insects on our fluffy-ruffle fern. What do we do?

This is a mealy bug and is difficult to control on the fluffy-ruffle fern. Cut the plant back severely and then wash the plant with a forceful stream of water. If this does not clear it up, use Diazinon. See Question 68.

73. Our Tahitian bridal veil is not doing well. What do we do?

The bridal veil is often called Spanish shawl and is *Schizocentron elegans*. It likes a semi-sunny to semi-shaded area, temperatures not over 70 degrees, fairly high humidity and a growing medium high in organic matter which allows for good aeration. Keep moderately moist at all times. As the plant becomes older, cut back as needed and withhold watering somewhat until new growth begins. Heavy growing plants need liquid fertilizer at regular intervals when growing actively. Propagate the plant from cuttings rooted in a warm area with high humidity.

74. What is the best soil to use when repotting a cactus plant?

The best soil is two parts sand and one part each of loam and leaf mold. Mix these together and add a small amount of superphosphate.

75. What is the best care for cacti?

Cacti like semi-sunny conditions. They do well in 60 to 70 degrees and average humidity of 30 percent with some fresh air. When replanting cacti, repot (see Question 74) and let them stay for several weeks before adding any moisture. Moisten the soil and allow to dry out between waterings. During the normal growing season, which is in early spring, water at regular intervals, being careful not to over-water. In late summer begin to withhold watering again, only watering once every three to four weeks. Fertilizing is not necessary unless plants are pot-bound.

76. Is March too soon to place cacti outside?

March is much too early in Zone 6 for placing the plants outside. Wait until all danger of frost is past.

77. My cactus plant has a graying, white material on it and when scraped, it comes off. Is this harmful to the plant?

The white material is scale which many cactus plants are subject to. Remove it by scrapping or by using a cotton swab dipped in alcohol. Apply a systemic spray such as Di-Syston to the soil.

78. How do I best trim or prune a cactus?

Cut back cactus plant when overgrown or when they have multiple stems by using a sharp knife. Remove the excess growth and sear the ends to prevent bleeding if it is a milk-type cactus. It seals in several hours. Trim immediately after flowering or in early spring before new growth begins.

79. We have a white, sticky substance on our cactus. What do we do?

This is a mealy bug and is brought under control by using a forceful stream of water and washing it off by using an insecticide under pressure to reach all areas, or by using a systemic insecticide. See Question 77.

80. My cactus is rotting to the ground. May I root the top?

This is caused from over-watering. Remove the plant from the growing media and throw away all decaying material. Let the plant sit for 24 to 48 hours to seal and then place back into the growing media, keeping it just moist until new roots begin to form.

81. How do I best care for a barrel cactus during the winter?

Keep the barrel cactus on the dry side during the winter months, giving it just enough water to keep it from shriveling. Water lightly once every three to four weeks. Place plants where temperatures are quite cool, as low as 45 to 50 degrees.

82. May I put a barrel cactus outside in the summer and indoors in the winter?

Yes. Put outside after danger of frost is past and bring indoors in late September.

83. Our milk cactus is shriveling up. What do we do?

The milk cactus (*Euphorbia*) is shriveling due to insufficient moisture. If only watering occasionally, water it more often; on the other hand, avoid over-watering which also causes loss of the root system.

84. How do I best care for a burro-tail plant?

The burro-tail plant (*Sedum morganianum*) is an attractive hanging plant. It likes the same growing medium as any other cactus. See Question 74. Water it enough to moisten the soil and allow it to dry out between watering. Avoid feeding the plant unless it is growing actively. Pinch the tips back to cause bushiness and to keep the plant compact.

85. How do I plant cactus seeds. How do I care for the seedlings?

Select a fine seed mix such as Jiffy Mix. Use fresh seed and sow lightly on top of the medium. Cover lightly. Moisten and then place a glass or cellophane over the mix. Place in a propagating house or warm moist area or other similar area. Seedlings start to grow fairly quickly. Several months are required before they are ready for transplanting. When seedlings are of sufficient size, carefully remove them with a pair of tweezers or tongs and place in the regular cactus mix of two parts sand and one part each of loam and leaf mold.

86. How do I make cuttings from cactus?

Take individual stems or leaves as cuttings. Allow them to sit for 24 to 48 hours to dry off and then place about one-third of the base in a cactus mix. Keep barely moist and cuttings will root in several weeks.

87. May I remove shoots on the side of a cactus and propagate them?

Yes. Remove the shoots with a sharp knife and allow them to sit for 24 to 48 hours before potting in the normal manner.

88. How frequently do I water cactus plants?

Start in February. Water enough to moisten the soil and water at two to three-week intervals when growth becomes active. In late summer, gradually withhold watering so that you are watering only once every three to four weeks. Avoid over-watering at any time.

89. How do I best water a pencil cactus?

The pencil cactus (*Pedilanthus*) is watered in the same way as you would any other cactus. See Question 88.

90. How do I best care for caladiums?

Caladiums are attractive foliage plants that like a growing media high in organic matter with good drainage and strong light but no direct sunlight. Water enough to moisten the media thoroughly and then allow to dry out somewhat between waterings but prevent the plants from shriveling. When first starting, temperatures are best between 75 to 80 degrees. Once growth becomes active, lower the temperature to 60 to 70 degrees. Occasionally feed them fish fertilizer at regular intervals.

91. How do I eliminate insects on a caladium?

Control insects by using an insecticide such as Diazinon. Apply at half strength to avoid burning of the leaves. Repeat as needed.

92. What is the best way to care for caladiums?

Caladiums continue growing actively if given sufficient moisture and food until late summer. At that time leaves start to yellow and die. Gradually withhold the watering until the foliage has died. Then remove the bulbs from the soil and place in an area where they receive good aeration and the temperature is around 45 to 55 degrees. Store the bulbs in moist peat moss with temperatures 75 to 80 degrees and high humidity until growth becomes active.

93. How do we get rid of a white powdery coating on our caladium plant?

This is mildew and is controlled by using a fungicide, applying it underneath and on top of the leaves and repeating in seven to 10 days.

94. How do I propagate a century plant?

The century plant (*Agave*) is propagated by off-shoots which emerge from the base of the plant. When these are of sufficient size, they are fairly well rooted. Sever from the crown plant with a sharp knife.

95. How do we best care for century plants?

Plants like a light sunny area, temperatures of 60 to 70 degrees and little water when soil is bone dry on the surface. Repot when they become too large for the container by using a good cactus mix.

96. The leaves on our Chinese evergreen are turning yellow. What do I do?

The Chinese evergreen (*Aglaonema*) is a plant that likes average potting soil. Keep moderately moist at all times. The plant grows well in average light or shaded conditions. Do not let it sit in water at anytime. Over-watering or lack of nutrients causes yellowing of the leaves. Occasionally feed when plant is actively growing.

97. May I air-layer a Chinese evergreen that is doing poorly?

Air-layering aids in starting new plants; however, Chinese evergreens propagate readily from cuttings. Allow the cuttings to sit for several hours to dry off and then place in a good rooting medium to produce roots in three to four weeks.

98. How do I air-layer a Chinese evergreen?

See article on Propagation at beginning of this chapter.

99. How do I plant a coconut?

The coconut (*Cocas nucifera*) is the common coconut palm. This is grown from seed. Set the unhusked nut of the coconut in soil so that most of it is above the soil with the stalk depression at an angle to allow some water to seep into it when you water the seed, which should be done daily. The coconut takes four to five months to germinate in a temperature of 70 to 75 degrees. It likes a sandy soil with equal amounts of organic matter. Keep constantly moist.

100. How do I repot a bamboo palm?

See Question 35.

101. How do I care for a coffee tree plant?

The coffee tree (*Coffea arabica*) makes an excellent potted plant and likes a soil well drained with plenty of organic matter. Proper lighting is essential. Place in a south or west window from late fall to early spring with some shading during the summer months. Keep the soil moderately moist but avoid over-watering. Check the plant periodically. It is subject to mealy bugs.

102. Our coleus plant has two and three leafy stems. Do I propagate them separately?

The coleus is a plant easily propagated from cuttings. Select cuttings with four to six sets of leaves, cutting just below the bottom leaf. Remove a few of the lower leaves. They root very rapidly in a regular medium. Each of these makes a new plant. As plants start to grow, pinch the center out to cause bushiness.

103. My coleus has started to flower and in removing these, keeps sending up new flower heads with no new leaf shoots. What do I do to make it branch out?

Coleus, once allowed to flower, usually does not come back with vegetative growth. Once flowering is finished, most plants are best discarded. Start with new ones.

104. How do I eliminate mealy bugs from coleus?

Mealy bugs are a problem on coleus and need to be checked at regular intervals to eliminate them before they become well established. Use rubbing alcohol with cotton swabs. In bad cases, spray with pressure with a good insecticide.

105. What are the best growing conditions for crassula?

Crassula likes the same soil conditions as most cactus plants. Good drainage is essential. Keep the soil moderately moist but allow to dry out between waterings. Plants like strong light. Keep in an east, west or south window.

106. What do I do to eliminate leaf drop from a croton plant?

The croton plant (*Codiaeum*) likes a growing medium high in organic matter with excellent drainage. Keep the plant moderately moist but avoid over-watering. Allow to dry out somewhat between waterings. Humidity needs to be fairly high when plants are first brought into the house. Occasional misting is beneficial.

107. Do I prune a croton in February?

Prune the croton in February by cutting back extra growth to encourage new breaks.

108. How do you trim croton plants?

Remove extra growth with a sharp knife and a pair of sharp pruners, cutting just above the leaf so that the shoots emerge as you choose. Pruning a leaf on the inside of the plant causes new growth inside the plant. If a leaf pointing outside is pruned, growth emerges from the center.

109. How do you care for a dieffenbachia?

The dieffenbachia is an attractive foliage plant in the home. It likes semi-sunny to shady conditions. Average humidity and temperatures of 60 to 70 degrees are ideal. Use soil high in organic matter that drains well. Moisten the plant thoroughly and then do not water until the soil has completely dried out. Avoid over-watering; this causes loss of plant roots. When the plant is growing actively and becoming pot-bound, feed occasionally with liquid fertilizer.

110. How do you root a dieffenbachia?

The dieffenbachia is propagated from stem cuttings usually about four to six inches long. Make cuttings and allow to sit for several hours to dry off. Then place in a rooting medium and keep barely moist. They root in three to four weeks. Cut long, bare stems into sections two to three inches long, place on their sides, cover up about halfway and keep moderately moist. They in turn send up new shoots in four to six weeks.

111. The tips on the dieffenbachia are browning and there are spots on the underside of the leaves. What do I do?

Check for scale insects. If these come off fairly easily by scrapping, then apply a good insecticide with an oil-base.

112. Do I grow dieffenbachia from seed and, if so, where do I obtain them?

Dieffenbachia flowers but rarely sets seed. It is normally propagated from either stem cuttings or tip growth. See Question 110.

113. How often do dieffenbachia bloom?

This depends on the individual plant. Some plants will flower more often than others. Often when the plant is pot-bound and reaches full growth, flowers are occasionally produced. These are not particularly showy. The plants are grown for the color foliage and not for the flower.

114. How do I get rid of the fungus moth in the soil of a dieffenbachia?

Give a light application of a mild insecticide. A repeat application in two to three weeks may be necessary.

115. What is the best care for a dracaena plant?

The dracaena likes a light to moderately light exposure. The best soil is equal parts of loam, sand and peat moss. Keep evenly moist. Avoid over-watering and do not let plant sit in water at anytime. Allow the plants to dry out somewhat between waterings. Wash the foliage periodically to keep it free of dust. This helps control any insects. Avoid feeding unless plants are pot-bound and making new growth. Two or three feedings of a balanced fertilizer for houseplants during the year is recommended.

116. How do I eliminate yellowing of leaves on a dracaena?

Yellowing of leaves is an indication of over-watering. Let the plant dry out between waterings. If watering is uniform and plant is pot-bound, yellowing may be caused by lack of nutrients. Increase feeding.

117. The leaf tips of my dracaena are turning brown. What do I do?

Browning usually occurs due to low humidity in the home. Remove the brown tips by using a sharp pair of scissors. Cut them off as they occur. Increase the humidity.

118. What is causing leaf drop on a dracaena massangeana?

Dracaena massangeana is extremely susceptible to over-watering. Moisten the soil and then let it dry out before watering again.

119. How do you treat tip blight on dracaena massangeana?

Tip blight is a blackening in irregular patches, starting from the tip of the leaf and working down the sides. This is a bacterial disease. Bring under control when first noticed by using a fungicide, such as Phaltan. Apply underneath and on top of the leaves down into the center growing tip. Cut away heavily infected leaves.

120. How do I propagate dracaenas?

Plants are propagated by stem cuttings or by root division when large enough.

121. What is the best culture for an elephant's-ear plant?

The elephant's-ear plant (*Colocasia esculenta*) comes from Hawaii and makes a popular foliage plant for growing outdoors. It likes a semi-shaded area for best growth and a soil well enriched with organic matter. Keep moderately moist.

122. May I grow the elephant's-ear plant as a houseplant?

Grow the elephant's-ear (*Colocasia esculenta*) indoors as a houseplant in a large container and allow a moderate amount of strong light.

123. Does an elephant's-ear plant over-winter outside?

The elephant's-ear does not over-winter outside in Zone 6 except in very mild winters if heavily mulched. Dig up in the fall and keep indoors until spring. An elephant's-ear over-winters in milder zones.

124. How do I carry over elephant's-ear plants through the winter?

Dig up plants in the fall as soon as they are affected by frost. Dry them off in a well aired area for several days and then remove all excess soil and dead plant material. Place them in a tray in peat moss for good air circulation. Check them occasionally in storage of temperature from 45 to 55 degrees and add a little water to keep them from drying out.

125. How do you propagate English ivy?

Take cuttings three to four inches long, root and repot.

126. Our English ivy is drying up. What do we do?

Keep moderately moist and allow strong light.

127. How do you care for an eucalyptus tree?

Use potting soil with a high amount of organic matter, temperatures of 60 to 70 degrees and strong light. Keep the soil moderately moist.

128. How do you best care for an elkhorn and staghorn fern?

Grow the elkhorn fern (*Platycerium*) on osmunda fiber or rough sphagnum moss attached to a board or piece of a tree. Give moderate light and keep moist at all times.

129. How do you care for staghorn fern so that the ends do not turn brown?

Keep the growing medium relatively moist with high humidity.

130. What is the best composition of a potting soil for ferns?

Any potting medium high in organic matter with good drainage is recommended.

131. How do you cultivate a resurrection fern?

The resurrection fern (*Selaginella*) dries up and if placed in water or a moist medium will open up. The plant does not continue growing if it has been dried for too long.

132. How do I root a fatsia?

Propagate from cuttings in early spring.

133. How do you care for a fiddleleaf fig?

Fiddleleaf fig (*Ficus pandurata*) should be given a growing medium high in organic matter. The plant likes moderately good light and soil kept moderately moist at all times.

134. How do I care for my ficus plant?

See Question 133.

135. Our ficus is losing leaves for the second time. What do we do?

Avoid over-watering. Allow the plant to dry out between waterings.

136. Our ficus benjamina is shedding its leaves. What do we do?

Avoid over-watering. If that is not a problem, increase feeding when the plant makes new growth.

137. We have marked defoliation on our fig plant. What do we do?

The fig plant needs a regular feeding program when actively growing. Avoid over-watering.

138. Our ficus benjamina has small spots on the leaves. What is the cause and how do we control them?

These are scale insects. Use an oil-base spray, applying under and on top of the leaves. Repeat as needed.

139. The leaves on our ficus are splitting. What causes this?

Increase humidity when plants are starting to make new growth. Splitting is caused by very dry conditions.

140. How deep do I plant a ficus benjamina indoors?

Plant the same depth as it was in the original container.

141. If we put a ficus tree outdoors, does it grow faster? If not, how do we encourage its growth?

Place ficus in a semi-shaded area during the summer months. Using a liquid fertilizer when plant is making new growth helps to increase growth rate.

142. My ficus is weeping. What do I do?

Some forms of ficus weep. You have a weeping variety.

143. Our weeping fig has spider mites. How do I get rid of them?

Use Kelthane once every three days for four applications.

144. What are the ideal conditions for growing a ficus elastica?

Ficus elastica (rubber tree) likes the same growing medium as any other ficus. See Question 133. The plant likes moderate light. Thoroughly moisten soil and allow to dry out between waterings.

GOLDEN BARREL CACTUS
Echinocactus grousonii
(Missouri Botanical Garden)

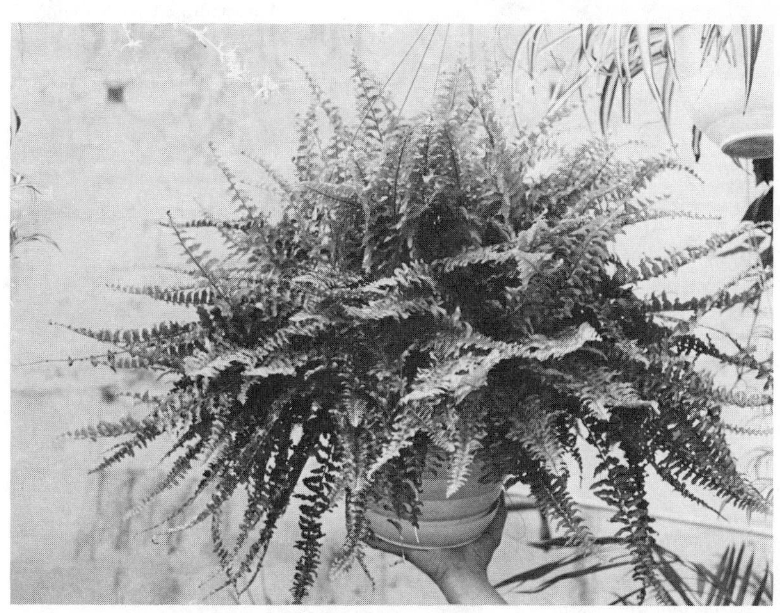

BOSTON FERN
Nephrolepsis exaltata
(Missouri Botanical Garden)

JADE TREE
Crassula argentea
(Missouri Botanical Garden)

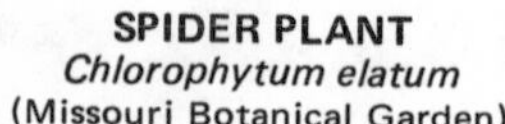

SPIDER PLANT
Chlorophytum elatum
(Missouri Botanical Garden)

145. Our rubber tree is losing its leaves after transplanting. What do we do?

Avoid disturbing the roots too much. Avoid over-watering and keep plant as cool as possible.

146. How is a rubber tree rooted?

Air-layer the plant in early spring.

147. The leaves on our rubber plant are turning yellow and dropping. What do I do?

Yellowing is caused by too much water or lack of food.

148. What do I do about a fungus on a rubber tree?

Spray with a good fungicide under and on top of leaves as needed.

149. How often do I water a rubber tree?

Water when soil is dry, two inches deep.

150. The leaves on our rubber plant are distorted in shape as they unfold. What do I do?

Increase humidity.

151. How do I air-layer a rubber tree?

See article on Propagation at beginning of this chapter.

152. Our rubber tree is too tall. How do we best trim off the branches?

Prune at anytime, cutting back to desired height.

153. How do I eliminate scale on a rubber plant?

Use an oil-base spray.

154. Is there any way to propagate a stem of a rubber plant that has broken off?

There is little hope of doing this except with bottom heat such as on a propagating mat.

155. Our rubber plant is failing. How do I revive it?

If over watering, repot by removing some old soil and placing in a fresh growing medium in a container slightly smaller than the present one.

156. How do I germinate orange, lemon and grapefruit seeds?

Citrus seeds are sown, as soon as available, in a seed mix at a temperature of 75 to 80 degrees.

157. How do I fertilize and water a grapefruit plant?

Fertilize when actively growing by using a regular houseplant fertilizer. Water when top soil becomes dry two inches below the surface.

158. The leaves are cracking on my grapefruit plant. What do I do?

Check watering and feeding conditions and for insects. Keep soil moist and spray if insects are present.

159. I have a lemon tree that is being attacked at the roots by soil bugs. How are these controlled?

Dilute an insecticide such as Diazinon and use in place of a regular watering.

160. My lemon tree is dropping leaves. What do I do?

Avoid over-watering. Check nutrient levels.

161. The leaves on our lemon tree are turning yellow and the lemons are dropping off. What do we do?

If watering is adequate, increase feeding with a balanced fertilizer and iron chelate, one tablespoon per gallon of water. Apply twice during the year.

162. Our orange tree is losing its leaves and is not growing. What do we do?

Depending on the growth habits, citrus trees shed some of their leaves. Less water is needed. Avoid applying fertilizers until the plants start to actively grow.

163. How do I care for an orange tree?

The orange tree likes the same requirements as any other citrus – strong light, moderate moisture and sufficient feeding.

164. How do I transfer my miniature orange tree indoors without injury?

Gradually move the plant from a strong light area to a weaker one by taking approximately four to six days to transfer it from outdoors into the indoor area.

165. What is the best care for a hen-and-chickens plant?

Use soil fairly high in sand and organic matter. Moisten lightly and let dry out between waterings. Allow enough light and house conditions of 60 to 70 degrees.

166. What do I feed hen-and-chickens plant?

Hen-and-chickens (*Echevarias*) need food only when pot-bound and when making new growth. Feed with a balanced fertilizer.

167. How do I fertilize Pothos ivy?

Use any liquid fertilizer when plant is actively growing.

168. What is the best cultural medium for a jade plant?

Jade plant (*Crassula argentea*) likes a soil high in sand and organic matter. Moisten the soil and let dry out considerably before watering again. Avoid over-watering. Give the plant strong light but not necessarily direct sunlight.

169. What causes leaf drop on my jade plant?

The jade plant is extremely subject to over-watering so avoid it.

170. My jade plant is turning soft and is wilting. How is this avoided?

Give plant plenty of light and just enough water to moisten soil. Allow it to dry out between waterings.

171. How do I eliminate white bugs in the soil of a jade plant?

Use Diazinon in place of a regular watering.

172. We have white fuzzy bugs on our jade tree. How are they eliminated?

This is a mealy bug. Use a pressure sprayer with a good insecticide. Repeat as needed.

173. How do I root a cutting from a jade plant?

Remove the cutting, let sit for several hours and then place in a rooting mix. Keep barely moist at a temperature of 70 to 75 degrees.

174. Our jade plant is shriveling up. What do we do to save it?

Shriveling is caused by lack of water. Increase watering.

175. How do I best grow portulacaria?

Portulacaria likes the same growing conditions as the jade plant. See question 168.

176. Is Japanese privet a good houseplant?

In Zone 6 this plant is not hardy in winter. Grow in a cool spot in the house.

177. How do I propagate a mango?

The mango is propagated from seeds.

178. How do I propagate Moses-in-the-cradle plant?

Moses-in-the-cradle (*Rhoeo*) is propagated by division or from seeds after the plant has flowered.

179. What is the best way to care for Moses-in-the-cradle plant?

Moses-in-the-cradle likes an average potting medium and strong light. Keep moderately moist at all times.

180. How do we best grow a monkey tree?

The monkey tree (*Araucaria*) likes a regular growing medium and strong light. Keep moderately moist and allow to dry out between waterings. Allow enough air circulation.

181. How big a ball is needed to transplant an Australian pine?

Transplant the Australian pine (*Araucaria*) as long as a good root system is secured with the plant.

182. The lower limbs of a 16-inch tall Norfolk Island pine are yellowing. What do I do for this condition?

Yellowing is caused by over-watering. Allow plant to dry out between waterings and increase light.

183. Our Norfolk Island pine is not flourishing. What do we do?

Check for spider mite with a fine lens. If present, use Kelthane. Increase the light on the plant.

184. How do we transplant Norfolk Island pine?

Transplant by removing one-third of the soil and by placing it in a container about two sizes larger.

185. What is the growth pattern of a Norfolk Island pine? How do you prevent it from losing lower branches?

A Norfolk Island pine sends out a new set of branches once or twice a year depending on the area that it is growing in. Lower branches usually are lost through over-watering or from lack of proper light.

186. What is causing leaf drop on my Norfolk Island pine?

Leaf drop is caused by spider mite or too dry conditions.

187. How do I propagate philodendrons?

Propagate from cuttings taken at anytime during the year.

188. What is the best media for rooting philodendron cuttings?

The best media is one-third part peat moss to two-thirds part perlite.

189. The stems on my tree philodendron are mushy and watery. What do I do?

Avoid over-watering. Remove the soft watery growth with a sharp knife.

190. Our split-leaf philodendron has spots. How do I eliminate this?

Spray with a fungicide underneath and on top of the leaves. Repeat in 10 days.

191. My philodendron is dying. How do I bring it back?

Take cuttings from the top growth and reroot.

192. What is the best way to encourage the growth of our philodendrons?

Increase light and move to a warm area.

193. What is the best culture for selloum?

Selloum is another variety of philodendron. The same cultural conditions apply.

194. Do I repot philodendron when pot-bound?

Yes, or increase feeding to keep it in good condition.

195. The leaves on our split-leaf philodendron are turning brown. What do we do?

Check for disease. Use a good fungicide if necessary.

196. Is it advisable to use ashes on philodendron plants?

Mix ashes with soil in small amounts to supply superphosphate.

197. How do I grow a philodendron on a pole?

Use the climbing variety and tie softly to the pole.

198. How do I root a split-leaf philodendron when the top leaves have stopped splitting?

Remove the top growth with three to four leaves attached and root.

199. How do I air-layer a Monstera deliciosa?

Monstera deliciosa is another type of philodendron. It is not necessary to air-layer. Cuttings are the best procedure.

200. Do I grow a palm tree from seed?

Yes.

201. We brought a palm tree home from Florida. When do I put it outdoors?

Put outdoors in spring when all danger of frost is over.

202. How do you maintain a palm in good condition?

Palms like average potting medium. Keep moderately moist and allow average light conditions. Avoid feeding when not actively growing.

203. What do you do about browning leaves on a palm?

Browning is caused by low humidity. Place plant on tray of water containing pebbles.

204. I have brown tips on a Kentia palm. How do I eliminate them?

Brown tips on a Kentia palm (*Howeia forsteriana*) are normal, caused by low humidity. When large enough, trim off with a pair of sharp scissors.

205. How do I start a Phoenix palm from seed?

Sow seed with a temperature of 75 to 80 degrees.

206. What are the light requirements for growing palms?

Palms grow in relatively little light; however, medium light but no direct sun is best.

207. What is the best fertilizer for palms?

Any household fertilizer such as 20-20-20 or 10-15-10 used when the plant is making new growth is ideal.

208. The green on our palm plant is diminishing in color. What is wrong?

Increase the light or apply iron chelate in April and again in October.

209. May I spray a palm plant with Malathion?

Yes, but keep the plant out of direct sun until dry.

210. How do I care for an elephant tree?

The elephant tree (*Beaucarnea*) likes average house conditions, preferably not over 75 degrees in winter and regular potting soil. Keep evenly moist.

211. How do I propagate a pony-tail plant?

Propagate by removing offsets in early spring.

212. What is the best potting mix for a Sago palm?

Sago palm (*Cycas*) likes growing media high in organic matter and well drained.

213. How do I cultivate a Sago palm?

Allow strong light and keep soil moderately moist.

214. May I grow a papaya from seed?

Yes.

215. How do I grow pomegranates?

Pomegranates (*Punica granatum*) are started from seed. Give enough light and keep moderately moist.

216. How long does it take to root peperomia?

The peperomia roots in three to four weeks.

217. What is the best culture for growing a peperomia?

Peperomia likes an average growing media, soil moderately moist and sufficient light but not direct sunlight.

218. The leaves on my peperomia are malformed. Why?

Malformation is caused by injuries to the plant. Also check for insects or diseases.

219. May I repot or reroot a peperomia plant?

If pot-bound, divide the plant or take cuttings, root and repot.

220. What kind of light and temperature does a piggyback plant need?

Piggyback plant (*Tolmiea menziesii*) likes good light but no direct sunlight and average temperatures not over 72 degrees.

221. We have scale on our piggyback plant. How do we get rid of this?

Spray a piggyback plant with an oil-based spray, such as Malathion. Keep the plant out of direct sun until thoroughly dry.

222. What is the best culture for a prayer plant?

The prayer plant (*Maranta leuconeura* 'Massangeana') likes growing media high in organic matter. Keep moderately moist at all times. Plants like high humidity and are best grown on a tray of pebbles in water. Allow enough light but not direct sunlight.

223. What do I do about leaves browning in spots and on edges on my prayer plant?

Increase humidity. Remove infected leaves.

224. My prayer plant never opens. What is wrong?

There is not enough humidity.

225. How do I propagate a prayer plant?

If the plant is large enough, divide; otherwise take cuttings from actively growing ends.

226. What is the best cultural medium for sansevieria?

Sansevieria likes a growing medium of equal parts sand, loam and organic matter. Moisten the soil and let dry out somewhat between waterings. Give sufficient light.

227. How do you divide a sansevieria?

Sansevieria is divided by separating the roots.

228. What is the best soil for growing schefflera?

Any good growing medium is ideal.

229. How do you eliminate scale and leaf spot on schefflera?

Spray scale with an oil-base spray. Use a fungicide on the spots.

230. How do you move schefflera from one pot to another?

Remove from container, loosen one to two inches of growing medium at the base and plant in a container two to three sizes larger than the present one.

231. Do I remove the new sprouts on a schefflera?

Do not unless you want to prevent the plant from becoming too full.

232. How do you eliminate spider mites on a schefflera?

Use Kelthane at three-day intervals for four applications.

233. What causes yellowing of leaves on a schefflera?

Over-watering or not enough nourishment are the causes.

234. What do I do about a schefflera that has been over-watered?

Avoid watering until plant has dried out considerably. Move to a cooler area or repot into a fresh growing medium.

235. How do I eliminate blackspot on a schefflera plant?

Use a fungicide.

236. What is a good fertilizer for a schefflera?

Use a houseplant fertilizer when plant is actively growing.

237. How much water does a schefflera need?

It needs enough water to moisten the soil. Then allow to dry out considerably before watering again.

238. How do I care for a screw-pine?

The screw-pine (*Pandanus*) likes regular soil, sufficient light and temperatures not over 72 degrees.

239. What is the best potting medium and care for Swedish ivy?

Swedish ivy (*Plectranthus australis*) likes a potting medium high in organic matter. Keep moderately moist and do not allow to sit in water. Allow average light and temperature around 70 degrees.

240. How do you propagate Swedish ivy?

Take cuttings from actively growing tips.

241. How do we stop the leaf loss on our Swedish ivy?

Leaf loss is caused by over-watering.

242. The leaves on my Swedish ivy are turning black. How is this controlled?

This is a bacterial disease and is controlled by removing infected parts. Spray plant with a fungicide. Isolate the plant until infestation is clear.

243. How do I encourage a thicker growth on a Swedish ivy?

Pinch the growing tips out periodically to cause bushiness.

244. How do you treat scale on Swedish ivy?

Use an oil-base spray and keep plants out of direct sunlight.

245. What is the best culture for growing a spider plant?

The spider plant (*Chlorphytum*) likes a good growing media with plenty of organic matter. Keep moderately moist and allow enough light.

246. My spider plant is not spreading shoots. What do I do?

The spider plant produces shoots when the plant becomes pot-bound.

247. We have mushrooms in our spider plant pot. Is this dangerous to plants?

No, but remove and destroy mushrooms.

248. How do you eliminate fungus on a spider plant?

Increase air circulation.

249. What do I do about leaf drop on a spider plant?

Increase air circulation.

250. How do I propagate string-of-pearls?

String-of-pearls (*Senecio royleyana*) is propagated by cuttings taken from the tips of the plants. Keep barely moist until well rooted.

251. What is the best care for a ti plant?

The ti plant (*Dracaena*) likes a regular potting media and sufficient light. Keep moderately moist at all times. Avoid over-watering.

252. What do I do about the browning leaves on my ti plant?

Check for spider mites and increase humidity.

253. How do I propagate an umbrella palm?

An umbrella palm (*Cyperus alternifolius*) is propagated by taking the stems and cutting the base off about one inch below the top. Place this in a rooting medium and keep moderately moist with high humidity.

254. What do I do about the browning of leaves on an umbrella plant?

Check for spider mite and increase humidity.

255. What kind of soil and how much watering does a velvet plant need?

The velvet plant (*Gynura aurantiaca*) likes a growing medium high in organic matter. When watering, use enough to moisten the medium and let it dry out between watering.

256. How do I encourage a bushier growth on a sparse velvet plant?

Remove the growing tips to cause bushiness.

257. How do I propagate a velvet plant?

Take cuttings three to four inches long and root.

258. May we use purple heart for hanging baskets?

Purple heart is ideal in a hanging basket.

259. Please describe how to pinch a purple passion plant?

Pinch to remove about one-half to one inch of the actively growing tips of the plant to cause them to bush out.

260. The purple passion plant we have is too large for the pot it is in. What do I do?

Plants outgrow their present containers through heavy growth and roots pushing through the top of the soil. Repot into larger containers by removing from present containers and by cutting off up to one-third of the old soil ball. Repot into larger containers as needed.

261. What is the best culture for a Venus flytrap plant?

Venus flytrap (*Dionaea muscipula*) likes a very rich, humus soil and high humidity. Grow in a terrarium and allow enough light. Water with rainwater or distilled water.

262. Why does the trap fall off of the Venus flytrap and how can this be prevented?

Increasing humidity prevents this. Grow in terrariums rather than in individual pots.

263. Do I feed a Venus flytrap bits of raw hamburger and when?

This is not necessary as the plant gets enough nourishment from the growing medium. The hamburger can contaminate the leaf, causing it to brown.

264. May I propagate a Wandering Jew and how?

The Wandering Jew (*Tradescantia*) is easily propagated from stem cuttings, taken anytime from active growth.

265. How much light is necessary for growth on a Wandering Jew?

The Wandering Jew plant likes strong light but not direct sunlight.

266. The leaves on our Wandering Jew look like a pinking shears has been used on them. What is the cause?

This is caused by a chewing insect. Examine pot carefully to remove all insects.

267. The leaves are dying on our Wandering Jew. What do we do?

Remove any dead or dying leaves. Keep plant moderately moist and feed with a balanced fertilizer at regular intervals.

268. Why is our Wandering Jew plant wilting?

The plant is not getting sufficient moisture or needs repotting into a larger container.

269. The roots on our Wandering Jew that I have in water are all tangled. What do I do?

Wandering Jew is propagated in water, but it is difficult to prevent the roots from tangling. Repot into soil immediately.

270. How do I take care of a yucca plant?

Yucca plant likes soil with equal parts of sand, loam and organic matter. Give enough water to moisten the soil and then let it become dry between waterings. Light from a south, east or west window and temperatures of 65 to 70 degrees are ideal.

271. The leaves on our yucca plant are drying up. What do I do?

Remove older leaves. Avoid keeping plant too wet.

272. Is there some way to make a yucca bloom?

When plants become pot-bond, they will start to flower.

273. Our yucca plant is rotting at the bottom. What do we do?

Rotting is caused from over-watering. Remove from present soil, repot into fresh soil and keep barely moist until new growth appears.

274. Do I remove seed pods from a yucca plant?

Unless seed is wanted for propagating, remove before seeds form.

275. How can we eliminate mold on a terrarium?

Give more ventilation or very carefully loosen the soil surface where the mold is present.

276. What causes plant tips to die and how can you prevent this?

This again is due to lack of moisture in the air. Tips can be very carefully pruned back with a pair of sharp scissors. Occasional mistings or increasing humidity by placing the plant on a tray of pebbles so the pot itself is just above the pebbles and keeping water over the pebbles to increase humidity is ideal.

277. What does it mean to top-dress a pot?

This means to remove one to two inches of the top soil from the pot, replacing this with a good potting soil with equal amounts of organic matter and some superphosphate added. Also on top of this could be placed a mulch such as fir bark or other suitable material to give a decorative effect.

278. What should be done about leaf drop on houseplants?

Check moisture levels and make sure that plants are not getting too much water or insufficient water. Also see that plants are not in a direct draft.

279. What effect does the reduction of sun have on houseplants?

Reduction of sun on houseplants tends to slow the growth down. Flowering will stop.

280. What kind of general fertilizer is best for houseplants like crotons, begonias, etc.?

Any of the houseplant fertilizers available on the market that are not high in nitrogen (nitrogen being the first number on the container) are ideal. One should try to get a balanced fertilizer such as one that can be divided equally by one number such as 20-20-20 which is easily divisible by five or ten.

Chapter Three
Outdoor Flowering Plants

General Information

This section deals with annuals, biennials and perennials. It does not deal with any material that is of a woody nature such as trees and shrubs.

Annuals are grown each year from seed, then flower and produce seed the same season. They need to be replanted each spring after all danger of frost has passed. There are, however, some exceptions of hardy annuals that can be put out earlier than the last frost.

Biennials are started from seed which form a rosette the first year and then proceed to flower early the following spring, taking two years to complete their growth cycle. These need to be replanted each year; although in some cases, if flower heads are removed before seeds have a chance to start, plants will grow into the next year.

Perennials are started from seed. They usually form a rosette the first year and then continue to flower each succeeding year.

Bulbs include many of the tender ones, e.g. Canna lilies. They are put outside in early spring and brought inside before severe frost in the fall. Bring indoors in temperatures that are between 40 to 55 degrees and keep where it is moderately dry so that bulbs do not dry out. Examples of these are the dahlias, gladioli and tuberoses. Other bulbs are spring bulbs, such as tulips, hyacinths and daffodils, which are planted outside in September and October and flower the next spring. Many of these carry over from year to year. There are the true lilies which are normally planted in the fall or early spring and continue to flower each succeeding year. The plants in this group have a wide use in flower and shrub borders and grow in various areas. Some are suitable for semi-shaded areas that receive filtered sun or sun for a limited part of the day. Example of these is the regal lily (*Lilium regale*).

Many of the spring bulbs are planted in areas that normally are shaded during the summer but receive sun during the spring. These plants flower and complete their life cycle before the trees branch out so that they are not affected by the shade once the trees are in full leaf. Nearly all members of the true lilies (*Lilium*) do best in semi-shaded areas as long as the bulbs are free of heavy tree roots. A wide selection of these is available and through careful selection, bloom from early May through late September. They come in a wide variety of colors and in sizes from one to six feet. Examples of spring bulbs are tulips, hyacinths, daffodils and crocuses.

Spring flowering bulbs are purchased in the fall, planted in September and October and form a root system during the cool days in the fall. They flower from February through early May. They all like areas which have sufficient drainage with plenty of organic matter and the addition of four to five pounds of superphosphate per 100 square feet of soil worked into the soil prior to planting. Methods of planting vary according to the size of the bulb. Small bulbs such as crocuses and snowdrops (*Choinodoxa*) are planted one to two inches deep. Tulips, on the other hand, are planted five to six inches deep. Narcissuses, jonquils and daffodils are planted six to eight inches deep, depending on the soil. When a heavier type soil is used, planting is shallower.

The bulbs are planted and allowed to remain in the ground for several years without having to be replanted; however, when the bulbs begin to multiply quite rapidly and flowering begins to decrease, it is time to dig up and redivide the bulbs. This takes place about six to eight weeks after flowering in the spring. Once the bulbs start to turn yellow, dig up carefully with a spade and allow to dry in the sun for a day or two. Then remove all the old soil, cut back the tops and place the bulbs in trays in an area where they receive good air circulation and where it is dry. Allow to remain there until early September. At that time, clean them. Sort the bulbs out according to their sizes and select the largest bulbs for replanting. Either discard the smaller bulbs or place them in nursery rows. Allow them to develop and mature to a sufficient size to flower again.

Impatiens also grow well in semi-shaded areas. They come in a wide range of colors and grow from five inches up to two feet tall. They bloom continuously throughout the summer months.

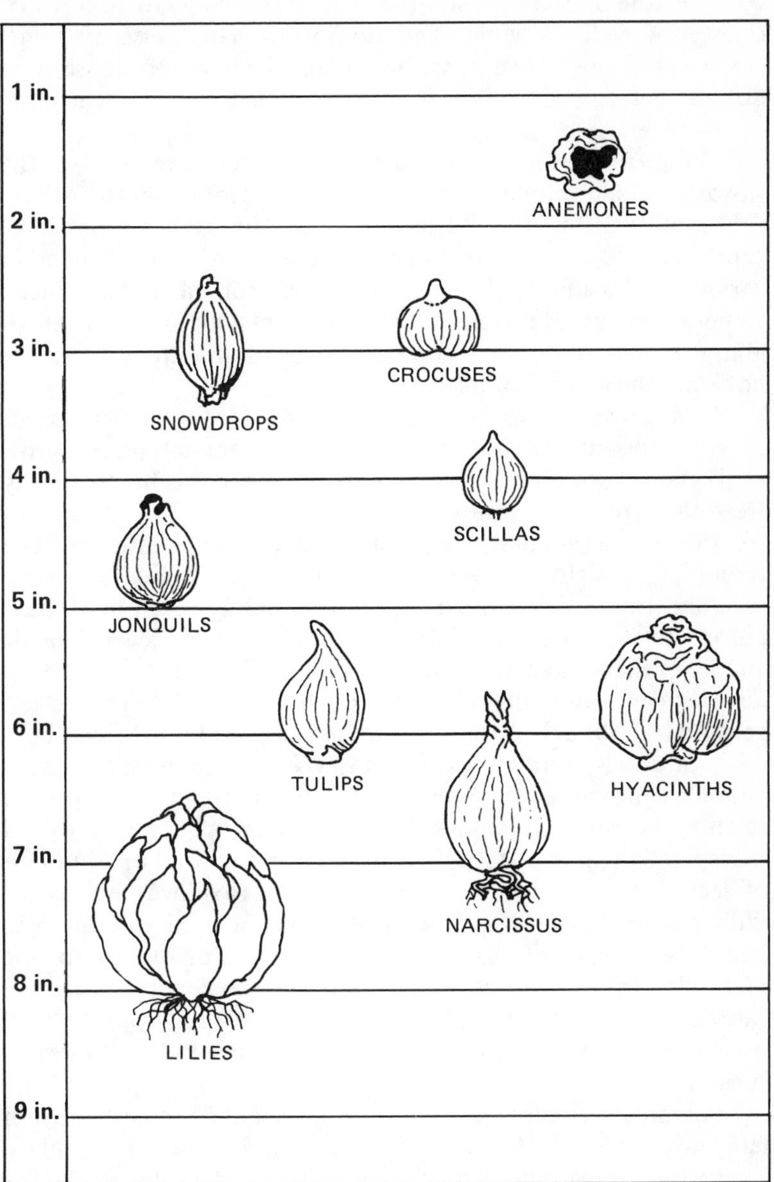

DEPTH FOR PLANTING BULBS

It is important when placing plants in a semi-shaded area to consider the amount of sun they are getting and to find which ones grow well and which ones do not. In many cases, all plants survive in semi-shaded areas but if the shade is too dense, you do not get the same flowering effects that you do when the plants receive more sunlight.

Good flowering plants in hot, dry areas are any of the flowers which come from Mexico or from South Africa. Practically all of the African daisies, the gerberas, arctotis, cape-marigold (*Dimorphotheca*), marigolds and the zinnias in various colors and heights that originated from Mexico are ideal. Experiment with different colored plants in hot, dry areas. Many of the stronger reds and deep blues stand up better in the hot sun than pastel colors do.

Is it better to grow flowers from fresh seeds or from seeds of your present plants? Most of the hybrid annuals do not grow well when sown from your own seed so that it is better to buy fresh seed from seed houses.

In growing annuals, start indoors and transplant later. Start them six to eight weeks before the last frost-free date in your area and then harden them off approximately seven to 10 days before setting them outside. Sow annuals using sterile media and keep them in an area where the temperature is around 70 to 75 degrees. Give them plenty of light once they start to germinate. About 12 to 14 hours per day under artificial light or in a good south or west window is sufficient. Not having enough light causes the seedlings to elongate and develop wide spacings between the nodes. Try to grow compact seedlings and transplant them at a stage when they have a second or third pair of leaves. Practically all of the biennials, foxgloves and Sweet Williams are best sown from seed. Sow the seed in Zone 6 in late July or early August. Use a cold frame or regular sowing methods, transplanting when needed. Transfer them to the garden about mid September when temperatures begin to cool off and more moist conditions prevail. Blooms will start in early spring.

Perennials usually are started from seed and are best sown in late July or early August, transplanting as you do biennials. They also are grown from cuttings which will be explained under Propagation. Nearly all annuals and perennials are available from nursery centers.

When transplanting bedding plants, use a liquid fertilizer at half recommended strength a day before transplanting. At transplanting time separate the seedlings out of their containers so as not to disturb the soil ball. In transferring them to the garden, water again with the same fertilizer. This prevents shock in transplanting. Plant most bedding plants when the weather is sufficiently warm and the night temperatures are uniform. In some cases, plant annuals late, sowing the seed directly into the garden or make successive plantings for continuous bloom until late fall. Plant most annuals in outdoor planters of various types of materials e.g. clay pots, aluminum, plastic and wooden containers. The essential thing is to have containers which have good drainage. Holes in the bottom or side of the container are needed to allow excess water to drain away. Containers which do not have drainage fill up with water, especially when it rains. Over-watering causes loss of the plants. In using wooden planters, make sure the wood has not been treated with materials which are harmful to seedlings. Railway ties which have been treated with creosote often burn the seedlings unless they have been weathered outdoors. If you are having a problem with growing plants in wood containers, leave the containers exposed for a year outdoors, subject to wind and rain to get rid of any detrimental material that is in the wood itself. Also, make sure that no injurious herbicides have been used around the wood.

In selecting flowering plant material for containers, consider color harmony, colors which blend well with one another and with their surroundings. Trailing plants are effective as they spill over the sides of the containers to give a full effect and de-emphasize the containers. Avoid bright containers that do not harmonize with flowering plants.

Soil Culture

Preparing the proper soil is important for growing flowering plants outdoors. Select areas which are well drained and incorporate plenty of organic matter, such as partially decomposed plant material or well rotted manure. Use peat moss and work into the soil. It is also essential to work in plenty of superphosphate which is essential for a good root growth and a factor in producing bloom. Work soil as deep as 10 to 12 inches and as much as 15 to 20 inches, particularly where plants are going to be growing for a number of years.

Each spring work in extra organic matter into the soil. This breaks down fairly rapidly in the soil and needs to be replaced at regular intervals. Also, work in additional amounts of superphosphate when growth is beginning. Follow, when growth becomes active, with a well-balanced fertilizer using a light application of three to four pounds per 100 square feet.

Mulching the plants with good leaf mold or wood chips is ideal to keep the soil open and to control temperature and soil moisture conditions.

Propagation

Most plants in this group are propagated either from seed or from cuttings. For cuttings, one should select plants which are heavy flowering and healthy. Take cuttings before flowering begins. Use ends that are six to eight inches long, cutting just below the node. Trim off several of the lower leaves and use a rooting hormone. Place these in containers with one-third part peat moss to two-thirds part perlite, keeping them moderately moist and out of the direct sun until rooted. Take cuttings from early June through late September. Properly rooted and cared for plants produce flowering material the following year.

Some of the bulb stalks, such as the true lilies (*Lilium*), are propagated by bulb division. When the plants develop several bulbs, dig them up in the fall, divide and plant. As the true lilies produce scale-like growths on the bulbs, remove the scales, allow to sit for an hour or two and then plant with the tip just showing in a well prepared media containing plenty of sand. Use a cold frame. Place the scales one to two inches apart and keep moderately moist. They will soon produce new roots and small tops. They need to remain in this area for approximately a year. Then transplant to the garden where they grow permanently.

Daffodils, tulips and other spring flowering bulbs (which are not true bulbs like the lily) are propagated simply by division. These tend to multiply each year and when they get to the stage where they become very thick and stop flowering, dig up and redivide. A good time to do this is just as the growth is beginning to yellow and die off. At that time, the plants are nearly dormant and one can dig them up (knowing just where they are), dry them off and store them in well ventilated areas until next September or early October. They are then planted back in the garden according to the sizes.

Potting Methods

Many annuals and perennials are ideal to grow in containers. Select soil which is extremely well drained with extra organic matter added which holds moisture and allows for good air circulation. Add plenty of superphosphate and a balanced fertilizer. When plants are established in the containers, add a light mulch to control soil temperature and moisture. Late in the fall move them to a protected area where they are heavily mulched with leaves or other similar materials to protect the ground from frost in the winter. Container-grown materials need fertilizer and water more often. Remove flower heads before they have a chance to set seed. This keeps them flowering over longer periods.

Watering

Outdoor flowering material needs adequate watering during periods of drought. This means two inches of rain at each watering. A watering once every eight to 12 days is sufficient. Water early in the morning through late afternoon, allowing the plants sufficient time to dry off before nighttime; otherwise, there is a chance of mildew affecting the plants if they are kept wet during the evening hours. Avoid heavy streams of water which break the plants down. A fine misting is ideal.

Fertilizing

Keeping the plants well nourished is important. In creating new flower beds, add superphosphate at the rate of four to five pounds per 100 square feet. Apply lime once every three to four years depending on the growth, which should be deep green. Add organic material when reworking the beds. Test the soil periodically to determine when lime is needed. Lime applied in the fall takes effect on the soil by early spring.

In early spring as plants begin to grow, work in superphosphate at the rate of four to five pounds per 100 square feet. Follow this, once growth is active, with a feeding of three to four pounds of a balanced fertilizer, such as a 5-10-5 or

6-12-12 per 100 square feet. Work this in lightly around the plants. Use liquid fertilizer after the beginning of August so that plants can harden-off and mature properly for winter growth.

Annuals or spring bulbs need specially prepared soil prior to planting, at which time, add superphosphate to the soil and work in to a good depth.

Insect and Disease Control.

Outdoor flowering plants are subject to the same insects and diseases as any other plants. Examine the leaves underneath and on top to see when insects first appear. It is not necessary to spray the whole garden if insects are only on one plant. Careful spraying with either water or insecticide brings the insects under control. If a disease becomes established, it is not worth saving the plant. Make sure that they are disease-free before planting in a garden. Watch mildew, which is a common problem in the garden, from the time growth starts in early spring until late fall. When first noticed, spray mildew with fungicide, applying it underneath and on top of the leaves. Some plants are more susceptible to mildew than others. Phlox is one that needs constant spraying starting early in spring when growth begins until after flowering.

Bacterial diseases, which affect the plants by causing buds to turn brown or black and stems to turn black, are controlled by using the proper sprays. Peony blight is one of the diseases. It causes buds to turn brown and stems to become soft and dark brown or black. Use a common spray, such as Bordeaux mix or Phaltan, when growth first begins. Repeat in 10 to 12 days.

QUESTIONS

1. How do you care for an alternanthera?

An alternanthera is treated as a foliage plant rather than a flowering one since the flowers are inconspicuous. This plant is used in carpet bedding and comes in various leaf colors. It likes a well drained soil and an area where one is growing other annuals. The plant does best under full sun. Set out after all danger of frost is past. Keep pinched or cut back for compact growing. It makes an excellent color accent used in the garden as a border or edging plant and remains in good color until late fall.

2. My sweet alyssum seeds sprout and then wilt before ready to transplant. Why?

The wilting is known as damping-off, a fungus disease. Make sure the medium used is sterile. Give the plant plenty of light and good air circulation. Avoid over-watering. If the wilting occurs, dust the tray immediately with a fungicide, such as Captan, which will bring this under immediate control. Remove the affected seedlings.

3. What is the best time to plant annuals and perennials?

Annuals are started indoors six to eight weeks ahead of last killing frost. Grow plants in good light and then transplant out as soon as all danger of frost is passed. Perennials may be started at the same time. They may be started from seeds sown in cold frames or indoor trays in early July and transplanted into permanent positions in mid September in the garden for flowering the following year.

4. How long do I hold annuals between receiving and planting?

If plants need to be held they should be given good light and plenty of air circulation until time to plant outdoors, otherwise loss will be very high.

5. What month is the best time in Zone 6 in which to set out annuals?

Most annuals can be planted out anytime from late April, depending on the season.

6. Is morning sun only the best for growing annuals?

Most annuals will grow best in full sun all day. Those which are semi-shaded ones will do better just in morning sun.

7. Is it too early to put out bedding plants and seeds in April?

Seeds may be sown as soon as the ground can be worked with many of the hardier annuals. Tender annuals should not be sown in seed outdoors until after danger of heavy frost is over. Plants started indoors can be put out in late April or once all danger of frost is over.

8. What is a biennial plant? Name some and when should they be planted?

A biennial is a plant which is started from seed. It forms a rosette the first year, over-winters, comes up and flowers early the next year and then produces seeds and dies. Good examples are: bell flowers (*Campanulas*), hollyhocks, foxgloves and Sweet Williams. A number of biennials make excellent additions to the garden for color and if started each year give continuous bloom from year to year.

9. May I bring fibrous begonias indoors in November?

Yes. Bring them inside in early October before the weather gets too cold. If allowed to remain out too long, flowering is reduced and plants are more difficult to bring back into bloom. Thoroughly water the ground if it is dry before moving them. Pot plants into containers and keep outdoors in a cool area for several days to allow new rooting to occur before bringing them indoors. Place them in an area where they receive full sunlight.

10. When do I buy Bells-of-Ireland?

Bells-of-Ireland (*Molucella laevis*) is an annual grown primarily for drying for cut-flower arrangements. It is available in early spring from the garden centers or shops selling bedding plants.

11. How do I separate Bleeding Heart plants?

Bleeding Heart (*Dicentra spectabilis*) has handsome cut-leafed, blue-green foliage and arching sprays of flowers like pink or deep-rose lockets. It grows 15 to 20 inches high. This plant is best divided when it begins to yellow, usually about six weeks after flowering. Dig up roots, divide the plant and replant about 18 inches apart in prepared soil. See Question 12.

12. How deep do we bury the roots of our Bleeding Heart plant?

Place the Bleeding Heart's roots about two inches below the top of the ground level. In dividing the plant, cut the roots into short sections about two inches long. Place in soil that is well enriched with organic matter. Cover them with one-half to one inch of soil and keep them moderately moist until new plants begin to emerge. At this time carefully lift and space them according to the space available in the garden. See Question 11.

13. May tulip and jonquil bulbs purchased in September be planted in May?

Plant in late September or early October. Do not carry them over through the winter until May or the bulbs will be of no value. If unable to plant bulbs in the fall when first purchased, carefully mulch the area to prevent the ground from freezing. Plant as soon as possible before winter arrives. Keep bulbs in a cool, dry area until ready for planting.

14. May I dig up tulip bulbs and narcissus bulbs in June?

Yes. See Question 13.

15. How do I best handle narcissus bulbs?

Purchase good-sized bulbs in early September and after preparing the soil, plant the bulbs no later than the end of October. In early spring, work in a light application of a balanced fertilizer. During periods of drought, keep well watered. If bulbs are planted sufficiently deep, you can plant annuals or other plants around them without disturbing them. Three to four weeks after flowering, cut foliage off one or two inches above ground level. It is not necessary to wait until the foliage yellows. If they have been given three to four weeks of solid growing, they form a bulb that is large enough for flowering again the following year.

16. When do I dig up my daffodils?

Dig up daffodils three to four weeks after flowering or when the foliage begins to yellow.

17. When do I cut daffodils back?

Cut back three to four weeks following flowering. See Question 15.

18. How deep do I plant daffodil bulbs?

Plant them so that there is five to six inches of soil above the top of the bulb.

19. How do I maintain the bulb size of my daffodils?

When planting in the fall, work in superphosphate and organic matter. See Question 15. In early spring follow with the feeding of superphosphate and fertilizer. This keeps the soil rich and allows the bulbs to remain a substantial size for a number of years.

20. My daffodils are not blooming. What do I do?

Daffodils usually stop flowering because the bulbs have become too thick or too small. To prevent this, dig them up every few years, divide them and plant them back in the fall in prepared soil.

21. Will cutting the flowers from daffodils and tulips harm the bulbs?

Removal of just the flower stalks without the leaves does not harm them in any way. In cutting the flowers, leave as much of the foliage as possible to allow the bulb to build up a new food supply for the establishment of a new bulb the next year.

22. When do I cut seed pods from daffodils?

Remove flowers from daffodils before they have a chance to set seed. Once the flowers begin to wither, cut flower stalks removing just the stalks without injuring the leaves.

23. Is it okay to replant last season's jonquil bulbs?

Plant them in late September or early October. See Question 13.

24. How do I distinguish tulip bulbs from jonquils?

If the bulbs are dormant, tulip bulbs are round and quite squat whereas the jonquils are round with elongated necks still attached to the bulbs. The tissues on the jonquils are a darker brown color than on the tulips.

25. May I uncover bulbs in March?

Gradually remove the mulch once heavy frost is over. Be very careful not to expose bulbs if they have become quite tall.

26. Will covering spring bulbs protect them from frost in March?

Spring bulbs mulched in the fall should have the mulch left on until all danger of heavy frost is over before removing mulch, to give good protection.

27. Are there any bulbs that can be planted at any other time than spring?

Yes. In September and October one should be planting spring flowering bulbs such as tulips, daffodils, crocuses, hyacinths and of course the true lily (*Lilium*) species which are also best planted in the fall.

28. Our crocus is not blooming. Is there anything we may do to encourage a bloom?

Once bulb starts to grow, apply a light application of superphosphate followed with a feeding of a balanced fertilizer.

29. May I separate and plant the autumn crocus, in November?

Divide the autumn crocus (*Colchicum*) once the foliage starts to turn yellow. The *Colchicum* bulbs flower in the fall and die after flowering. In early spring they send up the foliage which builds up the new bulbs. Allow the foliage to remain in good condition. Once it begins to yellow, carefully dig up the bulbs and separate them. Plant them back in late August in the garden.

30. How do I prevent squirrels or moles from eating the crocus bulbs?

Prepare the ground for planting. Once it is prepared, remove three to four inches of the soil and place wire netting with about one-fourth inch mesh on the bottom of the prepared area. Place the bulbs on top of this and then cover with three to four inches of the garden soil. Over the top of this place another layer of the netting. The squirrels or moles are unable to dig through the netting; therefore, they will leave them undisturbed. As the roots form, they penetrate through the wire netting, and the tops are also able to come up without any harm to the bulbs themselves.

31. May I plant crocuses in a lawn area?

Crocuses are ideal to naturalize in the lawn area. Carefully dig up a corner of the sod and plant the bulb about two inches below the surface. In early spring the crocuses bloom and send up new leaves. Leave the area unmowed for three weeks after flowering to allow the bulbs to build up sufficient nourishment to form new bulbs. Then cut the lawn without harming the crocus bulbs.

32. How do I transplant hyacinths?

Transplant hyacinths six to eight weeks after flowering or dig up for planting in late September or early October.

33. How do I handle hyacinth bulbs after the blooms have dried up?

Feed hyacinths when first beginning to grow. Immediately following flowering, remove the flower stalk and allow the bulbs to die down naturally.

34. May I plant hyacinth bulbs in May?

May is not the time to plant hyacinths but late September or October is the proper time. When hyacinths are forced into pots during the winter months and allowed to dry off, store their bulbs until early September. Clean them off and plant in the garden.

35. My hyacinths flowered very well for two years and then came up very small and failed to flower. What do I do?

Hyacinths are one of the few bulbs that do not last very long in the garden. They grow well the first year with some bloom the second year. They seldom bloom over a long length of time. It is much better to replace them with new bulbs when this occurs rather than trying to nourish the small bulbs.

36. How do I dig up and preserve our tulip bulbs?

Dig up tulip bulbs three to four weeks after flowering and place in the sun for a day or two to allow them to dry off. Then remove the soil, cut the tops off to within a couple of inches and place the bulbs in trays or other suitable containers where they have good air circulation and are kept dry. Leave until early September and then thoroughly clean off and sort. Then replant in the garden in late September or early October.

37. Do I cut spent flowers from tulip bulbs?

Yes. As soon as the flowering is finished, remove the stem down to the first leaf.

38. Is it too soon in March to uncover tulip bulbs?

Once the weather has started to warm up and all danger of severe frost is past, gradually remove the mulch over a period of seven to 10 days.

39. How do I care for tulips so that they will bloom next year?

When growth starts in the spring, incorporate a light application of superphosphate and balanced fertilizer. See Question 19.

40. When do you cut back tulips?

Cut back tulips to the first leaf as soon as the flower is finished. Once the foliage has started to turn yellow or three to four weeks after flowering, cut off tulips just above ground level. See Questions 21 and 37.

41. What is the best fertilizer to use on tulip bulbs?

Use superphosphate and a balanced fertilizer such as a 5-10-5 or 6-12-12.

42. How do I plant tulips that are already in pots?

Allow tulips to die down naturally in the pots. Once this starts to happen, withhold watering and place the pots in a cool, dry area. In early September remove the tulips from the pots, clean off thoroughly and plant in the garden in late September or early October.

43. Is there any way to increase the size of tulip bulbs?

Use a good feeding program and supplement with a liquid feeding of fertilizer immediately following flowering. See Question 19.

44. Our tulip bulbs are sprouting. When do I set them out?

Store tulip bulbs where they are perfectly dry to prevent any sprouting. Plant in the garden anytime from middle September to early November.

45. How do you transplant tulips?

Allow the tulips to dry out. See Question 44. Then plant in the fall. Another method, if they need to be moved early in the spring and are starting to grow, is to remove them with as much soil attached and replant then. Do not allow them to dry out. Follow by a light feeding with a liquid fertilizer to get them reestablished.

46. When do tulips bloom?

This depends on the variety and type of tulips grown. They come in a wide range of species. They flower in Zone 6 in late March through early May.

47. What are the cultural requirements for growing tulips?

Tulips require a prepared soil at a depth of 10 to 12 inches with plenty of organic matter and superphosphate. Once the bulbs are planted, use a light application of a balanced fertilizer over the top. Then in early spring come in with an additional feeding of superphosphate and fertilizer. See Question 19.

48. Some old tulip bulbs that have been in the ground for several years are coming up. Do I dig them up and separate them?

Yes. In late May dig bulbs up. Cut tops back and store bulbs in cool, dry area. When dry, clean and sort out large bulbs for replanting in late September.

49. How and when do I replant last year's tulip bulbs?

If bulbs were forced into pots, dry them off. See Question 42. Plant them in the garden in late September or October. If they were growing in the garden and were dug up after flowering, follow the same procedure.

50. How do I care for and use canna bulbs?

Cannas are attractive plants grown from tubers. Store tubers during the winter months and plant after danger of frost is passed in the spring. In some cases, start into bloom six to eight weeks ahead of time indoors. Clean tubers and cut back to growing tips. Then plant in potting soil in a temperature of 65 to 75 degrees with plenty of light. Keep moderately moist until they start to actively grow and then give regular waterings and occasional feedings of liquid fertilizer.

In early May, plant tubers outdoors where they are to grow all summer. Keep soil enriched with organic matter and superphosphate. Keep the tubers well watered during the summer months. Remove the flower heads once the flowers are spent to prevent them from forming seed. They will keep sending up new shoots which will flower until heavy frost.

As soon as they are partially frozen, dig up the tubers. Remove the tops two to three inches above the soil line and place them in an area where they can dry out for several days. Then remove all the old soil and old foliage back to within a couple of inches of the top of the tubers themselves. Store tubers in an area where temperatures are 40 to 50 degrees and where there is good air circulation. Leave them until next spring for planting.

51. How do we grow canna lilies?

Purchase canna lilies from garden centers in early spring once they have started to grow or tubers from seed firms early in the spring. See Question 50.

52. Do I start cannas in the house in pots?

Yes. Use healthy potting soil, keeping it moderately moist until growth starts and becomes active. Give them plenty of sun or

10 to 12 hours of good light per day until they can be placed outdoors.

53. When do I plant carnation seed to flower this year?

The carnation (*Dianthus*) is readily started from seed. Select fresh seed and start in six to eight weeks before the last frost-free date.

54. Do border carnations flower all summer?

The carnation flowers all summer. Set out after all danger of frost is past. Remove the spent flowers so that the plant cannot form seed. This keeps them from flowering during the summer. Occasionally feed liquid fertilizer and water regularly.

55. How do I ground-layer pinks?

Pinks (*Dianthus*) usually are not ground-layered. Take cuttings from active growth and root. See beginning of chapter under Propagation.

56. May I plant carnation seed before April for growing outdoors?

Plant carnation seed quite early. If one has space and good growing conditions are available, start as early as late February. Sow the seed and give them 12 to 14 hours of light per day. Grow in a cool area.

57. What is the best way to grow a Chinese lantern plant?

The Chinese lantern plant (*Physalis*) is often grown as an annual although in many cases it is a perennial. Start the plants from seed in the open ground in early spring or indoors. They prefer warmth and sunshine and enjoy frequent watering. They grow and spread so quickly as to become almost wild. Prepare soil with plenty of organic matter and keep them well watered during periods of drought.

58. What kind of care do I give a Chinese lantern plant?

The Chinese lantern plant is over-wintered by just leaving it in the garden and not disturbing the roots. If successful, it comes up again in the spring; however, it may be necessary to restart from fresh seed.

59. When do I divide chrysanthemums?

Divide in early spring, usually late April or early May.

60. Are the tops of chrysanthemums cut off or broken off in March?

Cut back dead material that was not cut off last fall to just above ground level.

61. Is it too early to divide chrysanthemums in March?

March is too early. Wait until plants are actively growing when new shoots are four to six inches long. At that time, carefully lift the plants and remove as much soil as possible. Take well-rooted pieces from the outside of the clumps, replant these and discard the centers which are the old parts.

62. How do I best divide chrysanthemums that are too crowded?

See Question 61. Replant new shoots out 18 to 24 inches apart.

63. How do I handle rooted chrysanthemum cuttings?

Once chrysanthemum cuttings are rooted, pot them in small pots and keep them in a frame or other protected area where they are well watered and regularly fed liquid fertilizer. In early May plant the cuttings in the garden. Pinch the tops out of the plants to keep them low and bushy.

64. When are chrysanthemums cut back?

Cut back chrysanthemums whenever the growth becomes farily long. Remove the tips of the new growth to allow them to branch out and become fuller. Cut back immediately after flowering to remove the flower heads.

65. When do I stop pinching back my chrysanthemums?

Stop pinching by late July. Let the ends develop to produce flowering buds for show from mid September on.

66. What is meant by pinching (or cutting) back the plants?

Pinching is removing the soft growing tip which is the top one-half to one inch of the plant when it is growing actively. Once this occurs, the plant sends out new shoots, making it bushier. Pinching is also used to control the height of many plants.

67. Is it okay to move my chrysanthemums from one place to another in May?

Yes, provided they are given a good watering and are protected from the sun for the first day or two. Also, chrysanthemums move easily in the fall once they come into bloom by soaking the ground thoroughly 24 hours ahead of time. Carefully lift them with as much soil attached as possible and move them to the desired area, thoroughly watering.

68. What do I use to spray the mums for aphids?

Use any insecticide. Be very careful to spray underneath and on top of the leaves.

69. How do you care for chrysanthemums in the winter?

Hardy chrysanthemums are readily over-wintered in an area that is well drained. If you have had a problem over-wintering in late fall after the first heavy freeze, lift plants with as much soil attached as possible and place in a cold frame or on top of the ground. As the weather becomes colder, mulch around them with leaves or other suitable material, being careful not to cover the tops of the plants. In this way they over-winter nicely. If they do not over-winter, they are too wet with insufficient drainage. Check plants occasionally to make sure that they do not dry out too much.

70. How do I propagate our columbine?

Columbine (*Aquilegia*) is propagated from seed early in the spring. As soon as the flowers are finished, seed has set and pods have turned brown, remove the seeds from the plant and sow. Another good method of propagation is to divide the plants when they become very large. Carefully separate them and plant them back in the garden. This usually is done in early September or early in spring just as growth is beginning.

71. Are Four-o'clock flowers poisonous?

The seeds and roots are poisonous if eaten in large quantities.

72. How do I care for Four-o'clocks in winter?

The Four-o'clock (*Mirabilis jalapa*) is usually grown as an annual. Occasionally it over-winters if given good protection with a heavy mulch. The seeds fall on the ground and germinate early in the following spring. Little or no special care is needed.

73. How do I best grow Easter lilies?

The Easter lily (*Lilium longiflorum*) is a hardy lily. It grows in an area where it receives some shade such as filtered sun or where it gets only morning or afternoon sun. Plant amongst low shrubbery or in a perennial bed. It likes a well drained soil. Fertilize at planting time with plenty of superphosphate worked into the soil. Then every spring as growth begins, add some additional superphosphate around the base. Work in a balanced fertilizer, such as a 5-10-5, into the ground after growth is several inches high.

74. When is the best time to plant lily bulbs?

Plant lily bulbs in late fall when they are nearly dormant. The best bulbs are found on the west coast and are dug in late October and then shipped out. With good storage conditions now available, bulbs are often stored and sold in many garden centers in early spring. For best results, plant as soon as possible to be ready for early spring.

75. Is it okay to plant bulbs on their sides so that water will not stand in the centers. If so, do they right themselves?

In cases where bulbs, such as the true lily (*Lilium*), are having difficulty becoming established, plant them by digging holes several inches deeper than required and putting in two to three inches of coarse sand. Then lay the bulbs on their sides and cover with the proper soil. The bulbs will quickly send out new roots in the moist soil and gradually right themselves. Placing them on their sides prevents water from collecting in the center and causing rotting. The bulbs are not harmed in any way by planting this way.

76. What kind of fertilizer is best for growing Easter lilies?

The best kind of fertilizer is superphosphate worked in the soil at planting time with an additional light application when growth begins in early spring, followed by a feeding of a regular balanced fertilizer when they are three to four inches high.

77. May I grow Easter lilies in containers? How do I do this?

Easter lilies grow in containers and are often purchased as gift plants at Eastertime. Then after flowering and when the ground is warm enough, transplant them directly into the garden where they often will flower again in the first year in late summer. The following year, they flower in many areas in late May or early June.

If you want to grow Easter lilies in containers, it is best to buy new bulbs from your garden center late in the fall, pot these in clay pots five to six inches in diameter, using proper potting soil and just lightly cover the bulbs. Place the bulbs in a cold frame or other cool area where the temperature runs around 40 to 45 degrees until they are well rooted. Then bring them into the house in late December or early January where they are given plenty of light and temperatures of 55 to 65 degrees. Keep watered as needed with occasional feedings of liquid fertilizer. They will bloom near early spring.

78. Do I plant imported Holland day lilies in March?

Holland day lilies can be planted anytime they are available. Prepare the ground in early March. Plant them in an area where they get either semi-shaded conditions or sun for three to four hours during the day.

79. How do I transplant day lilies?

Day lilies are easily transplanted at almost any time but preferably before they start to bloom. Once growth is active in early spring, carefully lift them with as much root system as possible. Remove as much of the soil as you can and separate the tubers so that you have two to three eyes to each division. Plant these back so that the growing tips are just barely covered and water them if needed. They soon become established.

80. What do I do about my day lilies? They are not sending up bud stocks.

If day lilies fail to flower, they are getting too much shade; however, if light conditions are proper, the bulbs are undernourished. By using plenty of superphosphate in early spring as growth is beginning and by following with a balanced fertilizer when growth is three to four inches high, good sized plants are produced which will bloom in summer.

81. The leaves on my day lilies are browning. What do I do?

Examine the leaves carefully for insects, particularly aphids, clustered along the under side of the leaves. They suck the juices out and cause discoloration. If no aphids are present, then look for disease. This produces browning of the leaves or an orange line between the green and the brown areas. If this is the case, spray with a fungicide or with a spray used for bacterial leaf rot.

82. Do I spray day lilies and with what?

If there are insects, spray with insecticide underneath and on top of the leaves. If it is a disease, find out what it is and use the correct spray.

83. How do I carry over shasta daisies from one season to another?

The shasta daisy (*Chrysanthemum maximum*) is an excellent garden perennial. Use soil well enriched with organic matter and superphosphate. Transplant the new plant and keep it well watered until it is established. Once flowering is finished, remove the flower stalk and keep it well watered during periods of drought. In the fall it forms a rosette of leaves which will over-winter without any difficulty. If you had a problem with wintering-over in the past, the ground does not have sufficient drainage. Move the plant where there is a lighter soil and no chance of it sitting in water.

84. When do I plant daisies?

Shasta daisies are available in early spring from most garden centers. They come in pots where they are growing actively or in plastic containers. Prepare the soil and plant. See Question 83 for watering procedures.

85. When are daisy seeds planted?

Sow the seed in March. See beginning of this chapter under Propagation. Give them plenty of light and a temperature of 70 to 75 degrees. They germinate in seven to 14 days.

86. What is the care and culture of dahlias?

Dahlias are grown over much of the country and make excellent late summer flowering plants. A number of the newer varieties, which are small, are available as flowering plants from garden centers in early spring. With good care they continue to flower until late fall. Select an area that is semi-shaded or where they get sunlight for only three to four hours, preferably in the early morning. Avoid the late afternoon sun which can cause the flowers to lose much of their color and cut their life span. Select an area that has good drainage. Work organic matter and superphosphate deep into the soil prior to planting. Dahlia tubers are available from local garden centers in early spring. Put outside after all danger of heavy frost is past. Plant dahlia tubers with the eye one to two inches below the ground level.

If they are the taller varieties, insert a sturdy stake at planting time. As the plants begin to grow actively, carefully tie them with a soft cloth material or soft tie to the stakes to keep the plants from bending. Pinch side buds and the center from the plants that are six to eight inches high to cause them to bush out and develop. Feed them occasionally. Watch for insects and spray as needed. Keep the plants well-watered particularly during drought periods of the summer. They will flower in late summer until late fall. After the first frost occurs and leaves start to turn black, dig up the tubers and allow to dry in a protected area for several days. Then remove excess soil. Place the tubers in an area where temperatures are between 45 and 55 degrees. Occasionally mist the tubers in winter to keep them from shriveling. In late March take them out of storage, thoroughly clean them and cut them up into new sections with each section having an eye. Then plant outside in late April in Zone 6.

87. How do you handle dwarf dahlia bulbs for winter storage?

Dig up tubers after the plants are hit with the first light frost, dry off and cut the tops off. Store in a temperature of 45 to 50 degrees. See Question 86.

88. Are dahlias grown from seed or roots?

Both methods are ideal for growing dahlias. A number of the dwarf varieties are readily available in seed and grow very well. Many are also available from garden centers as tubers, ready to start growing four to six weeks before they are ready to be planted outside after all danger of frost is past.

89. How do I plant a flower bed where I would have blooms all summer long?

Select annuals which bloom all summer such as asters, marigolds, petunias, snapdragons, zinnias and others which will give continuous bloom. Removing flower heads before they have a chance to set seed would also insure longer flowering spans. Geraniums are also excellent for all summer color.

90. What causes flowers to die in one area only in my flower bed?

I would suspect a bacterial disease. If so, have the plants treated accordingly. Send a sample to your nearest university extension division or botanical garden for diagnosis and treat according to results sent back to you.

91. When is the best time to plant gladiolus bulbs?

Plant gladiolus bulbs two to three weeks before the last heavy frost. Prepare the ground and plant the corms one to two inches below the ground level. These soon start to grow and can stand the early cold. Make repeated plantings at two to three-week intervals for continuous cuttings during the summer months.

92. Our gladioli grew six inches and then turned brown. Are they salvageable?

The browning is caused by a bacterial rot. Once the plants have started to turn brown, dig them up and discard them so the disease cannot spread to nearby corms. Select healthy corms or if growing your own corms from one year to another, thoroughly clean them in the fall and dust with fungicide. It may be necessary to dust with insecticide. At planting time, make sure that the ground is well worked with plenty of organic matter.

93. How do I handle gladiolus corms?

In late fall, dig up corms, cut back tops to within two inches of the top of the soil line and leave in an area that is well aerated to further dry out for one to two weeks. Then remove excess soil and place bulbs in trays in an area where the temperature is 45 to 55 degrees to further dry. In four to six weeks and if the tops are loose, clean all debris away. Take the corm in one hand and with the thumb and forefinger of the other hand, grasp the top and snap this away from the corm. If they are thoroughly dried, it will pull off easily. If not, try in another week or two. Remove all excess debris around the corm and dust with fungicide and insecticide. Store in a well ventilated area at a temperature of 45 to 55 degrees until ready for planting the next spring.

94. How do you grow gladiolus corms?

Gladiolus corms are obtained from garden centers or seed firms early in the spring. Plant two to three weeks before the last frost in soil which has been well prepared with plenty of organic matter and superphosphate and in an area where they receive sun most of the day. Watch the plants for aphids and other insects when they are actively growing and spray if necessary. Once the plants have flowered, remove the flower stalks to prevent seed from forming but allow the leaves to continue to produce food for the build-up of a new corm.

CANDY CANE ZINNIA
(Burpee Seeds)

WATER LILIES
(Missouri Botanical Garden)

DAFFODIL
(Missouri Botanical Garden)

ENGLISH LAVENDER
Lavandula angustifolia
(Missouri Botanical Garden)

95. When are hibiscus seeds planted?

The new cultivars of hibiscus are readily grown from seed, purchased from seed houses early in the spring. Start four to six weeks ahead of time indoors. Soak seed in hot water for two to three hours or in warm water overnight before sowing. Sow seed and transplant when the third pair of leaves have developed. Give the plants as much light as possible, preferably sun during the day or 12 to 14 hours of artificial light. As soon as all danger of frost is past, plant them outdoors where they will flower during the summer months.

96. When is the best time to transplant perennial hibiscus?

The best time is either in late fall or early spring just as growth is beginning.

97. What are the requirements for growing heather?

Heather is a very low spreading plant and can be grown in Zone 6 if given proper soil conditions. It likes a well drained soil enriched with organic matter and the same conditions as one would grow azaleas or rhododendrons where they are protected from the winter sun. Those that prefer an acid soil, add sulfur to the soil or use partially decomposed oak-leaf mold. Heather needs sun for several hours each day. Keep the plants well watered and plant in areas protected from wind and winter sun.

98. How do we grow hollyhocks?

Hollyhocks are a favorite of many people and are readily grown from seed. Purchase seed from a seed house preferably during mid summer when new seed is available. If seed is started in the month of July, it will germinate and be ready for transplanting into the garden in mid to late September. It will flower the following spring. Often plants that are established will self-sow in the same area if the ground is not worked too deeply. They prefer an area that is well drained with plenty of sun and ordinary garden soil.

99. Are hollyhocks planted in June?

Plant hollyhocks anytime from early spring through June as long as plants are available.

100. What are the best outdoor growing conditions for impatiens?

Impatiens like semi-shaded areas and soil which is well enriched with organic matter and well drained. Young plants are started indoors or purchased from garden centers in early spring after danger of frost is past. Water well during periods of drought with an occasional feeding of liquid fertilizer.

101. Do I put impatien plants in sun or shade?

Most impatiens do best when grown in a semi-shaded area although some of the newer varieties will grow well in the sun. However, their color is not as strong.

102. How do I carry impatiens over to next year?

Take cuttings in early fall before it becomes too cold and root in a mixture of one-third part peat moss to two-thirds part perlite. Keep moderately moist and they will root in two to three weeks. Pot and grow indoors in an area where they get plenty of light during the winter months. Another method is to cut the plants back early in the fall, bring them indoors and continue growing. Occasionally feed with liquid fertilizer and pinch back the plants to keep them compact.

103. How do we best care for irises? And when are they transplanted?

Irises like a well drained soil with plenty of organic matter added and an area that receives full sunlight. Iris plants are available and are best transplanted in late July or early August. Be careful to just barely cover the rhizomes. Plant three rhizomes facing out, spacing about six inches apart. These will root heavily by fall and over-winter. The following year they will start to send out new shoots and be in good bloom the second year, reaching their peak the third and fourth years.

104. Are flower stalks pruned from irises? How do you prune irises?

Flower stalks are removed as soon as the flower dies. Take a sharp knife and cut the flower stalks just above the leaves, leaving the leaves for the plant to manufacture more food.

105. Are irises fertilized? How and when?

Fertilize irises each year by using a light application of superphosphate followed in seven to 10 days with a balanced fertilizer into the soil in early spring as growth begins. Moisten soil when this is applied.

106. Are irises moved in May?

Irises can be moved in May but the best time to move them is in late July or early August.

107. What is the best way to plant and divide irises?

Irises are best planted in a sunny area with healthy soil and proper drainage. Irises are divided once they become very compact or stop flowering. Carefully dig up the large clumps and select new rhizomes from the outer edge by selecting three from each clump and placing these at six-inch intervals all facing outward. This is done in late July or early August.

108. What do we do when our irises fail to flower?

If this happens, plants are becoming too thick and overgrown. When this occurs, dig up plants and rework the ground adding plenty of organic matter and superphosphate. See Question 103.

109. My irises are very straggly. What do I do?

Give the plants plenty of sun and see that the ground is well enriched with superphosphate and a balanced feeding every spring when growth is beginning.

110. What do you do for iris borers?

This is an insect that bores into the base of the leaves just above the rhizome. Inspect plants at regular intervals. If holes are noticed, spray immediately with insecticide around the leaves and base of the plants, repeating again at 10-day intervals.

111. We have iris rootstocks that have been stored for two years. Will they grow if planted?

It is very unlikely that these will grow. If they do, they are going to be very weak. It is best to discard these and purchase new stocks which will be in a healthier condition.

112. When do I thin out the iris plant beds?

Irises grow well for three to four years. After that dig them up, redivide and plant. See Question 103.

113. The iris bloom stalks grow and then become limp and droop. What do I do?

Check the plants thoroughly to make sure that they are receiving plenty of nutrients early in the spring along with a proper feeding program. Spray to control insects and diseases. Flower stalks often droop over because they are top heavy. If this is the case, staking may be necessary.

114. What is the best method to store iris bulbs?

Bulbs are available in late fall and grown as potted specimens indoors during the winter months. After flowering, plants are allowed to continue growing until foliage starts to turn yellow. At that time withhold watering plant and allow bulbs to dry out. Plant iris bulbs outside in early spring after danger of frost is over and allow to grow and flower during the summer months. Dig up in the fall before heavy frost, allow to dry off thoroughly, clean and store in an area where the temperature is 45 to 55 degrees.

115. What is the best way to grow lavender?

Young plants are readily available from many garden centers in early spring. They prefer a soil that is well drained and somewhat sandy and an area where they receive sun. Set out plants after all danger of frost is over and water lightly. During the summer months see that they receive adequate watering during periods of drought. Late in the fall cut back plants, removing the old heads. In many areas in Zone 6 they will over-winter without any difficulty.

116. Does lavender grow successfully in Zone 6?

Lavender does very well in Zone 6 and under most cold conditions will over-winter without any problem. To be on the safe side, take cuttings in early fall or lift the plants, pot them up into pots and over-winter them in a frame or protected area.

117. How do we grow lupines?

Lupine seeds are readily available from most seed houses. The lupine is treated as a biennial so that its seeds are sown during July or early August. When seeds are ready for transplanting, pot in individual pots so as not to disturb the roots. New plants will be ready for planting in the garden in middle to late September. They form a rosette of leaves and over-winter if they are in an area that is well drained with plenty of organic matter in the soil. In the following spring they send up new leaves and flower quite early. In some parts of Zone 6 where it is very hot, they do not grow beyond the first year but in other cases, they produce side shoots which will flower the second year. It is best to start new ones from seed each year.

118. Is lily-of-the-valley planted in March or April?

Lily-of-the-valley (*Convallaria majalis*) is planted anytime in early spring. Plant the small buds in good soil in sunny or preferably semi-shaded areas. They like a rich, moist soil.

119. When are lily-of-the-valley transplanted?

Transplant in early spring or immediately following flowering.

120. Are marigold seeds planted outdoors in April?

Marigolds are planted directly in the garden in April without any difficulty. Also plant seeds indoors six to eight weeks before the last frost, grow under good light conditions and harden-off a week before transplanting outdoors.

121. How do I encourage the growth of our marigolds?

Marigolds like average garden soil. If the soil has been well enriched with organic matter and some superphosphate, they will grow readily. If plants are doing poorly in the garden, use a liquid fertilizer. If grown indoors, see that the plants receive plenty of sun or artificial light for 12 to 14 hours per day. Keep them moderately moist and well fed.

122. We have mold on our marigolds. How do we eliminate this?

The mold indicates a fungus disease. Spray with fungicide, repeating again in seven to 10 days. Give the plants plenty of air and space to keep the mold under control.

123. Do I save seeds from marigolds and plant again next year?

You may save marigold seeds; however, the hybrid seeds do not come true to form. It is much better to purchase new seeds from seed houses to be sure of the color and variety you want.

124. How do I transplant a Mayapple?

Mayapple (*Podophyllum peltatum*) is an attractive wild flower. Purchase it from nurseries which grow wild flowers. If you have them growing in your garden, transplant in early spring as growth is beginning. Give them a soil well enriched with leaf mold and transplant to a semi-shaded area, such as the edge of a woodland habitat.

125. How do I germinate morning glory seeds?

Morning glory (*Ipomoea*) seeds are best germinated by placing them in water with a temperature of 95 degrees for a period of several hours or leaving them in warm water overnight. Sow the following morning. Another method is to file one side of the seed until you break through the outer shell and then plant. This allows the moisture to get into the embryo and starts it germinating.

126. What is the best spray to use on nasturtiums?

Nasturtiums (*Tropaeolum*) are often infected with black aphids. Spray with insecticide under and on top of the leaves, repeat at seven to 10-day intervals if needed.

127. Will pampas grass grow in Zone 6?

Pampas grass is an attractive ornamental grass grown anywhere in Zone 6. It prefers a soil that is well-enriched with organic matter and well drained.

128. Are peony bushes grown from seeds?

Yes. It takes three to four years before they reach flowering size.

129. Our peony bushes are producing very small flowers late. What do we do?

Peonies like a rich soil made up of plenty of organic matter and superphosphate. Each spring as growth begins, work in a small amount of superphosphate around the base of the plant followed by a feeding in seven to 10 days of a balanced fertilizer. See that they receive plenty of water during periods of drought. Some species flower earlier than others.

130. Our peonies are not producing buds. What do we do?

Peonies, once they have been planted for two years and are not flowering, have been planted too deeply. If they are not flowering, take a garden fork or spade, dig down under each side separately, lifting the plant up partway. Firm down the soil underneath the spade. Raise the plant up so that the crown or eyes are just about an inch below the soil level.

131. Are peonies moved in June?

Peonies are best moved in September when they are nearly dormant. Allow them to go through the normal growing season and to build up as much nourishment as possible into the roots. If they must be moved in June, dig them with as much soil attached as possible and keep them well watered when replanting.

132. We have a sticky substance on peony buds. What do we do?

This is normal with the peonies and is a secretion produced by the bud itself. It attracts ants which feed on it and remove it.

133. How do we eliminate ants on peonies?

If there are not too many ants, do not worry about them. If there are a lot of them, find the source and use an insecticide to control them. Ants are attracted to the sticky substance on the buds and do not harm the plant itself.

134. When is the best time to divide peonies?

The best time is middle to late September.

135. How do we get rid of a fungus growth on our peonies?

When peonies start growing in early spring and become three to four inches high, spray with fungicide under and on top of the leaves, repeating in seven to 10 days. This stops it forming. However, once it has formed, spray with fungicide. Repeat in four to five days.

136. Our peonies failed to flower last year. How do we prevent this the next year?

If peonies have been planted for awhile, divide them in middle to late September. Feed early in the spring with superphosphate and a balanced fertilizer and water well during the summer months. Avoid cutting the flowers off or cutting the plants back until late summer. Allow them to grow as much leaf foliage as possible to build up nourishment. Remove flower heads as soon as the flowers are finished and do not allow to set seed.

137. What do we use on peonies to control insects?

Use insecticide under and on top of the leaves when insects are noticed. Peonies usually have few insects so that one to two sprayings is all that is necessary.

138. How and when are the flowers and seeds of the tree peony removed?

Remove just the flower head with a sharp knife or pair of pruners as soon as the tree peony, which is a shrub, is through flowering. Do not allow it to set seed.

139. What is a good fertilizer to use on tree peonies?

Use superphosphate worked around the base of the plant followed by a balanced fertilizer in early spring. Keep the plants well mulched with compost.

140. How do you eliminate mites on peonies?

Use an insecticide, such as Kelthane, as soon as mites are first noticed. Spray again in three days and apply thoroughly underneath and on top of the leaves. Often three to four applications are needed to bring this under complete control.

141. Is it too late to plant peonies in June?

It is best to wait until late September, obtaining healthy new root stocks.

142. How do I divide peonies?

Dig up peonies in the middle or late September with a heavy spade and remove as much of the root stock as possible. Wash the soil off. The top of the roots will contain small red eyes. Cut leaves off as close to the eye as possible. Then with a sharp knife or heavy spade, cut off sections containing three to four of the eyes with plenty of root attached. Set back in the ground in prepared soil with the eyes one to two inches below the soil level. Avoid planting too deeply.

143. Our peonies started to grow well in the spring and just as buds were forming, they turned black and the stems turned brown. How is this prevented?

The cause is a bacterial disease known as leaf blight. Spray with Phaltan or Bordeaux mixture in early spring as growth is beginning. Repeat in 10 to 12 days. Usually two applications are all that are necessary.

144. What is recommended for all summer bloom of perennial garden plants and bedding plants?

Perennials do not flower all summer therefore they are best inter-planted with a number of annuals for good color. Annuals such as marigolds, petunias, salvias and zinnias, depending on the height and color you want, are ideal to use with perennials.

145. Can perennials be mulched for weed control?

Yes. Apply the mulch as soon as plants are set in or as soon as the ground is cleaned up. Depth to three to four inches is best.

146. What do we do about slugs eating petunias?

Remove all debris around the petunias in the garden. Set out commercial slug bait early in the evening or use raw potatoes by cutting them in half and placing the cut side down. In the morning destroy the slugs collected in the potato.

147. How do we eliminate the aphids in our petunias?

Spray petunias at regular intervals with insecticide, applying it thoroughly under and on top of the leaves. Two to three sprayings may be necessary at four to five day intervals.

148. What do we do about wireworms in our petunias?

Prior to planting, redig the soil and treat with insecticides, such as synthetic Pyrethrin and Diazinon. If wireworms appear after planting, apply the insecticides around the plants.

149. What is the name of the disease that attacks petunias and how do you treat it?

Petunias are attacked by a fungus or by bacterial growth. Fungus appears as though the plant has been dusted with flour. With bacteria, the stems wilt and turn black. Spray the plants immediately with recommended fungicide and repeat again at 10 day intervals if needed.

150. My petunias do not look well. What do I do?

If not growing well, petunias may need additional feedings of a balanced fertilizer at regular intervals. Pinch the plants back to encourage bushiness. In mid summer prune the plants and follow with a feeding of a liquid fertilizer.

151. What are the best petunias to use in hot weather or in hot areas of the country?

The stronger colors, the deep reds and blues, along with some of the newer varieties of white stand up best under these conditions.

152. Our phlox is dying. Do I transplant the young shoots?

The phlox probably has a fungus disease, which is quite common. Spray the plant with fungicide, such as Captan, once growth becomes active. Repeat at 10 to 12-day intervals several times. In some areas the fungus does not become active until mid summer. As soon as noticed, spray under and on top of the leaves. Repeat at 10-day intervals.

153. How can I grow phlox from seed?

This is not recommended as many of the varieties are hybrids and do not come true from seed. It is better to propagate by dividing the clumps. Select outside divisions and plant these back. Remove flower heads as soon as flowering is through and before they have a chance to set seed. Often seed falls and the colors are not as vivid when grown from seed.

154. How do I propagate creeping phlox?

Creeping phlox (*Phlox subulata*) is an attractive, low plant used in front of rock gardens or as borders for flowering plants in early spring. Propagate by taking clumps, dug out with a trowel, and transplant into well prepared soil. Water well and protect from sun for the first day or two.

155. What does it mean to pinch back and how does this relate to removing dead flowers from begonias, petunias, etc.?

To pinch back simply means to remove a soft growing tip from the top of the plant. A soft pinch is removing approximately one-half inch and a hard pinch is removing several inches of growth. In removing dead flowers, one should pinch them off or cut them off to prevent them from forming seed and to increase better flowering habits.

156. How do I transplant Oriental poppies?

Oriental poppies (*Papaver orientales*) are transplanted in early spring as growth is beginning or after flowering when the foliage starts to die. Be careful to dig the roots out and separate into small divisions.

157. How do we get our poppies to rebloom?

The Oriental poppies flower early in the season. As foliage gradually dies down, the plant goes through a resting stage. In late fall it forms a rosette, flowering the following spring. See that the soil is well enriched with organic matter and add a light feeding of superphosphate with a balanced fertilizer. They will not bloom twice in one year.

158. The leaves of our Oriental poppies are dying. What do we do?

This is a natural with Oriental poppies after they flower; however, if it occurs before the plants flower, check for insect problems and spray. If no insects are apparent, check for disease.

159. How do I tell the top side of a ranunculus corm?

The bottom sides are pointed.

160. My ranunculus corms planted in early spring started to grow and then died back very suddenly. How is this prevented?

This usually indicates that the plants are growing where it is too warm. They like cool conditions. Place outside in the ground in the spring as soon as it is soft enough to prepare. Dust the plants or spray with fungicide when growth is active.

161. Can I plant roses where I had azaleas?

This is a common question and applies to a number of plants. In all cases if the area is well worked up and plenty of organic matter added, replanting of anything else in that area can be done without any harmful effect.

162. How do I grow salvia?

Salvia is available in early spring from garden centers as small plants ready for transplanting outside after all danger of heavy frost is over. You may also obtain seed to grow indoors six to eight weeks before planting outside. Allow plenty of light during the day or 12 to 14 hours of artificial light. Use soil enriched with organic matter and well drained in an area where they get plenty of sun. Use occasional feedings of liquid fertilizer.

163. I have yellowing leaves in the salvia. What do I do?

This sometimes happens when plants are too close together and not getting enough light or nourishment. Feed additional liquid fertilizer or work in a balanced fertilizer around the plants early in the season.

164. Does blue salvia grow in the shade?

Blue salvia is best grown where it gets full sun or sun for at least three to four hours. In shade, flowering is sparse and growth weak.

165. How is sage grown?

Small plants are obtained from garden centers early in the spring or you may purchase seeds. Sage likes the same conditions as salvia (see Question 162), i.e. soil well enriched with organic matter and a sunny location.

166. What is the best winter care of sage plants?

Dig plants up in late fall and bring indoors or start sage from cuttings taken late in the fall and bring indoors in winter.

167. How do I harvest seeds from flowering plants?

Many flowering plants are hybrids therefore seeds will not come true to form. In collecting seeds, let the seeds mature fairly well on the plants then very carefully remove the seed heads and store them in a cool, dry area until thoroughly ripe.

168. Is it okay to take a sempervivum out of the pot and plant outside in September?

Yes. Place in an area that is well drained with a light sandy soil.

169. How do I propagate snapdragons?

Start snapdragons from seeds readily available in most garden centers early in the spring. Sow eight to 10 weeks before it is ready to plant outdoors. Grow indoors where they can get plenty of light during the day or grow under artificial light for 12 to 14 hours. Pinch plants to produce compactness. Plant outdoors after all danger of frost is over.

170. Are snapdragons propagated from stem cuttings?

Take cuttings from healthy plants before they start to form buds, root in perlite and peat moss and then plant outside when heavily rooted. Protect them from the sun for the first day or two.

171. What is a good mulch to use for sweet peas?

Any form of decaying plant material or leaf mold is ideal. Apply three or four inches of it. Avoid peat moss or grass clippings as they shed water.

172. When are tuberoses planted?

Plant the tuberose (*Polianthes tuberosa*) outside in late April or early May in Zone 6 in an area that is well enriched with organic matter and where it receives sun.

173. My tuberoses failed to flower over the past two years. How do I get them to flower?

Storage of tuberoses is extremely important. Store them above 50 degrees. Dig up bulbs in the fall before the weather gets too cold, dry off and then place in an area where it is relatively dry. Leave until ready to plant outside again in the spring. Put outside in Zone 6 the latter part of April for flowering during the summer months. Cold storage delays flowering.

174. How often are tuberoses divided?

Divide only when the individual bulbs separate freely. Do not force them, but leave them in clumps. They flower well this way.

175. How do I grow verbena?

Verbena is an annual started from seed. Many of the seed houses now carry a number of the newer varieties. Germinate in seed media in temperatures of 75 to 80 degrees. Once the plants have established their second or third set of leaves, transplant into other pots. Start this about six weeks before planting outdoors. Do not place outdoors until all danger of frost is past and then space at about 12-inch intervals.

Some varieties are readily propagated from cuttings taken before the plants start to flower while the growth is still soft. Take cuttings and root them in a mixture of peat moss and perlite. When plants are growing actively, water at regular periods when needed and occasionally feed them liquid fertilizer. Remove flower heads when flowering ends. If plants are allowed to set seed, flowering is delayed in many of the varieties.

176. What is the general care needed for growing water lilies?

Water lilies are grown successfully in almost any area of North America. Select tubers in early spring and place outdoors once all danger of frost is past and the water temperature has reached approximately 60 degrees. This is very important as far as the tropical ones are concerned. Place hardier water lilies outside earlier. Tropical water lilies, if planted out too early, go dormant and will not start back into growth until very late in the season and will seldom flower.

Water lilies are grown in any pool where there is about six to eight inches of water over the top of the bulb. Use a potting soil with a balanced fertilizer, such as a 5-10-5, used at the rate of about a five-inch potful to one wheelbarrow of soil. Start tubers indoors in early March and grow in four-inch pots in tanks where the water temperature is around 75 to 80 degrees. Then place the plants outdoors by removing them from the pots and placing them in planters, such as plastic tubs, where they have about one foot of soil. Put two inches of sand over the top to keep the soil from becoming disturbed when adding water. Slowly lower the tubs into the tanks or pools where the lilies are to be grown. Avoid sudden plunging which causes growing media to rise. With water temperatures of around 60 degrees, plants will grow actively and even better when the soil warms up.

Plants set out in Zone 6, usually from the middle to the end of May, will be in full bloom by late June and will continue to flower until late fall. Remove any dead or partially destroyed leaves as close to the soil line as possible with a sharp knife. Remove old blooms at regular intervals if not wanted for seed. Six weeks after planting, add a handful of a well balanced fertilizer into the tub in which the lilies are growing to keep them in good condition. Occasionally hose off the water to remove any insects that get on the buds or leaves.

When weather becomes cool, remove tropical water lilies from the growing area and carefully dry off the tubers and store in a moist sand in glass jars at a temperature of 40 to 45 degrees. Leave until early March and start back into bloom.

177. What is the best fertilizer to use on water lilies?

A well balanced fertilizer, such as a 5-10-5 or well rotted cow manure is ideal.

178. Aphids are a problem on water lilies. What is used to bring these under control?

Hosing with a strong force of water is sufficient to remove the aphids from around the leaves and bloom stalks; however, if this does not keep them under control, use an insecticide, such as synthetic Pyrethrin or Diazinon, at about half strength. Use insecticides with extreme care.

179. Are water lilies grown from seed?

Yes. Flowers that are left to form seed pods drop down in the tank. As soon as the seed is ready, pick it off. Allow seed to thoroughly mature and ripen, remove from the seed pods and place in small containers. Keep moderately moist by putting water or another moist media with it. Store the seed in a refrigerator at some other area at a temperature of around 38 to 40 degrees until ready for planting. Plant seed in late February or early March indoors in containers where the seed is sown in a regular media and then place in tanks of water at approximately 80 degrees. Germination occurs fairly rapidly. As soon as seedlings are of sufficient size, carefully transplant into individual 4-inch pots and place back into the tanks where they are allowed to grow until planting outdoors in May.

Plants started from seed flower the first year and are not necessarily the same as the parent plant because many of them are hybrids. Seedlings vary in flowering characteristics.

180. I purchased water lilies last year and left these out in the tank all winter. They did not grow this spring. What is wrong?

The water lilies were probably tropical. In Zone 6 if left in the tanks, they will die since they are unable to stand the cold weather. Remove from the tanks in middle October and store indoors. See Question 176.

181. May I leave hardy water lilies outdoors all year?

If hardy water lilies in Zone 6 are growing well, leave outdoors all winter in a tank or area where water remains above the crown of the plant at least six to eight inches. These plants start to grow in early spring once the water reaches a temperature of around 50 degrees and bloom a little ahead of the tropical water lilies.

182. Do hardy water lilies need any special care?

Hardy water lilies left in the tank year round do well but need an occasional feeding of a balanced fertilizer. Apply the first application when growth begins and then another light feeding in middle to late June. If they are growing in containers, replace the soil at least every other year with a growing medium well enriched with organic matter. Use a balanced fertilizer at planting time.

183. What is the best culture for water hyacinths?

The water hyacinth (*Eichhornia*) is a plant commonly found in the South and in some areas is a pest. It is not allowed across state lines, where it does not grow, at any time. The plant needs as much light as possible, preferably sun for several hours. If growing outdoors, make sure water temperature is warm before placing it outside. The proper water depth is eight to 10 inches in the tank over the soil.

The water hyacinth makes long fibrous roots which float around the water. Some of these take the nourishment from the water and even root in soil where they come in contact with it. Plants without enough nutrients will be yellow and not grow very well. Plants are produced by sending out off-shoots which root. When large enough, remove from the parent plant and grow as individual plants.

For winter storage in Zone 6 move plants indoors to tanks where the water temperature is around 55 to 65 degrees and where the plants get as much light as possible until ready for planting outdoors again next spring.

184. How do I transplant wild flowers in bloom?

Wild flowers should not be dug up when in bloom as this results in the loss of the plants. In most states it is illegal to dig wild flowers and move them from one area to another unless special permits are obtained. It is much better to leave the plants growing where they are and if desired, to purchase seeds of wild flowers and start these as you would other plants, transplanting them when large enough to the woodland area where you want them to grow.

185. When are yuccas transplanted?

Yuccas make ideal accent plants in the garden and are planted in early spring as new growth is beginning or in late summer.

186. What is the best culture for yuccas?

Yuccas like garden soil well enriched with organic matter and some superphosphate added to it. Set plants outside in early spring or in the fall to establish a good root system. They are hardy in winter in Zone 6. Plants form a series of leaves in the fall called a rosette. In early spring, depending on weather conditions, they start flowering. They form offsets, which when large enough are removed from the parent plant with a sharp spade and planted the same way as the parent plant.

187. Are yuccas grown indoors?

Yes. These varieties are different than the hardier ones grown outdoors. They like a good potting soil and the same cultural conditions as any cactus plant.

188. How do I make my yuccas bloom?

Yuccas bloom once they reach a certain size; however, if they are propagated from plants which produce little bloom, there is little likelihood of them blooming at any time. To increase the flowering, work in superphosphate around the base of the plant in early spring and avoid high nitrogen fertilizers. Plants do well with poor soil with only superphosphate added.

189. Are bloom stalks cut from yuccas?

Remove bloom stalks immediately when the flowers are finished. Plants produce seed quite easily. If you have no desire for the seed, remove the flower stalks and allow the plants to build up a vigorous root system with new growth for flowering again next year.

190. How do you trim yuccas?

Remove the flowering stalk with a sharp pair of shears, cutting it down as close to the crown of the plant as possible without injuring any leaves. Remove older leaves on the outside or base of the plant with a sharp knife by cutting the leaves off as close to the ground level as possible so they do not show.

191. What do I do with a rotting yucca plant?

Remove all infected parts of the plant. If grown in a poorly drained area, replant in an area where drainage is better. If the plant is badly infected, dig it up and destroy it. If only rotting a little, remove the diseased or infected portions. Keep the plant dry and dust with fungicide.

192. Are zinnias planted outdoors in May?

Plant zinnias outdoors in May once danger of frost is past if they were grown from seedlings inside. Harden-off plants for several days before placing them permanently outdoors. Start zinnia seeds in Zone 6 as early as the first week of April. Sow again at two to three-week intervals to produce continuous blooms throughout the growing season. Pull out small, weak seedlings to allow plenty of room for the others to grow.

193. How do I transplant my zinnias?

Transplant when they are quite small with only three to four sets of leaves. Select a cloudy day and keep moderately moist. With a garden trowel, dig down and get as much of the root system as possible and move them to the desired location. Give them a feeding of liquid fertilizer at half the recommended strength. Shade them for the first 24 hours until the new root system is established. Keep them moderately moist for the first few days.

194. My zinnias grow well but have mildew. How is this prevented?

Mildew appears on zinnias like a dusting of white flour. If allowed to continue, it causes leaves to wither and brown. Use fungicide, such as Captan, underneath and on top of the leaves at regular intervals.

Chapter Four
Roses

General Information

Grow roses where they receive four hours of sunlight. Morning sun is preferable; the afternoon sun is stronger and bleaches the colors out of the roses. Some varieties bleach more than others. Select an area free of tree roots and with good drainage.

Roses prefer soil on the heavier side. Prepare to a depth of at least two feet. Remove some of the top soil and add organic matter to the subsoil. Replace good top soil with more organic matter. Add approximately five pounds of superphosphate per 100 square feet to the beds and work into the top five or six inches of soil. Add lime if needed. Secure healthy rose stalks. Plant floribunda, a small clustered type, near the front of the bed with hybrid tea roses next to this and grandiflora at the back. Use climbing roses to frame the outer edges of the rose garden and grow on trellises.

Select healthy roses in early spring and plant immediately when the ground is prepared. If roses are received before the ground is worked, store in an area which is 40 degrees. Keep the roots moist. Light is not a factor at this stage. If roses have dry bare roots, take a bucket of water, mix some soil into this and place the roots in the bucket in a cool area for at least 24 hours before planting. This allows the roots to receive quick nourishment.

Prune roses heavily at planting time. Retain only three to four sturdy canes, removing all weak growth. Cut back remaining canes to within six to eight inches of the ground, cutting to an outside bud. The growth will come out and away from the center of the bush. Allow good aeration.

When planting, dig a hole larger than needed and make a cone shaped area at the base so that roots can be spaced out evenly throughout the area. Prune back any roots that are damaged to good wood. Firm soil about halfway up the plant and then water well. As soon as the water drains away, finish filling the hole. In planting, make the graft, which is the knob just below where branches start, approximately two inches below the finished soil line. Growth coming below this is from understock and is undesirable growth. Roses with the graft planted two inches below soil level gradually establish their own roots and eventually become very hardy. If the graft is planted above the soil, the understalk starts to grow and will kill the graft that grows above the soil.

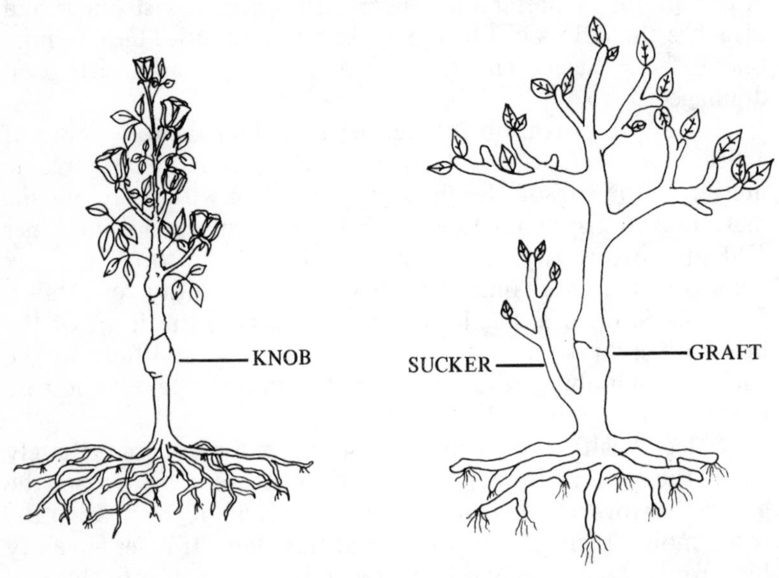

SUCKER BELOW A GRAFT

Once the roses are planted, feed a light application of a balanced fertilizer, such as a 6-12-12, around the base of the plants. Add compost around the new plant for a week to 10 days. Once growth starts gradually remove the mulch and work into the surrounding area. As soon as leaves begin to emerge, use fungicide, such as Captan. Watch for black spot which starts with irregular dark circles appearing on the leaves. Control with spray, such as Acti-dione. Spray again in 10 days underneath and on top of the leaves. Repeat the spray after any rain or when plants have made six to eight inches of new growth.

When flower buds first start to show, give an additional

feeding of a liquid fertilizer. If the color is light green, use a liquid fertilizer, such as a 20-20-20, dissolved in water. Apply two to three gallons around each rose bush. Color on the new growth is a rich green or tinted slightly red if plants are getting the needed nutrients.

Roses generally bloom around the middle to the end of May. When the roses have flowered and the blooms start to fade, remove the old blooms. In cutting roses back, leave five full leaflets from the base of the stem up. Remember to cut to an outside bud so the growth comes up and away from the center of the plant. Prune back weak growth. Following the removal of the spent blooms, use more liquid fertilizer in about two weeks to stimulate the plants into better growth.

Immediately following pruning, use epsom salts, using one tablespoon per gallon of water around each rose bush. Repeat again in three weeks with another application three weeks after that. The epsom salts improves color and perfume of roses and prevents bacterial die-back which sometimes occurs when roses are pruned back.

Once roses are actively growing, check them on a daily basis for insect control. Aphids are usually the first insects to appear on the soft growing tips. They suck the juices out. Use insecticide underneath and on top of the leaves to bring these under control.

During the hot, dry weather roses are subject to spider mites, tiny insects which feed by sucking the juices out from the underside of the leaves and moving on to the top of the leaves. They produce a fine webbing over the plant. To control mites use a good spray for mite control, such as Kelthane, at three-day intervals for three to four applications. Use preventative sprays at regular intervals. If roses are properly sprayed for both insect and disease control during the summer months, they remain in active growth until heavy frost starts.

After the first heavy frost in autumn, mulch the roses for winter protection. Use partially decomposed compost eight to 10 inches around the roses. Prune the plants to prevent damage from winter winds; however, roses will over-winter much better if most of the old growth is left and then pruned in the spring. Add a cup of superphosphate around the roses just before mulching. Roses continue to make root growth as long as the ground is not frozen. After mulch is applied and heavy frost sets in, the ground begins to freeze. In mid or late December, use additional mulch of two or three inches of wood shavings. Apply uniformly over the bed to protect the mounding. Do not take soil from around the base of the plants. You expose the roots which will cause damage to the roses.

Occasionally roses produce stalks which are blind. (The stem forms but no bud develops.) When it is first noticed that the bud is not there, remove one to two inches of the stem tip; it will send a new shoot which in turn produces a bud. If the growth is weak and blind, cut back to the main trunk.

BLIND STALK

Prune roses to control the height of the plant. Prune floribunda, which do not grow as tall as other roses, severely in early spring, hybrid tea roses six to 10 inches above the ground and grandiflora roses up to a foot above ground. New canes which shoot up will flower. Then cut back heavily to produce good side breaks. Prune in early spring after danger of heavy frost is past. The first half of April is recommended in Zone 6 to produce flowers by the third week of May. Do not prune too early even though the weather is mild.

QUESTIONS

1. Can I remove mulch and prune roses in March?

Do not prune roses in March because frost may occur in late March or early April. Wait until after late frost ends.

2. How do I store roses that have been ordered from out of town and arrive before the ground is suitable for planting?

Keep the roots moderately moist and store in an area where temperatures are not over 40 degrees until planting time or keep roses outdoors covering them completely with soil until planting time.

3. How do I care for climbing roses?

Prune climbing roses immediately after flowering. Remove the oldest canes and cut back the other canes that have flowered. This encourages them to send out new growth from the base. Stake or fasten to a trellis. Mulch climbing roses in the fall after the first heavy frost. In very cold areas bend the canes and cover them with burlap or other suitable insulation to protect them from winter cold. Feed with superphosphate, approximately one cup around the base of the plant when growth first begins. Follow this in about two weeks with a light application of a balanced fertilizer, such as a 5-10-5. Use liquid fertilizers during the summer to keep them healthy. Do not feed after the first of August in Zone 6 to allow the plants to harden-off for winter.

4. What is wrong with climbing roses that do not bloom?

This sometimes is due to poor soil conditions. Work in plenty of organic matter and superphosphate in early spring and follow with regular feeding and pruning of excess weak growth to encourage better flowering.

5. What is a good mulch for roses?

Any partially decomposed compost is ideal for mulching roses. Put on the beds in early spring to control weeds during the summer months.

6. Can cuttings from roses be rooted?

Yes. Select cuttings six to eight inches long in mid June and root them in a mixture of three parts perlite to one part peat moss. Keep the cuttings moderately moist and in an area out of direct sunlight. Rooting will occur in about six weeks. Cuttings will flower the next season.

7. When are roses moved?

Move roses in early spring just before growth begins. Also move in the fall when they start to go dormant. Keep as much of the root system attached as possible and mulch heavily to establish healthy root systems.

8. Do you fertilize roses just planted?

If soil is properly prepared at planting time, add another light application of a balanced fertilizer, such as 5-10-5, or a liquid fertilizer, such as 20-20-20.

9. Is soil improved by adding cow manure to the rose bed?

Fresh cow manure burns the roots. Use dried cow manure by working into the top two to three inches of the soil.

10. Is it okay to plant dry root roses in April?

Yes. Soak roots in water overnight first.

11. Are roses uncovered in early April and how far are they cut back?

Remove the mulch over a period of seven to 10 days by working this back from around the base of the roses. When this is completed, prune roses back according to the variety and growth of the roses. Prune floribunda within six inches of the ground level, hybrid tea roses eight to 10 inches and grandiflora roses 12 to 14 inches. Remove all weak growth, and if plants are poor leave only one or two good canes. With a good feeding program these will develop into sturdier roses early in the season. Good sturdy bushes have as many as six sturdy canes left after pruning.

12. Are roses transplanted in May?

If roses are grown in containers that are available in many areas, plant at any time; however, prepare the soil ahead of time and when removing them from the containers avoid breaking the soil up too much. Loosen the roots at the bottom so they will quickly spread into the surrounding soil. In many cases container grown roses are planted too high. Set in the ground so that the graft is just below the soil level.

13. How do I counteract the over fertilization of roses?

Water heavily leaching much of the fertilizer out into the surrounding area.

14. The leaves of some of our roses are a purplish color. What is wrong with them?

The purplish color indicates that roses are getting the proper nourishment. New growth shows a purplish tinge with a dark glossy green on the older leaves just below this.

15. Should rose canes be painted after they are cut back?

It is not necessary if they are well fed and cared for.

16. We have leaf spot on our miniature roses? What do we do?

Leaf spot is caused either by a fungus or a bacterial leaf spot. Check the plant carefully and spray on a regular basis.

17. Plants are heavily infected with black spot and yellow leaf coloration. What do we do to eliminate this?

Spray the plants immediately, getting the spray underneath and on top of the leaves. Repeat again in five to seven days. Follow this with a feeding of a liquid fertilizer up to the first of August.

18. Is there a particular time when it is not wise to feed rose bushes?

Do not feed after the first of August.

19. The leaves of the roses are turning yellow and brown even after regular spraying and fertilizing. What do we do?

Apply sprays thoroughly underneath and on top of the leaves. Keep the ground moderately moist when applying the fertilizer. During the summer months liquid fertilizer is faster acting and easier to apply than the powder. Also check the plants thoroughly for spider mites. Control with Kelthane rather than by other general insecticides.

20. I cannot control the aphids on our roses. What do I do?

Use a spray, such as Diazinon. Follow in four or five days with Malathion or another general insecticide. Alternating between these gives excellent control.

21. What do I do with the flowers on roses once they start to fade?

Remove them. Cut the stems back leaving five full leaflets from the base where they emerge.

22. What do we do about leaves falling off our miniature rose plants?

Make sure plants are receiving adequate moisture, proper feeding and control of mildew and black spot.

23. Where can I buy a Paul's scarlet rose?

This is a climbing rose and is usually available from many of the garden centers and nurseries carrying rose stock.

24. Our cabbage rose is wilting. What do we do?

Check to make sure there is plenty of moisture and no insects in the soil around the base of the rose. If so, use a regular insecticide. Mulch the plant during extreme hot weather.

25. How do we eliminate rose borers?

Immediately following pruning in early spring spray the stems thoroughly with insecticide, such as Diazinon or Malathion. Repeat as needed.

26. In transplanting our old roses the roots seem very large. Can they be cut back part way?

Prune back excess root growth. Do not allow to dry out and plant immediately or keep moist until ready to plant again.

27. How do you remove suckers from roses?

Suckers on roses is the growth which appears below the bud graft. Remove the soil so that the base of the rose stem is visible. With a pair of pruners or a sharp knife, cut flush with the main stem. Plant so that the flower bud is two inches below the soil to prevent suckers from forming.

28. The petals on the outside of my roses are not as nice as the inside. What is done to improve this?

Spray flower buds thoroughly during periods of high humidity or following periods of rain. Discoloration or deformed petals are due to fungus disease. Repeat the spray as needed.

29. Can I grow roses in a big container in the patio?

Roses respond well to container growing provided they are given adequate drainage. Extra watering and extra feeding with liquid fertilizer are needed. Mulch the top of the container with two or three inches of good compost. Follow the normal routine for insects and disease.

30. May I send rose buds to another state?

Roses are transferred from one state to another; however, make sure they are free of insects and diseases. If there is any question, have them inspected by someone from the local extension division of your university.

DOUBLE DELIGHT-HYBRID TEA
AARS award winner for 1977
(All-America Rose Selections)

31. What do we do to save our rose tree (standard rose) which is dying?

Make sure soil is well enriched with plenty of organic matter. Give regular feedings of liquid fertilizer while in good growth up to the first of August. Work in some extra superphosphate into the soil. Do not over-water but keep the soil moderately moist. Follow normal procedures for insect and disease control.

32. Our tea roses are falling over. Do we trim or stake them?

Avoid the problem by pruning back heavily in the early spring to within eight to 10 inches of the ground. When first blooms are finished, cut the stalks back leaving five to seven full leaflets from the base. Remove weak growth.

33. How do we eliminate Bermuda grass which is invading the rose bed?

Dig a small trench around the edge of the bed leaving a neat edge. As Bermuda grass grows over the bed, keep it trimmed and dig any runners which come up through the bed.

34. Our rose bushes are dormant in August. Why?

Roses may lose all their leaves in August due to fungus and bacterial spot.

35. Should roses be mounded?

Yes. Following the first heavy frost apply eight to 10 inches of good top soil or partially decomposed compost around the base of the plants.

36. Are tree roses left outside during the winter in Zone 6?

Yes. Where extremes of temperature exist it is much better to carefully dig the plants up with as much root intact and lay them down covering them with soil after the first heavy frost. If container grown move to protected areas and protect the tops by covering with burlap or another insulating material.

Chapter Five
Trees and Shrubs

General Information

Trees and shrubs add much to the value of a home so carefully select the appropriate ones. The following are the major considerations: freedom from insects and disease, shape and form, good autumn color and flowering and fruiting habits. Trees and shrubs are used as screen for privacy, as specimen plantings and to control the wind and temperature fluctuation.

Deciduous trees and shrubs lose their leaves in the fall and grow new ones each spring. Evergreen trees and shrubs retain their foliage year round; however, evergreens shed some of their needles in late spring. If evergreens retain foliage for two or three years, they are a healthy specimen. If they lose needles within one year of growth, there is a problem. In selecting these plants, consider the location for planting and select the plants in proportion to the height that one wants them to be. Select various plants with interesting shapes, colors, textures, leaf forms, bark and flower and fruiting habits.

Plant trees and shrubs when they are in a dormant state or before growth becomes too advanced. In Zone 6 this occurs from middle October until early spring. Move plants as bare-root specimens, which have no soil attached to the roots, or as balled and burlapped specimens with a soil ball attached, well wrapped in burlap or plastic. Plant at the same depth that they were at the nursery. Avoid deep planting which causes the roots to smother. If planting balled and burlapped specimens, remove the cord or ties around the top of the soil ball which can cut into the tree and eventually kill it. Prepare the planting area, place the specimen at the desired depth and then fill in about halfway with good soil mixed with equal parts of organic matter. Water heavily and when the water has drained away, cut the tie around the top of the soil ball. It is not necessary to remove the burlap. Fill up the rest of the hole with equal parts of soil and organic matter. Do not use fertilizer at this stage. Commercial fertilizers burn the new roots. After the plants are well established, use fertilizer, if needed, to stimulate growth.

Check new plants, particularly if they are bare-root, for damaged roots. If they are, carefully prune. Pruning is required to offset the loss of the roots. Remove some of the weaker growth from the main stem or thin out some of the weaker branches. Avoid cutting the leader on the main stalk of the tree. Once the leader is cut back, it will dwarf the tree considerably. If the leader has been damaged, replace with a new one or create a new one on the tree. Take a stake long enough to protrude above the top and tie in two areas to the main trunk. Take one of the remaining top branches and bend up slowly and tie to the stake to create a new leader.

New trees and shrubs need a good watering when planted. Once planting is completed, use mulch of four to five inches of partially decomposed compost. Place 12 to 18 inches beyond the hole to control soil moisture, ground temperatures and weeds. As the mulch breaks down, it releases nutrients into the soil. Add more mulch yearly.

Once the plants are established, prune occasionally to control the shape of the plant and to open it up for good air circulation. Prune flowering material according to its flowering schedule. Prune early spring flowering plants immediately after flowering. Flower buds are produced on growth following the flowering. Prune late flowering trees and shrubs in late fall or early spring before growth begins. They produce their flower buds early in the growing season. Forsythia, azaleas, rhododendrons and mock-oranges are pruned in early spring following flowering. Prune late flowering plants, such as the *Althaea*, commonly called hibiscus, in early spring before they leaf out. This gives them time to produce new wood and flowers for late summer flowering.

Old shrubs can be renovated by removing up to one-third of the old canes at ground level each year. Check back in six to eight weeks to remove any excess weak growth. After a three-year period, plants are replenished with new growth. After pruning, feed with superphosphate or a balanced fertilizer placed around the base of the plants.

Prune to control the height of the plant and to remove any bad or damaged material. Remove the old flower heads to prevent the plant from setting seed, which in some cases can weaken the plant considerably. Trees require less pruning than shrubs. In most cases just remove any branches which cross one another or cut back branches to control the shape of the plant.

Most evergreens need pruning during the second or third week of June and again around mid September. It is needed to control the height of the plant. Remove the growing tips or cut some of the branches back to cause them to become bushier and more compact. In pruning hedges, whether deciduous or evergreen material, consider the height of the plant you want. Remove one-third to one-half of the growth to encourage the plants to make heavy but compact growth from the base up. Each year as the new growth slows down in mid June, remove up to one-third of the current season's growth until the plants are at their desired heights. Prune hedges of all sizes so that they are narrow at the top and wider at the bottom. This allows for good light exposure and for the plant to absorb and divert rain down to the center of the plant where it is needed.

Deciduous material is planted as soon as plants shed their leaves in the fall and until new leaves begin to emerge in the spring. Plant evergreens from early September in Zone 6 through May. Container-grown stock of both types of plants is available. Plant at any time of the year as long as the soil is well prepared. Carefully remove the plants from the container without damaging the soil ball. Heavily water and add mulch. Water adequately until established.

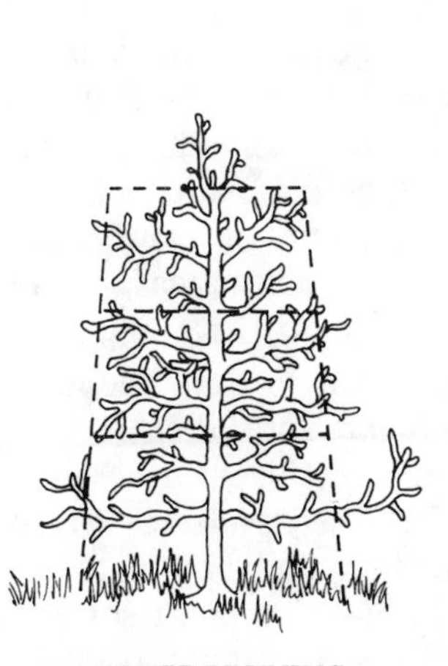

HEDGE PRUNING

DRIPLINE

If plants are damaged in winter, remove the bad material once the plants make new growth. Only prune if necessary but in some cases, cut the plant back severely about a month after plant starts making new growth to reshape it. If ends are larger than an inch in diameter, apply a tree paint over the cut ends. The paint prevents moisture from entering and causing the plant to rot. Make cuts as close to the main branch as possible. Do not leave a stub which causes decay.

Plants which have been winter damaged and have been carefully pruned need a feeding of balanced fertilizer in mid to late April to stimulate growth; however, avoid over-fertilizing which causes soft growth. Feed trees and shrubs in early spring as they make new growth. Apply it evenly around the base of the shrub out to the dripline. With heavier specimens, dig a series of holes one-third of the way from the trunk to the dripline at 18 to 24-inch intervals and about one foot deep. Continue the holes out to the edge of the dripline. In each hole place a handful of a balanced fertilizer. Leave the holes open. Moisture penetrates down and allows air into the root system. This encourages deep rooting of trees and shrubs. Root feeding keeps the roots down low away from the grass. It is needed every three to four years from mid November through late April. Avoid feeding during the summer months. This stimulates too much growth, preventing the plants from hardening-off and making them more susceptible to winter damage. Commercial tree spikes are useful since they feed over a long period of time.

Also use liquid fertilizer, applied through root feeders to the root system, on trees and shrubs anytime the plant is growing up to the end of June. The amount of fertilizer depends upon the size of the plant. Very large trees require anywhere from 50 to 150 gallons of solution to be effective. Plants which are chlorotic, lacking in green color which occurs on plants such as the broad-leafed evergreens and on oaks in many areas, need the addition of iron chelate added to the fertilizer.

If plants are in poor condition, avoid feeding them. This sometimes causes further damage. Make sure the trees have adequate root growth before applying fertilizer; otherwise, it burns the roots. Avoid chemical fertilizer on trees in areas where drainage is exceptionally poor and the root systems are not extensive. Either improve the drainage or plant somewhat higher than is normally done. This allows the plants to establish root systems and grow into the surrounding areas where drainage is not so good.

Plants, such as the hollies, rhododendrons and azaleas, may need an acid soil. Incorporate partially decomposed oak leaves, or other acid type material such as pine needles, or sulfur into the soil which lowers the pH level considerably. In areas where the soil is alkaline, the additional use of sulfur or acid-type fertilizers may be needed at regular intervals.

The following is a list of small shade trees suitable for homeowners with patios or limited space (Check your zone for hardiness.):

Birch, cut-leaved European (*Betula pendula*) 30 to 40 feet.

Birch, slender European (*Betula pendula* 'Gracilis' sometimes listed as *Betula pendula laciniata*) approximately 40 feet.

Cork tree, amur (*Phellodendron amurense*) approximately 35 feet.

Crab apple, various (*Malus* species and cultivars) 12 to 40 feet.

Chinese dogwood (*Cornus kousa chinensis*) 15 to 25 feet.

Flowering dogwood (*Cornus florida* and cv.) 15 to 30 feet.

Golden-rain tree (*Koelreuteria paniculata*) 25 to 30 feet.

Hawthorn (*Crataegus* sp. and cv.) 35 feet.

Holly, American (*Ilex opaca* and cv.) up to 45 feet.

Holly, English (*Ilex aquifolium*) 40 feet, approximately.

Honey locust, thornless cultivars (*Gleditsia triacanthos* and cv.) up to 45 feet.

Hornbeam, pyramidal American (*Carpinus caroliniana* 'Pyramidalis') 40 feet.

Magnolia, species and cultivars, 15-40 feet.

Mimosa or silk tree (*Albizia julibrissin*) 25 – 30 feet.

Olive, Russian (*Elaeagnus angustifolia*) 25 to 40 feet.

Pagoda tree (*Sophora japonica*) 40 feet.

Silver bell, Carolina (*Halesia carolina*) 25 to 30 feet.

Snowbell, fragrant (*Styrax obassia*) 25 feet.

Snowbell, Japanese (*Styrax japonica*) 25 feet.

The following are medium to tall trees. These are used to line streets or placed near one and two-story homes where more space is available. They are:

Ash (*Fraxinus* sp. and cv.) 40 to 60 feet.

Basswood linden tree (*Tilia* sp. and cv.) 60 feet.

Catalpa (*Catalpa speciosa*) 40 to 60 feet.

Chestnut, Chinese (*Castanea mollissima*) 50 to 60 feet.

Horse chestnut (*Aesculus hippocastanum*) 75 feet.

Katsura tree (*Cercidiphyllum japonicum*) 50 to 60 feet.

Magnolia, southern (*Magnolia grandiflora* and cv.) to 75 feet.

Maples, silver, red and Norway species and cultivars (*Acer* sp.) 25 to 80 feet.

Oaks in species and cultivars (*Quercus* sp.) 60 to 90 feet.

Pagoda tree, Japanese (*Sophora japonica*) 75 feet.

Pine, Austrian, red, black (*Pinus* sp.) to 90 feet.

Red cedar, eastern (*Juniperus virginiana* cv.) 35 to 75 feet.

Sourwood tree (*Oxydendrum arboreum*) 75 feet.

Spruce, Colorado, Norway (*Picea pungens* and cv.) to 90 feet.

Tupelo, black gum, sour gum (*Nyssa sylvatica*) to 75 feet.

Yellowwood (*Cladrastis lutea*) to 50 feet.

Zelkova, Japanese (*Zelkova serrata*) to 90 feet. A good substitute for American Elm and disease resistant.

For further information on trees and shrubs I would suggest the studying of various trees and shrubbery growing in the area in which you are located and through the selection of local nursery catalogs to see what is available as well as many good books on trees and shrubs suitable for your zone.

Soil Preparation

In planting trees and shrubs properly prepare the soil for planting. The area should be well drained; otherwise, select plants which grow in low, wet areas. Dig twice the depth required for the tree and replace part of the soil with new top soil mixed with organic matter which is any form of partially decaying plant material; however, avoid using fresh manure which burns the roots of the plants. Fill the hole with water to test for drainage. If water drains immediately, there is no problem; if it stays, fill the hole halfway with coarse gravel, then a layer of coarse hay or sphagnum moss and several inches of rich soil followed by the soil ball with the plant. Fill in the rest of the hole with soil. Keep at the same depth as at the nursery. You must slope from the top of the soil line out to the surrounding area. Keep the plant heavily mulched and moderately moist until roots are established. If there is no drainage problem, firm down the soil around the soil ball in the center and fill up halfway with well prepared soil mix. Firm and water well. When the water has drained away, add more soil and water. After the water drains, use four to five inches of mulch one foot around the plant.

Pruning

Check new plants for damaged roots and branches. After planting, remove weak branches, up to one-third of the total growth; however, avoid damaging the leader which can dwarf the plant. Prune again each spring after any winter or storm damage or immediately following flowering.

Feeding

Do not use fertilizer on new plants. It burns the new roots as they begin to emerge. Instead, use well prepared soil with equal amounts of organic matter and allow the tree to become well established for the first year. At the beginning of the second year as new growth begins, use a balanced fertilizer, such as 6-12-12 or 5-10-5, as a light application of top dressing around the top of the plant to stimulate extra growth; however, avoid over-feeding or fertilizers high in nitrogen. This stimulates a lot of top growth at the expense of little or no root growth. It is more important to have a solid root system. Most plants planted in good soil have sufficient nutrients to carry them along until they become well established.

Root feed well established plant every two or three years by using a balanced fertilizer from late November until the end of April. Use liquid feeding from early April to the end of June. It stimulates extra growth on the plant and helps correct the lack of iron or other nutrients. Normally, it is important to consult with a tree specialist and follow his recommendations in regards to this type of feeding. Late feeding stimulates late growth thus causing the plant not to harden-off in the fall and making it more susceptible to winter damage.

Propagation

Most trees and shrubs are propagated in various ways. One of the more common ones is to use seeds. However, plants which are cultivars or hybrids do not come true from seed. Select seeds from trees with heavy flowering habits, good growth patterns and good autumn color. Collect seed, once it is ripe, during the late summer months. Store in a dry cool area until planting time in early fall. Plant most tree and shrub seeds in a protected area, such as a cold frame, where squirrels and other insects will not touch them. Plant in a good seed mix, thoroughly water and place outdoors in late fall. Winter months, the freezing and thawing breaks the seeds down. Many of them will start to germinate early the next spring; some take as long as two years before growth begins. Once the seedlings are large enough to handle, transplant into individual rows in a small nursery.

Another common method is using stem cuttings. Most plants root readily from stem cuttings from the middle to the end of June. Root cuttings in a cold frame, under a misting system or in a high humidity area where temperatures are around 75 degrees. Hormones may be needed to induce extra rootings on the cuttings. Protect cuttings for the first year or two until they are well established.

Propagate some shrubs by division. Dig the shrub up, carefully select rooted ends and plant them. Cut back to encourage new growth near the base of the plant. Many plants are also propagated from cuttings taken from root sections. Take sections of roots that are two to three inches long and place these in a propagating medium to grow. Take hardwood cuttings from late January to early March. Root indoors where temperatures are 40 to 45 degrees with bottom heat of 75 to 80 degrees. They will root in four to six weeks. Plant outside in protected areas in the spring for a year before planting permanently.

Insect and Disease Control

Select plants which are insect and disease-free; however, sometimes these problems are unavoidable. Trees in many areas suddenly wilt before leaves have fully matured. This is caused by a fungus disease called anthracnose. As soon as the wilting is noticed, spray with fungicide underneath and on top of the leaves to prevent the disease from further spreading. The anthracnose disease affects the plants in early spring as leaves are maturing and again in late summer; however, it is not as noticeable when the leaves begin to fall. Remove the diseased parts immediately on any plants and check at regular intervals for leaf spotting or other symptoms of disease.

Insects are fairly common on plants when leaves begin to grow. Most insecticides keep these under control if used when the insects first appear. Spray at 7 to 10-day intervals until under control.

When insects attack trees or shrubs, the first indications are holes or sections eaten out of the leaves. Many trees and shrubs are damaged by borers. These feed on the old wood of the tree by drilling into the main stems, anywhere from three to four inches up to 18 inches above ground level. They make small round holes about one-fourth inch in diameter with a trace of sawdust at the base of the plant. Insect borers are very damaging to certain trees, e.g. dogwood. Keep under control by using insecticide applied with a pressure sprayer up and down the tree trunk. Repeat at seven to 10-day intervals for three or four applications. Keep weeds around plants under control by spraying the ground, as they attract insects.

Scale is a common insect found on many trees and shrubs. It is a grayish, scale-like material along the main stem and sometimes on the leaves. The scale is a hard-shelled material with numerous small sucking insects underneath it. Control by using an oil-based spray, preferably a dormant oil, applied before the leaves begin to emerge sometime in February or early

March when temperatures reach at least 45 degrees for several hours. Use more than enough spray and allow the excess to run off the plant. Scale is also fairly active in early June. Control by using a summer oil or oil-based spray on a cloudy day or early in the morning so that plants have a chance to dry off before the sun fully shines.

Special Problems

Some trees fail to leaf out when first planted or grow leaves very slowly. Often they have been damaged prior to planting time. Keep the soil roots as moist as possible. Make a solution of mud and water and place bare root plants into this solution in a cool, shaded area for up to 24 hours before planting. Mist the plants with water two or three times a day to encourage new growth. Cut back up to one-third of the growth to offset the loss of the root system. If plants have been damaged by lawn mowers, cut away the damaged bark with a good sharp knife by making an oval cut with a "V" at the bottom and at the top. This also allows moisture to readily drain. Most of these plants heal with time, but if the damage is large, treat with a tree paint applied over the wound once cleaned up. When plants have been split by freezing or damaged by lightning, cut the bark back to solid areas and use tree paint.

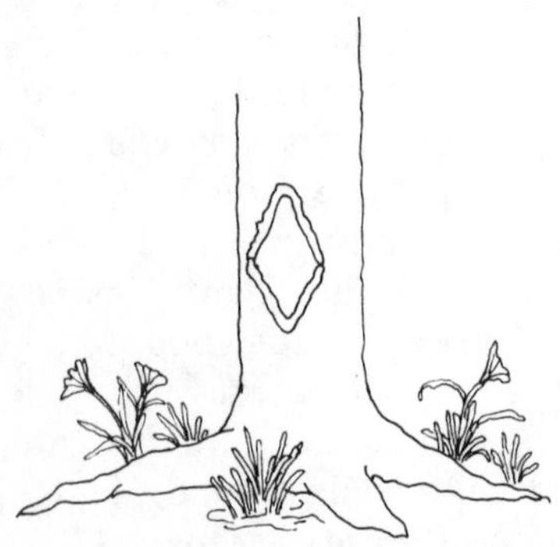

"V" CUT ON DAMAGED WOOD

If trees have damage from improper pruning, holes, or branches that have broken away, treat as soon as noticed. Remove all damaged parts back to solid wood and apply cement or special tree filling to the cavity. Do not allow moisture to remain in the cavity; clean thoroughly, properly fill and seal.

Often damage occurs where tree roots are dug up and exposed. If part of the root system has been removed, feed in late fall or early spring around the rest of the tree.

Black topping around the trees needs drain tiles laid below the surface to allow air and water to penetrate to the ends of the roots. In this way, black topping can be done fairly close to the tree without damage; however, if black topping has been applied to the surface around the tree, the tree will gradually die through lack of moisture and air.

In planting where water or electric lines are below the ground, avoid heavy rooted trees where wires or pipes may have to be dug up. Use shallow-rooted specimens.

If planting trees and shrubs as windbreakers or to provide privacy, select plants which are as pollutant resistant as possible and are able to withstand exhaust. Pines, maples and viburnums are some that are useful. When planting, avoid a direct draft from an air-conditioner on the plant. Many of the viburnums make ideal subjects for planting within three to four feet of an air-conditioner. If plants are too close, they prevent the air-conditioner from working effectively; on the other hand, if the air-conditioner is shaded by the plants, it will function much more efficiently.

Many people like to buy live Christmas trees such as fir, spruce and pine to plant out later. Avoid bringing the plants inside too early. They should be very carefully dug and tubbed up in late fall and then stored in an area outdoors where they are away from prevailing winds and freezing conditions. Bring the plant in a day or two before Christmas and do not keep it in the house anymore than a week. High temperatures soften the growth and start sap flowing through the plant if allowed to stay inside too long. Once the plant is ready to move outside, put it in a well protected area. If the weather is severely cold, avoid placing it outside until warmer. Dig the hole in late fall, heavily mulch and cover to prevent freezing. At planting time, remove the mulch and cover and place the plant in the hole at the required height. Mulch the plants four to six inches when through planting and water well. Protect evergreens by spraying with an anti-dehiscent such as Wilt-Pruf which cuts down evaporation. Place a screening of burlap or other material around them to protect from the winter sun and prevailing winds.

In areas where climatic conditions vary considerably, offset damage to plants by mulching heavily. As the mulch decomposes, it releases nutrients into the surrounding soil. Mulch prevents severe freezing of the ground in winter and controls soil temperatures by keeping them 10 to 15 degrees cooler than air temperatures in summer. The plants continue growing over a longer period. The mulch absorbs moisture into the ground and releases it gradually. It also prevents weeds from growing. Any type of decaying plant material is ideal. If using fresh wood chips or sawdust, add extra nitrogen in the form of Milorganite or bloodmeal to compensate for the nitrogen which the chips use when first decomposing; however, avoid applying too much because once the material begins to decompose, it releases the nitrogen back into the soil.

Water plants during periods of drought and allow to penetrate deep into the soil. A heavy watering once every two to three weeks is adequate during periods of drought. Add additional water in late fall, if dry, and in periods of thaws from late January through February. Evergreens which start turning brown in the spring are suffering from a lack of water earlier in the year.

Premature leaf drop in the late summer or fall is also caused by insufficient watering. Plants shed some of the leaves to offset for the lack of moisture received. Make sure the roots have plenty of moisture.

Many plants may have cankers on the stems or the growing tips of plants. They are gall formations caused by insects or disease. Spraying is not recommended. Remove small galls by hand. A maintenance program of root feeding trees every two to three years and watering sufficiently keeps plants in good condition. Avoid planting trees which have a tendency to form galls. Many of the oaks and maples have galls which are formed on the leaves by insects during the summer. Spray when the insects are first noticed; however, once the damage is done spraying is not recommended.

In selecting hedges, pick material which holds its growth near the base. Prune and occasionally feed. See General Information and Feeding Sections in this chapter. Many of the evergreen shrubs make ideal hedges. The yew (*Taxus*), cedar

(*Arborvitae*), juniper, viburnum, weigela and mock-orange (*Philadelphus*) are suitable in many areas. Suitable hedges in shaded areas are some of the yews and hemlock (*Tsuga*). Many of the viburnums, azaleas and boxwoods (*Buxus*) also grow under varying degrees of shade.

QUESTIONS

1. Can the top be cut from an ash tree to make it bushier?

Yes. It also shortens the height of the tree.

2. What causes an ash tree to drop its leaves?

The disease anthracnose causes leaf drop in early spring.

3. There are tiny holes in the ash tree which is losing bark. What do we do?

Check for insects which are probably doing the damage. Woodpeckers cause holes in the bark.

4. Should the sprouts on trees, such as the ash, be cut off?

Remove sprouts caused by extra soft growth if protruding along the main branches. Cut as close to the main branch as possible.

5. The leaves are falling off our ash tree. They seem to have been chewed on. What is recommended for this?

The leaves are being chewed by insects. Use an insecticide.

6. How do I care for a green ash tree?

Water regularly during periods of drought, keep mulched and root feed every two to three years.

7. Some branches of our green ash are not leafing out. What do we do?

Wait several weeks and if not in leaf, prune back to the main branch.

8. Do I prune a green ash tree?

Yes. Prune in June or during the dormant period in winter.

9. Is the climate in Zones 2 through 6 good for European mountain ash trees?

Yes.

10. When is the best time for removing mulch from azaleas?

Do not remove from azaleas because it interferes with the fine root system. Add mulch yearly.

11. When is the best time to transplant azaleas?

Transplant in early spring as leaves begin to mature or in late fall. Follow with a good mulching.

12. Are azalea cuttings moved outside in April?

Yes.

13. When is the best time to cut back azaleas?

Prune azaleas immediately following flowering to remove excess growth, to shape the plants or to remove dead material.

14. What do we feed azaleas?

Feed azaleas a balanced fertilizer, such as a 5-10-5, or an acid-type fertilizer in early spring as new growth begins. Occasional feedings of iron chelate correct chlorosis.

15. Do azaleas grow on the south side of the house with some shade?

Yes, but protect them from winter sun.

16. I have long neglected azaleas. How do I trim and fertilize them?

Trim back heavily in early spring as soon as flowering ends and follow with a feeding of a balanced fertilizer or cottonseed meal. Mulch carefully and avoid disturbing roots.

17. Why is an azalea planted near a hickory tree not doing well? Is there any connection?

The hickory tree may be taking extra nourishment from the azalea. Give the azalea additional fertilizer.

18. What do we do for winter damage on an azalea?

As soon as new growth begins, prune azaleas back to healthy wood.

19. We planted azaleas where a juniper had been. Will they bloom?

They will bloom if the ground is properly prepared.

20. When is the best time of the year to prune azaleas and rhododendrons?

Prune immediately following flowering.

21. Is there a special way to prepare soil for planting azaleas?

Incorporate plenty of organic matter, preferably oak leaf mold or pine needles, along with some additional sulfur to acidify soil.

22. Are azaleas mulched in the fall in Zone 6?

Mulch anytime during the year until late fall. Do not remove the mulch.

23. What do I use for mulch on azaleas?

Use any decaying plant material, such as partially decomposed leaf mold or wood chips.

24. How do I tell if our azalea is the hardy type?

If pot-grown and no name, check with a florist to find out what kind, or place in a protected area and check for hardiness.

25. Which variety of azaleas best withstand the sun?

Nearly all azaleas prefer semi-shaded conditions; however, most grow well if they receive sun during part of the day or all day.

Flowers last longer if they receive sun during either the morning or afternoon.

26. What fertilizer is used on barberry bushes?

Use a well balanced fertilizer, such as 5-10-5 or 6-12-12.

27. How do I root cuttings of red barberry?

Barberry is propagated from seed but if cuttings are used, take in mid June.

28. What arrests the curling of leaves on our American basswood?

American basswood (*Tilia americana*) is usually infected with aphids which cause the curling. Spray with insecticide underneath and on top of the leaves.

29. The last five feet of our 25-foot white birch tree are dead. What do we do?

The white birch (*Betula alba*) is probably infected with dieback, a bacterial disease. Prune back to good wood. Fertilize the tree in late fall and keep well watered during periods of drought.

30. Will Jobe's tree spikes burn roots of a birch tree?

Jobe's tree spikes do not burn the tree roots.

31. When is the best time to plant birch trees?

Plant birch trees anytime from late October through late April.

32. What is the best fertilizer for birch trees?

Use any well balanced fertilizer.

33. There are borers in our birch tree. How are they eliminated?

Borers in birch trees are fairly common. Spray the trunk of the tree with a good insecticide, such as Diazinon, starting in late April. Repeat at 10 to 12 day intervals for three to four applications.

34. What causes brown leaves on our birch tree?

Brown leaves early in the season is caused by a fungus disease. Spray with fungicide when first noticed and repeat in 10 days.

35. Our birch tree has spots with a pulpy mass. What do we do?

Cut back, open to allow material to drain away. Remove all infected parts and apply tree paint. Spray trunks in early spring with insecticide.

36. Our birch tree is defoliating. What do we do?

This is often caused by inadequate nutrient levels or from drought. See that tree is well watered and fertilize every two to three years.

37. How do we eliminate bugs on our birch tree?

Spray with insecticide when first noticed.

38. Our birch tree is doing poorly. What do we do?

Check to make sure that drainage is proper and that the tree has healthy soil. Apply mulch and keep watered during periods of drought. Feed lightly with a balanced fertilizer in early spring.

39. How do we best care for a river birch?

Plant in an area that is well drained with soil enriched with organic matter. Keep heavily mulched and water during periods of drought.

40. We have a 15-year old white birch which is losing sap through brown spots on the trunk. What do we do?

Remove infected areas with a sharp knife, and if necessary, spray with Diazinon to control birch borers.

41. I pruned a white birch and the wound is bleeding through the paint. What do I do?

Prune a white birch when the tree is dormant before sap starts to run or in late June and early July.

42. The leaves on our boxwood are turning yellow. What do I do?

The yellowing of leaves is probably due to drought. See that the plant is watered heavily and avoid feeding with high nitrogen fertilizers late in the season.

43. What is the best method for cutting back stringy boxwood?

Prune in early spring and cut back heavily to encourage new growth from the base of the plant. Follow this with a feeding of a well balanced fertilizer worked in lightly around the base of the plant.

44. What is the best care for boxwood?

Boxwood (*Buxus*) likes well drained soils with a good supply of organic matter. Plant in sun or semi-shaded areas. Mulch heavily and avoid cultivating around the base of the plant. Water well during periods of drought.

45. What do I do about boxwood that has died back to the ground?

If new shoots are showing at ground level, prune back all dead wood and allow new growth to develop.

46. How do we propagate boxwood?

Boxwood is readily propagated by taking cuttings in mid June.

47. Is boxwood pruned back in April and how is it fed?

Prune from April through June. Use a light feeding of a balanced fertilizer in early spring.

48. Is boxwood planted in sun or shade?

Either condition is correct if protected from the prevailing winter winds and from winter sun when first planted.

49. How do I cultivate broom as a hedge?

Cytisus, commonly called broom, likes a sandy, well-drained soil planted in full sun. Cut back about one-third of the growth each year immediately following flowering.

50. Our buckeye tree does not seem to be thriving. What do we do?

Keep buckeye trees (*Aesculus glabra*) heavily mulched. Occasionally feed with a balanced fertilizer in early spring when growth begins.

51. Can bushes be transplanted in June?

A great deal of material is now container-grown and can be moved at anytime during the year. Very carefully remove the plants from the container and loosen up some of the roots at the bottom so that they can spread out into the surrounding area. Be careful not to remove all the soil as this can be injurious to the plant. Water plant well and mulch immediately.

52. Is dormant spray used on Japanese cherry trees?

Spray Japanese cherry trees (*Prunus* sp.) with dormant oil before they leaf in early spring for control of insects and scale.

53. How do I best trim a Japanese cherry tree?

Prune a Japanese cherry tree immediately following flowering by removing weak growth and branches that cross one another. Also prune during the dormant winter months.

54. Are flowering cherry trees fertilized in late fall?

Do not feed in late fall. Avoid feeding until early spring when new growth begins.

55. We have a vertical crack in a cherry tree. What do we do?

Cracking is caused by winter freezing and thawing. Carefully remove damaged bark along the sides of the crack and apply tree paint.

56. I forgot to remove the plastic wrap around the ball of a cherry tree and it is dying. Do I do anything to revive it?

Dig up, remove plastic and replant.

57. The branches on our weeping cherry tree are dying. What do we do?

It is caused by bacterial blight. Check the base of branches and if black material oozes out, cut back to good wood; otherwise, remove damaged or dead material and spray with fungicide in early spring as growth begins. Repeat at 10 to 12-day intervals for two or three applications.

58. Why are the leaves on our cherry tree turning yellow?

The leaves are turning due to either insects or insufficient nourishment.

59. I have a Kwanzan cherry tree. Something is eating the leaves. What do I do?

Kwanzan cherry (*Prunus serrulata* cv. 'Kwanzan') should be checked to see what is causing the damage and spray accordingly.

60. How do we prevent ants from feeding on our white cherry tree?

Find the source of ants and eliminate by spraying or pouring boiling water in the ant hole. Spray tree with insecticide at regular intervals.

61. Will a wild cherry tree poison a newly built pond?

It will not poison the pond.

62. When does a cottonwood tree shed cotton?

The cottonwood tree (*Populus*) sheds cotton or the seed in early summer in most areas.

63. Our cottonwood tree is losing its leaves. How is this prevented?

The cottonwood loses leaves when suffering from drought.

64. When are flowering crab apples pruned?

Flowering crab apples (*Malus*) are pruned during the winter months such as February or immediately following flowering in late May or early June.

65. We have scales and holes in the back of our crab apple tree. What is wrong?

Scale is caused by insects and is controlled by using dormant spray in late February or early March before leaves emerge or by spraying in mid June with an oil-base spray. Holes are probably caused by borers. Spray with Diazinon along the trunk.

66. What spray do we use on a flowering crab apple?

Spray flowering crab apple with fungicide when leaves begin to emerge. Repeat at 10-day intervals until flowering ends. Spray as needed for insects.

67. How do I control crab apple rust?

Use fungicide in early spring as leaves begin to emerge. Repeat at 10-day intervals until leaves are fully mature.

68. Is there a flowering crab apple that does not bear fruit?

All flowering crab apples produce fruit. Some fruiting is controlled by spraying the flowers when in full bloom with a concentrated solution of Sevin.

69. When is the best time to prune a high bush cranberry?

Prune high bush cranberry (*Viburnum trilobum*) in early spring by removing two to three of the oldest canes to encourage new growth. Cut back some of the taller branches to cause bushiness.

70. My crape myrtle was winter damaged. When is this removed?

Prune crape myrtle (*Lagerstroemia indica*) as soon as new growth begins to show. Cut back heavily to remove all dead or dying wood.

71. Is crape myrtle transplanted in September?

Yes. Plant with as much of the original soil attached as possible and water well.

72. When is the best time to move crape myrtle?

Move in early spring before growth begins.

73. Our crape myrtle has no buds in early May. What do we do?

Crape myrtle usually flowers from about mid summer on. Plants have to be a certain size to flower.

74. When and how are crape myrtle pruned?

Prune as a shrub by cutting back to within 15 to 18 inches of the ground each spring or by training it as a single stem, small tree by removing all side shoots and allow only one stem to mature. Cut back side branches in early spring just as growth begins.

75. Crape myrtle is getting lanky. How is fuller growth encouraged?

Head back growth by removing up to one-half to two-thirds of thy previous year's growth.

76. Does crape myrtle grow from old wood?

In Zone 6, crape myrtle is a borderline plant and in some cases, may be partially frozen back. Remove all dead growth back to new ends.

77. Will roots come out of the ground on a bald cypress?

Bald cypress (*Taxodium distichum*) often have the roots appear above the ground. They are called knobs.

78. The leaves on our cypress tree are turning brown. What do we do?

The cypress browning is caused in most cases from spider mites which feed on the needles. Bring under control by using insecticide for mites.

79. Does a dogwood tree need morning or afternoon sun?

Dogwood (*Cornus florida*) does best with sun during part of the day, however, it also grows in full sun.

80. We have grown a dogwood in a pot. Do we plant it outdoors? When and how?

Dogwood is planted outside in early spring by preparing soil normally. Water and mulch well.

81. When is the best time of the year to transplant a dogwood tree?

The best time is in late fall after the plants are dormant or in early spring before they leaf out. Select nursery grown stock that is balled and burlapped.

82. How do we transplant a dogwood?

If the dogwood has been growing in the same area for several years, prune the roots at least a year before transplanting. Make a straight cut with a spade six to eight inches down to cut the roots back. Do this in early June and repeat again in mid September. Transplant the following spring.

83. Why are we unable to grow dogwood trees? They die after planting.

Prune the roots one year prior to moving. Moving dogwoods after they are in full leaf is seldom successful. Select nursery-grown stock in early spring or late fall.

84. Is a dogwood tree pruned before planting?

Prune dogwood (*Cornus*) prior to planting or following planting. Remove up to one-third of the growth. See Section on Pruning.

85. The leaves of our dogwood tree are not leafing out. What do we do?

The dogwood grows leaves by early May. If not in leaf, it was winter-killed.

86. The leaves on our dogwood tree are coming out and then wrinkling up. What do we do?

Check the tree to make sure that no borers are present and no damage has been done to the root system. Water adequately during periods of drought.

87. Our red dogwood blooms with only two petals. Is there something wrong with it?

Some cultivars of red dogwood (*Cornus florida* cv.) have only two petals. Little can be done to improve this situation.

88. I have leaf curl on my dogwood. What do I do?

Check for insects and spray as needed.

89. Our dogwood tree is doing poorly. Do I root the top?

Cuttings taken from the dogwood in mid June root if given bottom heat.

90. Is it okay to feed a dogwood tree with muriatic acid? What is the best fertilizer for a dogwood tree?

Muriatic acid is used on acid-loving plants and will not harm the dogwood tree if not overused. Apply in early spring as growth begins. A balanced fertilizer such as 5-10-5 or 6-12-12 is ideal.

91. My dogwood tree is dying. What do I do?

Prune the dogwood tree back to good wood. Improve drainage if needed and avoid cultivating around the base of the tree.

92. What do I do for winter damage on a dogwood tree?

Prune back all dead or dying material by mid April.

93. Our box elder has beetles on it and is shedding leaves. What do we do?

Use an insecticide under and on top of the leaves. Repeat again in four to five days.

94. Does trimming a box elder which causes sap to run out hurt the tree?

Do not prune the box elder (*Acer negundo*) after it has developed new leaves but while the tree is dormant during early February or as late as June or July.

95. We have a bleeding canker on our elm and the ants are feeding on it. What do we do?

Remove the canker, if possible, by careful pruning. Hire a qualified tree surgeon to do this. Ants feed on the sap which has sugar in it.

96. How do we eliminate slime flux on our elm tree?

Tap the tree with a copper pipe placed into the wood to allow the sap or water to run out. Use a tree surgeon to do this work.

97. Our elm tree leafed out and is now dying. What do we do?

Check the elm (*Ulmus*) and if dying back rapidly, it probably has Dutch elm disease. If heavily infested, remove the tree. If less than five percent is damaged, call in qualified people to have the tree treated for Dutch elm disease.

98. We have rust on the trunk of our elm tree. What do we do?

Spray the trunk of the elm with a fungicide once or twice during the early season.

99. There are bugs on the leaves of our American elm and it is losing sap. What do we do?

Spray bugs with insecticide when first noticed. Insects secrete material which seeps out.

100. Is the eucalyptus a good tree to plant in Zone 6?

No. Very few eucalyptus trees are hardy in this area and are not recommended for planting without further experimenting. They have been successfully grown in California.

101. What do we do about the leaves rolling up on our euonymus?

Check the stems for scale and use oil-base spray to control.

102. When and how are euonymus hedges trimmed?

Trim euonymus hedges from mid to late June so that they are narrow at the top and wide at the bottom. Remove approximately one-third of each year's growth until the hedges reach the desired height. A second pruning may be needed in mid September to keep them uniform.

103. Our winged euonymus is dying in early May. What do we do?

The problem is caused by winter damage. Prune back heavily to new growth. Follow this with a light feeding of a balanced fertilizer and keep well watered.

104. How do I identify winged euonymus. Why is it doing poorly?

Its twigs have bark protruding at an angle from the wood, giving it a cocky appearance. Its problems are due to winter damage.

105. How do you control scale on evergreens?

Spray with a dormant oil during late February or early March and again in mid June when insects are active. Make sure sprays are compatible with the evergreens.

106. Is December too late for planting balled root evergreens?

December is ideal as long as the ground is not frozen. Mulch well.

107. What fertilizers do I use on evergreen seedlings?

Use any balanced liquid fertilizer when evergreen seedlings are making new growth.

108. Some branches on our evergreens are wilting and dying. What do I do?

Remove all damaged plant material. Send samples to your nearest botanical garden or university extension center for diagnosis.

109. Our evergreens are bleeding after being cut back. What do we do?

Avoid pruning when evergreens are making soft growth. Prune before growth begins or as growth is hardening-off from mid to late June.

110. Is it okay to plant all species of evergreens, such as spruces, yews and junipers, together?

Yes. These can be easily mixed.

111. Is it possible to move a five-foot evergreen tree?

Yes. Keep a solid soil ball attached.

112. Last year our evergreens had many of their branches turn brown. Do you prune these and does feeding make them more vigorous?

Prune browned branches anytime. It is caused by insects, such as mites, or by disease. Check plants thoroughly and occasionally feed in early spring with a balanced fertilizer. Water adequately during periods of drought.

113. Our evergreens are dropping their leaves. What do we do?

Some leaf drop in early summer is normal when they shed their third or fourth-year needles.

114. When is the best time to prune evergreens for shaping?

Prune from mid to late June. Remove the center tips of growth. Be careful not to cut back too severely.

115. What species of evergreens grow best in complete shade?

The amount of shade depends on the density of the area. If moderate shade, grow hemlock species, the yews (*Taxus*) and many of the broad-leaved evergreens, such as azaleas, rhododendrons and viburnums.

116. Is March a good time to plant evergreens?

Yes.

117. What do you do about winter damage on broad-leaved evergreens?

Remove winter damage when new growth begins. Prune back all old growth. Prevent winter damage by screening the plants with burlap or other suitable material to protect them from the winter sun and wind. Spray with Wilt-Pruf in late fall.

118. How do we use forsythia cuttings to produce new plants and how long does this take?

Propagate forsythia from cuttings taken from mid to late June. Root and plant outside in protected spots in early fall.

119. Are forsythia pruned before planting?

Yes.

120. When is the best time of the year to prune forsythia?

Prune immediately following flowering.

121. In trying to root forsythia, the cuttings were dead at the tips. What is wrong?

The atmosphere is too dry. Increase humidity around the plants by covering with plastic.

122. Does cutting straggly limbs from my forsythia keep it from blooming?

Cut straggly branches immediately following flowering. It does not interfere with flowering.

123. We have a ginkgo tree with long shoots in the middle. Do we remove them?

Cut these back to the main stem.

124. Is it okay to plant a potted ginkgo tree outdoors in September.?

Yes.

125. Our sweet gum shade tree is drying out. What do we do?

The sweet gum tree (*Liquidambar styraciflua*) should have all dying branches cut back to good wood. Keep the plants well watered during periods of drought and root feed in late fall.

126. Why is our gum tree slow in leafing out?

The gum tree (*Liquidambar*) is a borderline tree in many areas in Zone 6 and is often affected by freezing temperatures. Select plants from hardy stocks.

127. Is a hawthorn tree a good tree to plant in Zone 6?

The hawthorn tree (*Crataegus*) has numerous species and cultivars that make excellent street or specimen trees.

128. How do I improve soil for the best growth of a hawthorn hedge?

The hawthorn hedge needs organic matter worked in lightly around the base. Feed regularly with a balanced fertilizer.

129. In what month does the hawthorn tree bloom?

The hawthorn tree blooms from mid April through early June, depending on the spring weather.

130. How do I care for a hazelnut shrub?

The hazelnut (*Corylus americana*) requires an area with good drainage, a soil well incorporated with plenty of organic matter and full sun.

131. How do I start hazelnuts?

Use fresh seeds sown in pots outdoors or in cold frames in the fall. Stratify seeds in October or early November.

132. How do I trim the winter damage on our hemlock trees?

Prune hemlock (*Tsuga*) by removing damaged ends with a pair of sharp pruners or shears.

133. How do I plant hickory nuts?

Select fresh seeds, planting in October or early November. Stratify seeds during winter months.

134. When is the best time of the year to transplant small holly seedlings?

Plant them when large enough to a protected spot and care for until large enough to move into the permanent border.

135. Our holly tree is dying back but leafing out at the bottom. What do we do?

Prune back all dead material to good growth.

136. There are suckers coming from our holly tree. Are these removed or left alone?

Prune back all dead material to good growth.

137. Holly trees are shedding leaves. Why?

Shedding of leaves is normal on holly in late spring. As it sheds old leaves, new ones emerge.

138. What causes yellow spots on a holly tree?

This is often caused by damage or chlorosis, a lack of iron. Use iron chelate in early spring.

139. Our holly trees do not leaf out. Why not?

Holly (*Ilex*), if it has lost all of its leaves and no leaves reappear, is dead. Dig up and remove.

140. Is fertilizer applied to hollies that appear dead?

No.

141. Our holly tree is doing poorly. Is it planted too deeply? If so, what do we do?

If planted too deeply, raise the plant up and avoid over-watering. Keep the ground moderately moist. Avoid using chemical fertilizers until well established.

142. What is the best way to trim holly trees damaged by the winter cold?

As soon as new growth begins, prune hollies back to good growth. In some cases, severe pruning may be required on varieties that are not as hardy.

143. What causes a brown leaf on a holly?

Holly leaf miners often attack holly (*Ilex*). Apply a spray, such as Malathion, in early May. Repeat at 10 to 13-day intervals for at least two more applications.

144. What is the best way to remove a dead holly tree?

Dig it out.

145. Do I plant a holly tree in the fall?

Yes. Mulch well.

146. How do I tell if holly trees are dead?

If trees do not leaf by early May, they are probably dead. Remove them.

147. How much growth is there each year in holly trees?

It depends on the species and cultivars. It usually grows anywhere from three to four inches up to 18 inches.

148. What is the hardiest holly that is grown?

Holly (*Ilex*) has a number of species and cultivars that are hardy. Check with local nurseries, botanical gardens and other display areas to see what is recommended for your particular area.

149. Are new holly shoots planted in May?

Yes.

150. How much iron chelate and how much epsom salts are put in the ground around a holly tree?

Use iron chelate and epsom salts at the rate of one tablespoon per gallon water. Apply approximately two gallons of water for every six-inch growth of tree.

151. How and when do I prune holly?

Prune anytime; however, many people prefer to prune in December and use the cuttings for Christmas decorations.

152. What do we do about holly trees that are half damaged by winter conditions?

Cut back to good growth and maintain trees in vigorous condition by feeding in early spring. Keep well mulched and watered during periods of drought.

153. How do we eliminate moths in and around our holly tree?

If they are laying eggs, spray with an insecticide when first noticed.

154. Do I root American hollies from stem cuttings in March?

Wait until mid to late June.

155. When is the right time to cut back an American holly?

The proper time is in early spring just as new growth is beginning.

156. Our burford holly is not doing well. What do we do?

Burford holly is a borderline plant in Zone 6. Plant where it is well protected from winter winds and sun. Keep plants well mulched and watered during periods of drought. Avoid cultivating the soil around them at all times.

157. Can burford holly be cut back to the ground to encourage new growth?

If severely winter-damaged, cut back burford holly as much as possible. Wait until signs of new growth appear and prune accordingly.

158. Our burford holly is showing signs of life. Do I feed it, how much and with what?

Remove damaged growth. When growth becomes active again, feed it with an acid-type fertilizer applied lightly around the base. Avoid working it in too deeply; this destroys the fine root system at the surface level.

159. How do I prune a Chinese holly?

Prune as you do any other holly. Trim to encourage compact growth.

160. What do we do about a dwarf holly that is sun-scorched?

Give the plant some shade. Keep well watered.

161. When is the best time to trim Japanese holly?

Prune in mid to late June as growth is hardening-off.

162. What is the best kind of fertilizer for Japanese holly?

Use a balanced fertilizer or acid-type fertilizer.

163. How do I care for my hibiscus plant?

Hibiscus (*Hibiscus syriacus*) is commonly called shrub althaea and blooms in late summer. Plant normally, prune in early spring before growth begins and cut back heavily as plants produce buds on new growth.

164. What is the best way to reset or move our hibiscus?

Move plants in early spring before growth begins or in late fall after leaves shed.

165. How do I prune a hibiscus?

Cut plant back heavily in early spring to control height and encourage new shoots.

166. Does Rose of Sharon grow in a shady area?

Plant where it receives full sun for best flowering.

167. Our hibiscus is dropping leaves after spraying for scale. What do we do?

The dropping is caused by burning from the insecticide. Spray when temperatures are below 75 degrees and keep the plants out of the sun until they are thoroughly dry.

168. When is the best time to prune a honeysuckle?

Prune immediately following flowering.

169. Is honeysuckle fertilized in September to encourage growth?

No. Feed in early spring.

170. We have white fly on our red honeysuckle. Can I transplant it?

Control white fly by use of synthetic Pyrethrin spray. Transplant in early spring before growth begins.

171. How do I propagate a honeysuckle shrub?

Take cuttings in mid to late June.

172. Are honeysuckle bushes mulched in October?

Mulch anytime mulch is available.

173. How do we change the color of our hydrangea from blue to pink?

Add lime around the base of the plants in early spring.

174. Our hydrangea was rooted from a cutting on a plant with blue blossoms. Why do the new plants have pink flowers?

Hydrangeas require acid soil for blue flowers; flowers turn pink in an alkaline soil.

175. Our hydrangea bush is changing from pink to blue. Why?

Soil is becoming more acid.

176. How and when do I prune hydrangeas?

Prune hydrangeas in early spring. Cut back heavily and remove any weak or small growth.

177. Why do we get lots of foliage on our hydrangeas and no bloom?

Hydrangeas like a well drained area and plenty of superphosphate. Avoid high nitrogen fertilizers.

178. How do I propagate the outdoor type of hydrangea?

Take cuttings in mid June or divide the bushes in early spring as growth begins.

179. How do I care for hardy hydrangeas?

Prune plants back heavily in early spring, work in plenty of superphosphate around the plants and give them a sunny location.

180. Are the roots of a hydrangea pruned when applying acid feedings?

No.

181. Why does one hydrangea bloom and another one does not?

This depends on cuttings taken from parent plants. A plant which produces a lot of bloom continues producing. Cuttings from plants which produce little or no bloom do not produce flowers.

182. How do I winter a colored hydrangea?

Place plants in a well drained area and if pot-grown, put in a cold frame or other protected spot.

183. Our hydrangeas failed to flower last year. Why and what do we do?

Failure to flower depends on the conditions under which it is growing. Prune back heavily each spring and incorporate superphosphate to encourage plenty of bloom.

184. When is the best time to plant a container-grown juniper?

Do it anytime the ground can be prepared.

185. What causes needles on our juniper to turn yellow and drop?

Needles lighten in color and drop in mid summer. Keep trees well watered and feed every two to three years with a well balanced fertilizer.

186. We have pea-size soft growth on our juniper trees. What is it and how do we eliminate it?

This may be cedar apple rust which starts out small and in the fruiting stage, turns a bright orange. Prune off or spray with fungicide when they first start fruiting.

187. We have bugs on our juniper tree. What are they and how do we get rid of them?

Use insecticide applied under pressure to the trees.

188. How do we get rid of a Kentucky coffee bean tree and minimize the shoots that come up?

Cut the tree down to ground level, carefully dig around the stump and remove as much of the stump as possible. If the tree is growing in a lawn area, spray shoots that come up with ordinary 2, 4-D.

189. Is it harmful to prune lilacs in September?

No, but you will remove the flowers that will appear next spring.

190. We have leaf curl on our lilac bushes. What do we do?

Leaf curl is usually caused by mildew. Spray with fungicide when it first appears and repeat after heavy rain or at regular intervals.

191. What is the best fertilizer for lilacs?

Use fertilizer high in superphosphate or work in superphosphate or wood ashes around the plants in early spring.

192. Is it okay to transplant a white lilac in November?

Yes. Transplant if a solid root system is attached.

193. When do I plant a lilac bush I received in February?

Plant as soon as the ground can be worked.

194. Are seed pods cut from lilac bushes?

Yes. Remove as soon as flowering is finished.

195. The leaves on our lilac bush are turning brown on the edges. Is it okay to water in October?

Leaf browning is caused by a fungus disease. See Question 190. Keep lilacs watered during any period of drought.

196. The tops of our lilac bushes are green but about 12 inches down they are all brown. What do I do?

This also is caused by a fungus. Use a spray. See Question 190.

197. Is it possible to grow a lilac bush in the shade?

Lilacs need full sun.

198. When is the best time to divide lilac bushes?

Divide in early spring just before growth begins by keeping as many roots as possible.

199. How do I plant French lilacs?

Secure healthy plants and put outside in early spring before growth begins or in late fall once they are dormant.

200. How do I propagate lilac bushes?

Take cuttings in late June or by division in early spring.

201. When is the best time to prune lilacs?

Prune immediately following flowering.

202. May I successfully transplant a large Persian lilac and how?

Yes. Keep a large root ball attached to the plant. Prepare the soil well in early spring or late fall.

203. How tall does a linden tree grow?

The linden tree (*Tilia*) grows anywhere from 45 to 90 feet.

204. Our small leaf linden tree is infected with moths. How do I get rid of them?

Spray with insecticide by applying it underneath and on top of the leaves.

205. Our moraine locust is not doing well. What do we do?

Cultivate lightly around the base of the plant and work in a well balanced fertilizer, such as 6-12-12, in early spring as new growth is beginning.

206. How do we eliminate borers in our globe locust?

Spray the trunk of the tree in early spring with insecticide, such as Sevin, Malathion or Diazinon. Repeat at 10-day intervals for at least two more applications.

207. One-half of our locust tree appears dead and the other half is living. What do we do?

Prune out all dead parts back to good wood. If necessary, cut back other branches partway to balance growth. Feed in early spring. See Question 205.

208. When is the best time to plant a magnolia tree?

Plant magnolias from late October as long as the ground is not frozen and in early spring before growth begins.

209. What are the names of the magnolia tree species that do best in Zone 6?

The following are some of the magnolias that do well in Zone 6: *Magnolia acuminata*, the cucumber tree; *Magnolia grandiflora*, southern magnolia; *Magnolia stellata*, star magnolia; *Magnolia soulangiana*, saucer magnolia, and *Magnolia virginiana*, sweet bay magnolia.

210. Our magnolia is not budding. What do we do?

Magnolia that fails to bud in early spring has probably been affected by frost. If wood is not damaged flower buds will form next year.

211. Our magnolias are blooming in June for the second time. Is that usual?

Magnolias often flower into the early summer.

212. Is it too late to plant a magnolia grandiflora in May?

If the tree has been carefully dug with a solid soil ball attached or if it is container-grown, move in May; however, heavily mulch and keep well watered during the first year.

213. How do I encourage the growth of a magnolia grandiflora?

Keep the plant heavily mulched and once established, apply a balanced fertilizer, such as a 5-10-5, in early spring as new growth is beginning.

214. Our magnolias are doing poorly. What do we do?

Water heavily during periods of drought and apply a balanced fertilizer in early spring.

215. How do I germinate a southern magnolia tree?

Start southern magnolia (*Magnolia grandiflora*) from seed. Sow in October and leave it in a protected spot outdoors to make it germinate the following spring.

216. Is it okay to cut back a magnolia tree in April?

April is a poor time for pruning because you remove many of the blooms which occur. It is much better to wait until after flowering.

217. What is causing the leaves to fall off our magnolia trees?

Magnolias, like many other trees, shed some leaves if temperatures are too high and the soil too dry. Shedding cuts down on the rate of evaporation.

218. The leaves on our magnolia trees are turning brown. What is wrong?

Browning of leaves may be caused by anthracnose.

219. What do I do for winter damage on our magnolia tree?

As soon as new growth begins, prune back to good wood.

220. Our crimson king maple has buds that keep falling off. Why and what is done to prevent this?

Acer, crimson king maple, has flower buds which form and bloom in early spring. If these are winter damaged, they drop before opening up but do not affect the growth of the tree.

221. What causes leaf drop on a maple and what do we do about it?

Leaf drop occurring early in the spring is the result of anthracnose. If occurring later, the tree is shedding leaves that its root system is unable to support.

222. How do we kill sprouts shooting up from a hard maple tree that has been cut down?

Carefully paint 2,4-D on the new shoots. This is absorbed into the trunk and causes the tree to die. Another method is to pour boiling water over the new growth.

223. The leaves on our maple tree are turning brown. What do we do?

Browning early in the season is usually caused by insects or anthracnose disease. If insects are present, use spray.

224. My maple tree is planted close to an azalea and is not doing well. Is there any connection between the proximity of the two which accounts for this?

The maple (Acer) is not affected by the azalea. Azaleas make very shallow roots and do not compete with the maple. The plant is doing poorly due to poor soil and needs extra feedings early in the spring.

225. The bark is peeling on a maple tree, what do we do?

Bark is peeling because of damage. Remove all loose bark back to solid material and apply tree paint over the cutaway area.

226. The pruning cuts on our maple are bleeding. What do we do?

Do not prune when buds begin to swell or after growth begins. Prune when plants are completely dormant, from late November through early February and also in late July when they are starting to harden-off.

227. Is March too late to fertilize a maple tree?

No.

228. What is the best fertilizer for a maple tree?

Use any well balanced fertilizer.

229. Does a broken limb from a soft maple tree heal?

It depends on the break. Remove the limb as close to the trunk as possible.

230. Our maple tree is being eaten by ants. How are they eliminated?

Spray the branch with insecticide when ants are first noticed. Repeat if needed.

231. Is it better to plant a silver maple or sugar maple?

The silver maple (*Acer saccharinum*) and the sugar maple (*Acer saccharum*) grow equally well.

232. What do you do for a silver maple whose bark is splitting?

The splitting is due to freezing. Protect the trunk of the tree during winter months by wrapping with paper or burlap. Remove all loose bark and use tree paint.

233. What do you do about wilt and disease on a silver maple tree?

Anthracnose affects the silver maple. Do not spray unless it is a fungicide used when the disease first starts. Silver maples are also subject to a soft rot, which usually is not diagnosed until too far advanced to control with a spray.

234. How do you trim and feed a silver maple?

Trim when the tree is dormant and feed with a balanced fertilizer from late November to the end of April.

235. We transplanted a red maple late in the season and it is doing poorly. What do we do?

Red maple (*Acer rubrum*) should be kept well watered during periods of drought and heavily mulched. Growth improves the second year. Avoid using a strong fertilizer.

236. Is a red maple fed in April?

Yes.

237. Do we prune our Japanese maple to one stem?

Prune the Japanese maple to a single stem if desired to have a small shapely tree, or it can be left with several stems which will be somewhat lower but fuller.

238. Why are the leaves turning gray on our Japanese maple?

It is caused by too much sun.

239. Our Japanese maple leaves are turning wheat color. What do we do?

Leaves are bleaching due to too much sun.

240. Is sun or shade better for coloring a Japanese maple?

Plant in a semi-shaded location.

241. My Japanese maple had red leaves last year but this year the leaves are green. What do I do to keep them red?

To retain good color, it needs more light, preferably sun.

242. How do we prevent our Japanese maple from losing leaves?

Japanese maple (*Acer japonicum*) loses leaves early if getting too much sun. Mulch plant heavily and keep well watered.

243. May I grow a Japanese maple in a container?

Yes.

244. How do we fertilize a trident maple?

Fertilize like any other tree. See Section on Feeding.

245. Can a mimosa tree be transplanted in March?

The mimosa tree (*Albizia*) can successfully be transplanted in early March before it leafs out.

246. What do I do about a split in our mimosa tree?

The mimosa tree splitting is caused either by branches being too heavy or by freezing. If caused by branches separating, brace them. If caused by freezing cut back to good wood and use tree paint on the cut area.

247. How do I best encourage the growth of a mimosa tree?

The mimosa tree grows well in healthy soil. To increase growth, apply a balanced fertilizer in early spring.

248. Our mimosa tree seems to be dead. How can I be sure?

A mimosa tree in Zone 6, under severe winter conditions, sometimes freezes back partway or severely. Wait until new growth begins and then prune back to breaks in tree.

249. There are borers in the mimosa tree. How do we destroy them?

Spray the trunk for borers. See Section on Insect and Disease Control.

250. How do I discourage the growth of sprouts on a mimosa tree?

Prune new sprouts with a sharp pair of pruners as soon as they emerge, or rub them off with your hands.

251. Do small mimosas come from the roots or seeds?

Most come from seeds.

252. Can mock-orange be grown in a container?

The mock-orange (*Philadelphus*) can successfully grow in a container if given winter protection.

253. How do I best divide a large mock-orange?

Dig the plant up when dormant in late fall or early spring and divide into sections. Cut the plant back heavily.

254. Our mock-orange bushes have leaves that are browning. What do we do?

The mock-orange browning is caused by a fungus disease, controlled by using a fungicide when it first appears.

255. Why did our mock-orange defoliate while still green?

The mock-orange is affected by fungus. If not controlled, it causes defoliation fairly rapidly.

256. We have mulberry bushes on our property. Are they edible?

Yes.

257. How do you prune a mulberry tree?

Prune in late summer or during winter months when dormant by removing excess growth or any branches which cross one another. Thin out the small weak growth.

258. What can be planted on the north side of the house where there is no sun?

The north exposure in many areas is excellent for planting azaleas and rhododendrons which are protected from the winter sun. These plants will flower well during the early spring. Foliage plants such as yews and boxwoods are also ideal.

259. What is the best type of cinquefoil?

The bush cinquefoil (*Potentilla fruiticosa*) is hardy from Zone 2 on down. There are a number of cultivars: 'Farreri,' called Gold Drop; 'Grandiflora' and 'Mt. Everest,' which is white. Check with local nurseries for what is available in your area.

260. Why do some pin oaks shed their leaves in the fall and others in the spring?

Some pin oaks (*Quercus palustris*) have some leaves which are quite persistent and they will hang on until early spring. Others will fall at the normal time in the fall.

261. Our pin oak leaves are coming out red. Why?

The pin oak often has reddish-colored leaves when it first emerges but then the leaves turn their normal color. This is dependent on the amount of nutrients available.

262. What is done about borers in the oak tree?

Spray the trunk with insecticide early in the spring, repeating at 10-day intervals as needed.

263. Our oaks are partially killed back by winter damage. What do we do?

As soon as new growth begins, prune back all dead or dying branches.

264. When is a pin oak pruned?

The pin oak can be pruned anytime during late summer or winter. Remove dead or damaged branches, or head back to control growth.

265. We have a large cavity in our oak tree. What do we do?

Call in a qualified tree surgeon to fill the cavity.

266. Do we fertilize a one-year old oak tree?

Use light application in early spring.

267. May I plant an oak tree in a tub and keep it small?

The oak tree is a very large growing tree and survives in a container if pruned on the top to balance the lack of a full root system.

268. We are losing bark off our oak trees and they are dying. Is it salvageable?

Remove any dead or dying material, root feed every two to three years and keep well watered during periods of drought.

269. The roots of our oak tree were cut when we were building. What do we do to save it?

If only part of the root system is damaged, root feed in late November to late April to offset the lack of roots.

270. Our 80-year old oak tree has sap running out of the bark on the trunk. What do we do?

Remove bark around areas where sap is dripping and if needed, call in a qualified tree surgeon to examine it.

271. Is it all right to use Volck oil spray on pin oaks?

It is better to use a dormant oil when trees are dormant or a summer oil which is light weight, to control scale insects.

272. The buds are brown and dry on a three-year old pin oak. Is it dead?

If the tree fails to leaf, assume it is dead and remove it.

273. How do you trim and feed an oak tree?

Remove dead or diseased parts of the tree, or head back to control the growth. Feeding for large trees are root feedings done from late November to the end of April, or use tree food spikes.

274. How do I plant oak acorns?

Sow seed in late October.

275. What is the best way to transplant oak seedlings?

Transplant in early spring before they leaf. Keep as much of the root system as possible with some soil attached.

276. Oak trees have galls. How are these eliminated?

Galls on oak trees, once established, are difficult to eradicate. Prune in early stages to keep them under control. Spraying is not recommended.

277. How high will a willow oak grow and what is the rate of growth of oak trees?

The willow oak (*Quercus phellos*) grows 80 to 90 feet. The rate of growth of oak trees depends on the location, but it can be expected to be anywhere from six to 18 inches of growth a year once trees are established.

278. There is a hole about the size of a dime in the trunk of our pin oak tree. What does this signify?

Examine closely and if the hole is not too far in the tree, suspect woodpecker damage.

279. What is causing perfectly green leaves to fall off of a black oak tree?

The black oak (*Quercus velutina*) is probably dropping leaves due to insufficient moisture.

280. What spray is used on a black oak tree?

Use a dormant oil or any insecticide.

281. How do I treat a wound on a red oak tree?

Thoroughly clean the wound and cut back the bark to healthy bark. Remove damaged wood and if needed, fill with cavity filling. Otherwise, cut back to solid wood and use tree paint.

282. How do we move a thundercloud plum tree?

Move in late fall once it is dormant or in early spring. Keep solid soil ball attached.

283. How do you eliminate leaf drop on a hardy-orange?

Poncirus trifoliata is the hardy-orange that does well in Zone 6. Leaf drop is usually caused by poor drainage and drought.

284. What are the soil requirements for the Bradford pear tree?

The Bradford pear tree (*Pyrus calleryana* 'Bradford') likes ordinary garden soil with good drainage.

285. Our Bradford pear tree is not leafing out. What do I do?

It probably is dead.

286. How is a Japanese pagoda tree best removed?

Move with a large soil ball attached once the tree has gone dormant in late October or in early spring before it leafs out.

287. What is the best way to grow a Japanese pagoda tree?

The pagoda tree (*Sophora japonica*) likes garden soil that is well drained.

288. Where and when is a flowering peach pruned?

Prune before the plant starts to grow, preferably in late February or in mid summer. Remove excess growth or branches which are rubbing against one another. Pruning controls the height and shape of the plant.

289. Can fruit formation on a flowering peach tree be prevented without damaging the flowers?

Yes. Remove fruit by handpicking when it begins to form. Another method is to spray the plant with Sevin when in full bloom which, in many cases, keeps some of the flowers from setting seed.

290. Are papershell pecans grown in Zone 6?

Yes.

291. What are some of the varieties of pecans that are grown in Zone 6?

'Busseron,' 'Green River,' Indiana, 'Major,' 'Niblack' and 'Posey' are grown in Zone 6. Check with local nurseries for recommended varieties.

292. When is the best time to prune a pecan tree?

Prune a pecan tree when the top has made enough growth to shade the trunk. Prune to control shape and size of tree when the tree is dormant.

293. How long after planting pecan tree seeds do I have to wait before they begin to produce nuts?

It depends on the trees. Generally, four to five years is required.

294. What do the long panicles on my pecan tree mean?

These are flower buds.

295. What is done about spittlebugs on pfitzers?

The pfitzer is a juniper. Spittlebugs are controlled by using any insecticide when first noticed.

296. What is the best way to transplant and transport white pine seedlings.

Seedlings are transplanted in early spring, when making new growth, into a well drained, sandy loam. In transporting seedlings, wrap them in moist paper or cloth until ready to replant. Keep as cool as possible.

297. What do you do about winter damage on pine trees?

If just tips of needles are brown, do not worry about it. If some freezing back of branches has occurred, prune back to good growth.

298. We have just planted a 10-foot pine tree. Does it need water?

Yes.

299. What is causing the needles to dry out on our pine tree? What do we do about it?

Drying of needles is due to several things: excessive drying winds, dry soil or disease. See that plants are well watered and heavily mulched. Check for disease.

300. When is the best time to trim long-needle pines?

Trim from mid to late June as the new candles are beginning to slow down. Remove the center candle to cause bushiness.

301. Is May too late to transplant an unballed three-foot pine?

Yes.

302. A loblolly pine in southern Missouri looks very brown. Will it survive?

The loblolly pine (*Pinus tada*) browning is caused by windburn. Most plants outgrow this as new needles develop.

303. Our pine trees are losing needles and branches, and there are holes around the bark. How do we save them?

Holes in the bark are usually caused by woodpeckers after insects. Spray trunk of tree thoroughly in early spring with insecticide. Repeat in 10 to 12 days. Prune out all dead or diseased material.

304. How do I make a pine tree cutting?

Pine trees are grown from seeds not from cuttings.

305. Sap is running out of my pine tree. Is this all right?

Check where sap is coming from and cut around the area so it can drain well.

306. How do I prune pine trees to encourage the density of a foliage?

Prune out the main candle, which is the new growth produced at the tips, in mid to late June. This causes others to elongate and give a bushier effect.

307. Our Austrian pine is dying from the bottom up. What do we do?

Examine carefully. Remove all dead or infected branches. Keep plants well mulched and watered during periods of drought.

308. What are the features that make planting a black Japanese pine worthwhile?

The Japanese black pine (*Pinus thunbergii*) is very hardy. It serves as a windbreak in specimen trees and is relatively fast growing. It is an excellent plant to train for bonsai work and for use in the Oriental garden.

309. What causes brown needles on a Japanese black pine and how are they eliminated?

Browning needles on any pine is usually caused by windburn or sunscald and is difficult to prevent. Use Wilt-Pruf on plants in late fall. Keep the plants well watered during periods of drought and in severe cases, handpick the needles.

310. Our pine trees are shedding needles after spraying for bagworms. What do we do?

Make sure insecticide is suitable for pines. Avoid spraying when temperatures are over 80 degrees or when a full sun is out.

311. How do we best care for a ponderosa pine?

Ponderosa pine (*Pinus ponderosa*) likes average soil conditions in an area that is well drained. Keep plants well watered during periods of drought.

312. How do I grow Scotch pines from seeds?

Plant them in a well drained soil as soon as the cone opens up and releases the seed.

313. Are Scotch pines planted in rough rocky soil?

Yes. Add plenty of organic matter at planting time.

314. Our Scotch pine tree has recently been transplanted and is losing needles. What do I do?

Heavily mulch and keep adequately watered until well established.

315. How do I eliminate white scale on a Scotch pine?

Spray with dormant oil in late February or with a light summer oil in mid June.

316. What is the best way to grow white pines?

All pines like well drained areas and average garden soil with plenty of organic matter.

317. Our white pine tree seems to have some kind of disease. What do we do?

Take specimen of diseased material to the botanical garden or university extension service for diagnosis and treatment.

318. May I successfully transplant pine trees from one place in the garden to another.

Yes. Transplant from mid October to mid April.

319. We have just moved a 20-foot pine. Will it survive?

Yes. It will survive if well dug and watered during periods of drought until re-established.

320. What do we do about pine needle rust?

Pine needle rust is prevalent in early spring. Spray with fungicide, such as Benlate, Phaltan or Bordeaux mixture when new growth emerges.

321. Our yellow poplar tree is not blooming. What do we do?

The plant may be too young. If growing well, do not be concerned.

322. How do I care for a hybrid poplar?

Plant in any average garden soil, water well and keep watered if needed until well established.

323. What kind of spray do we use for anthracnose on a yellow poplar tree.

Spray with a good fungicide when it first appears.

324. How do I get rid of the insects chewing the leaves of our poplars?

Poplars (*Populus*) are usually attacked by aphids and other small insects. Use insecticide when first noticed and repeat as needed.

325. How do I cut dead growth on a privet?

Remove dead wood back to good wood or to ground level early in the spring as growth is beginning.

326. How far back do we prune our privet hedge?

If a hedge is sparse and thin, cut back up to two-thirds of growth and gradually allow it to grow back to the normal height.

327. What is the best way to root pyracantha cuttings?

Take cuttings of half ripened wood in mid to late June and root in a mixture of three parts perlite to one part peat moss in a cold frame.

328. Pyracantha flowers have turned black. What is the cause and how is it controlled?

This is caused by a disease called fire blight. Use a spray such as Phaltan or Benlate as new leaves are forming and again as flower buds are beginning to open.

329. Our pyracanthas are not coming out in growth in April. What do we do?

Leave plants until early May. If growth is beginning to emerge, cut back to where best growth appears. Plants may be partially killed by winter damage.

330. When is pyracantha pruned?

Prune immediately following flowering or in early spring before growth begins to shape the plants.

331. Is a flowering quince moved in April?

Yes. Mulch and water well.

332. Leaves are turning brown on top of a flowering quince. How is this prevented?

Spray with fungicide as new growth begins and at intervals after any heavy rain.

333. Can we transplant an eight-year old golden-rain tree?

Transplant with a heavy root ball attached.

334. Can a redbud tree be moved in October?

Move anytime from late October on.

335. Do you wrap the trunk of a redbud tree?

Wrap the trunk for the first year or two until established.

336. Does a redbud branch root?

Yes. It roots in mid June.

337. When is the best time to trim a redbud tree?

Trim immediately following flowering.

338. Our redbud tree has shoots coming off the side. Do I trim them?

Some heading back controls growth.

339. The flowering limbs of our redbud tree are dying. What do we do?

Trim dead portions back to good wood. Keep well watered and feed a balanced fertilizer in early spring.

340. How do I prevent our redbud tree from losing its leaves?

The cause is probably anthracnose. Use fungicide when first noticed.

341. Our redbud tree, which was recently planted, is sending up multiple shoots. Is this normal and do I leave them?

If you want a bush, leave them. If you want a single stem tree, remove all shoots except the most sturdy one.

342. Our dawn redwood is losing sap from holes up and down the trunk. What do we do?

Do not prune when leafing out. The losing of sap stops once the season progresses and is not harmful to the tree. If the problem persists, call in a qualified tree surgeon to examine the tree.

343. When are rhododendrons and azaleas transplanted?

Transplant in early spring before they start to flower.

344. When are rhododendrons and azaleas trimmed?

Trim immediately following flowering to remove flower heads and head back growth.

345. When do I spray rhododendrons and azaleas?

Spray immediately when attacked by insects.

346. When are rhododendrons and azaleas fertilized?

Apply fertilizer as new growth emerges. If growth is yellow, use iron chelate along with epsom salts, one tablespoon of each mixed with fertilizer and applied lightly around the base of the plants.

347. Can tall, thin rhododendrons and azaleas be cut back and if so, how much?

Cut back straggly plants immediately following flowering by removing up to two-thirds of the growth. Keep plants well mulched and watered.

348. What causes browning leaves and leaves to drop on rhododendrons and azaleas?

Browning is often caused from winter burning and when leaves become dry, they fall in early spring. Keep plants protected from the winter sun and wind, and keep well watered during periods of drought.

349. Our rhododendrons are doing poorly. What do we do?

Avoid cultivating around the base of the plants as they produce shallow roots. Mulch plants well with organic material, such as decaying leaves, and apply a light dressing of sulfur to help acidify the soil. Use an acid-type fertilizer from mid to late April.

350. We have sparse blossoms on our rhododendrons. How do we encourage heavier flowering?

Keep plants well mulched and fertilized. See Question 349.

351. What particular varieties of rhododendrons do best in Zone 6?

A very wide variety of species and varieties are available. Check with local nursery or garden center for types hardy in your particular area.

352. Do I remove old flowers from rhododendrons and how?

Yes. Remove flower heads immediately after flowering with a pair of sharp pruners.

353. The new leaves on our rhododendrons are becoming discolored. What do I do?

This is caused from lack of iron. Apply iron chelate and epsom salts, one tablespoon each to a gallon of water. Use a gallon of water for approximately every six to eight inches of plant growth. Apply this in early spring. A second application may be necessary in early September to correct chlorosis.

354. Rhododendrons are not flowering and are lanky. What do we do?

Prune plants back early in the spring. Mulch and apply a light application of cottonseed meal.

355. Is it okay to plant a Rose of Sharon in March?

Transplant successfully in early March to mid April.

356. How does one care for Rose of Sharon?

Prune the hardy hibicus back heavily in the spring as it flowers on new wood. Plants like average garden soil in a well drained area with full sun. Keep well watered during periods of drought.

357. Is a Russian olive tree good to use as a screen?

The Russian olive tree (*Elaeagnus angustifolia*) is used in many places as a hedge or screen for protection.

358. Is the Russian olive tree poisonous?

No.

359. How do I prune a Russian olive tree and what do I use as a spray on it?

Prune tree in early spring as growth is beginning to keep it at desired height. Identify insect and use recommended spray for its control when first noticed.

360. Our Russian olive tree is wilting after transplanting. What do we do?

After transplanting, keep plant well watered and mulch heavily.

361. How do we encourage the growth of a sassafras tree?

Apply a well balanced fertilizer lightly around the tree in early spring as growth is beginning. Keep tree well watered during periods of drought.

362. What is best to plant in a shady area among oak trees?

Plant azaleas, euonymus, ivy, rhododendrons and ground cover plants.

363. What is the best method of propagating a smoke-tree?

Propagate by sowing seed as soon as ripe or by taking half-ripe wood cuttings in mid June.

364. When do I plant a bare root snowball bush received in February?

Plant as soon as ground is soft. In the meantime, place plant in a cool area and keep roots moist.

365. How do I propagate a snowball bush?

Propagate from seed or from cuttings taken in mid June.

366. How do I prune a snowball bush?

Prune immediately following flowering by removing some of the older canes and/or cutting growth back to control height and growth.

367. Is southernwood shrub toxic?

Southernwood (*Artemisia abrotanum*) is not considered toxic.

368. How and when do I transplant spiraea?

Transplant from mid October through late April. Select a well drained area and average garden soil with organic matter. Water well.

369. Our spiraea bloomed last fall and is not blooming in April. What do we do?

Some spiraea shrubs flower in late fall and not again in the spring because flower buds do not form. Flower buds form on current season's wood usually in mid summer.

370. Will the spraying of trees harm birds?

Many sprays are harmful to birds. Spraying should only be done when needed.

371. How do I best care for a spruce tree?

The spruce tree (*Picea*) likes a well drained location. Established trees need occasional feedings of a balanced fertilizer applied in early May as growth is forming. Keep plants well watered during periods of drought and avoid cultivating around the base because roots are shallow.

372. Is it too late in May to plant a spruce tree?

Move in early May with heavy root ball attached. Keep well mulched and well watered.

373. Is it necessary to keep trimming a spruce tree?

It depends on the height and growth you want.

374. What kind of spray is used for bagworms on our spruce tree?

Use Diazinon or Sevin.

375. The low branches on our blue spruce are too long. Do we cut them back?

The blue spruce (*Picea*) cannot stand heavy pruning. Remove just the growing tips to keep the plants from spreading too much. Long growth removed does not grow back in.

376. May I transplant a blue spruce only 18 inches high?

Yes. Water and mulch. Shading is not necessary.

377. Blue spruce is losing its needles. How is this prevented.

Some shedding of inner needles occurs in mid summer. If current season's needles are shedding, it is due to drought or damage.

378. What is the best method for moving a blue spruce?

Move anytime from mid October to late April. Dig the plant with as large a root ball attached as possible. Plant in a well drained area with plenty of organic matter in the soil. Water well and keep plant well mulched and watered during periods of drought until re-established.

379. We have grown blue spruce trees from seeds. They are now two feet tall. What do we do?

Transplant in early spring before growth begins. Allow them plenty of room to develop.

380. What do I do for a blue spruce tree whose tips are drying up?

Check tips to see that damage is not caused by spruce budworm. If curled under, larvae is in the center. Spray with insecticide. Otherwise, mulch and water well.

381. Blue spruce is not holding color. What is wrong?

The blue spruce varies in coloration depending on the stock. Koster spruce is a grafted plant and holds color throughout the season. Colorado blue spruce, on the other hand, is grown from seed. It is blue in the spring and turns to normal green during the summer. Nothing is done to change the color.

382. How do I prune a sweet gum tree?

Prune during the dormant season or mid to late summer by removing any dead or diseased branches. Remove excess growth to thin the tree out.

383. What is the best way to get rid of borers on sweet gum trees?

Spray trunks in early spring with insecticide. Repeat as needed.

384. We have holes in the bark of our sweet gum tree. How do we treat this?

The usual cause is borers. See Question 383.

385. With what do we spray a sweet gum tree?

Use insecticide on insects when first noticed. If a disease, identify and use a recommended spray.

386. Sweet gum trees appear to be winter damaged and are not leafing out to the ends of the branches. What is causing this and how is it controlled?

Sweet gums in some areas are borderline trees and in severe winters partially die. Remove all growth back to where new growth is developing. Avoid feeding trees after late May so that they can harden-off in the fall.

387. Is the American or English plane tree hardier?

Both are equally hardy.

388. Our sycamore tree is doing poorly. What do we do?

A sycamore tree is subject to anthracnose and in many areas this hits as new leaves are beginning to form. Spray with fungicide when this first starts. Keep tree well watered during periods of drought and root feed every two to three years.

389. What do I do about bark peeling from our sycamore tree?

This is normal and does not hurt the tree in any way.

390. How can I prevent tree roots from penetrating the garden area?

This is very difficult. The best method is to dig down along the edge of the beds every spring and cut back roots which penetrate into the beds. Avoid locating gardens where tree roots are a problem.

391. How do I start a tulip tree?

Start from seed selected in mid summer. Sow the seed in early fall. It will germinate rapidly the following spring.

392. What causes leaf drop on a tulip tree and what do we do about it?

This is caused by anthracnose. No spray is recommended.

393. Our tulip tree died, was cut down and new shoots are coming up. Will they become a tree?

It is better to start with a new tree rather than trying to retrain one of these shoots.

394. Is the tulip tree a kind of poplar?

The tulip tree (*Liriodendron*) is not.

395. How do you eliminate aphids on a tulip tree?

Spray as soon as noticed with insecticide applied underneath and on top of the leaves.

396. What do I do about a fungus on a tulip tree?

Spray with fungicide as soon as noticed. Repeat in 10 days.

397. Is a tulip tree transplanted bare-rooted or balled?

The tulip tree (*Liriodendron*) is best moved balled and burlapped.

398. What is the care for a walnut tree?

Start from seed stratified in the fall. Transplant it or a new small tree from the nursery from late October through late April. The tree likes average garden soil in a well drained area. Water well.

399. Do I grow a black walnut tree from a nut?

Yes.

400. What do I do to prevent a black walnut tree from producing walnuts?

There is nothing you can do.

401. There are brown spots on the wood of a black walnut. What kind of disease is this and how do you treat it?

This is a fungus disease. Remove infected parts back to good wood and treat with fungicide. Repeat as needed.

402. Does a willow tree clog sewers?

The willow tree (Salix) produces a heavy root system and may clog old sewers.

403. How do you keep roots of a willow planted in your patio out of the sewer?

It is impossible to keep roots out of old sewers. New sewers are usually tight enough so that roots cannot get into them.

404. What is the care for a weeping willow?

Plant in an area near water, prune occasionally to keep the plant in good shape and remove old or dead wood. Spray as needed for insects.

405. How do I eliminate a fungus that is growing into the roots of a willow tree?

Spray roots with fungicide early in the spring. Repeat in three to four weeks.

406. What are the growing habits of a corkscrew willow?

The corkscrew willow (*Salix*) grows like any other willow except that the branches are twisted and curled as it grows up.

407. How do I grow pussy willows?

Take cuttings anytime from early spring through late summer. Place in moderately moist soil or root in perlite and peat moss.

408. What is the best way to prune a pussy willow tree?

Prune in early spring just before growth starts or in late summer. Remove all excess wood.

409. Do I transplant a pussy willow tree in May? What is the best way to do this?

Yes. Move with a solid soil ball attached and water well.

410. Parts of the leaves and branches on a weigela bush are dying. What do we do?

Prune all affected branches back to healthy wood. Prune out up to one-third of the old canes each year and allow plenty of air and light to circulate through the bushes.

411. When is the best month to plant weigelas?

Plant in late October through late April.

412. Is a bare rooted weigela planted in May?

Yes. Cut back heavily, mulch well and keep moderately moist until established.

413. Does the heat from an air-conditioner hurt a nearby yew?

The yew (*Taxus*) may be affected by the draft from an air-conditioner. Place a screen or other apparatus to direct the air from the yew.

414. Are yews poisonous to work around?

No.

415. What is the best way to trim yews?

Use a sharp pair of hand trimmers and remove leader growth on the ends to shape the plants. If used as a hedge, use hedge shears. Trim the plants narrower at the top than at the bottom.

BONSAI PINE
(Author)

MAGNOLIA TREE BLOSSOMS
Magnolia soulangeana
(Author)

416. I have a row of yews and the one end dies out constantly. What do I do?

Check the area for drainage. If excess water is there, try raising the plants up six to eight inches. Also check for nematodes which are nodules on the roots.

417. Are Texas yews adaptable to areas other than Texas?

Yes. Buy in early spring to acclimatize during the summer months.

418. Are yews fertilized in March?

Yes. Use a balanced fertilizer.

419. Is it okay to spray yews for red spider mites in March?

No. Red spider mites are not active until mid summer.

420. How do you prune the winter die-back from Japanese yews.

Prune with a sharp pair of hand pruners.

421. Yew trees are yellowing. Is this caused from over-watering.

Yes.

Chapter Six
Lawns

Soil Preparation

In establishing a lawn, the preparation of soil is one of the most important things. The following procedures are outlined for the building of a new lawn or for a lawn that needs to be reworked.

The soil in which grass is going to grow needs to be loose to allow air to flow through it freely and to contain plenty of organic matter to hold the moisture and to release it gradually. Soil should be well drained and through the addition of fertilizer will maintain good growth. Work the soil to a depth of six to eight inches with a rototiller which breaks up the soil.

Areas for lawns should be rough graded and then worked up. Add three to four inches of organic matter for every six to eight inches of soil. Any type of decaying plant material, such as peat moss, partially decomposed animal manures or leaf mold is ideal. Work thoroughly into the soil. Then add lime if needed, about three to four pounds per 1000 square feet. Spread over the top of the prepared soil. Add a balanced fertilizer, such as a 6-12-12 or 12-12-12, at the rate of four to five pounds per 1000 square feet. Work in with lime. Lime is fairly stable and stays in the area in which it is worked. It is slow acting and is best applied in the fall to allow time for it to break down and have effect on the lawn in the early spring when growth begins. Do not lime too often as it raises the pH level of the soil too high. Grass likes a pH level of 6 to 6.5 for best growth. If it is too high, the phosphorus, needed for good growth, is lost in the soil. Apply lime every three to four years unless soil tests indicate otherwise.

Take soil samples several weeks before you are ready to plant a lawn so that you will know what nutrients are needed. Once material is added and worked in, thoroughly rake to have a uniform tilth and to avoid any heavy lumps. In raking, consider the grading so that no hollows are left in which water may sit. If working around a building, leave the ground high enough around the building to divert water away from the foundation.

Once the area is thoroughly raked, you are ready to plant the seed. Select a blended mix of seeds, preferably two or three different cultivars, to have more resistance to insect and disease. Also, the area being seeded determines what type of seed to use. See also Types of Seed section in this chapter.

Use seed on a new lawn at the rate of two to three pounds per 1000 square feet. To renovate a lawn use one to two pounds. Broadcast uniformly over the whole area. Divide the seed in half, first applying it east to west. Then apply it from north to south. Rake the seed in lightly and follow with a light rolling to firm the seed into the soil. Keep moderately moist; seed germinates in seven to 10 days.

Cut grass when it is approximately one and one-half to two inches high, removing about one-third of the growth. Cut again when needed, removing about one-third of the growth each time. This helps the grass to fill out and become well established. Keep short into late fall to prevent tall grass from falling over and matting, which makes it disease prone during winter.

Fertilization

On an established lawn, use adequate fertilizer. Apply fertilizer such as 5-10-5 or 6-12-12 for the first time in Zone 6 in early March as growth is beginning. This is relatively low in nitrogen, of which most soils contain enough when they warm up. It is important to have a high amount of superphosphate which encourages root growth. Most grasses grow best during the cool season; therefore feed in early March. Repeat in about six weeks. Apply a third feeding in mid June and a fourth feeding in mid September. In September use a 12-12-12 fertilizer, which is higher in nitrogen, when temperatures are lower and nitrogen is tied up in the soil. (Zoysia grass starts growing in May; apply fertilizer in early May as growth is beginning. Repeat once again in six weeks if needed. Zoysia does not require heavy feedings.)

When fertilizing lawns, keep the soil moderately moist and the grass dry. Follow with a light watering to prevent the fertilizer from sitting on the plants and burning them. Applying fertilizer just before a rain is also beneficial. Use three to four pounds of fertilizer per 1000 square feet each time.

When using sod, prepare soil as described above. Place sod down over the area and roll lightly. Follow with a light application of fertilizer. Keep the sod moderately moist until it has a chance to establish new roots. It receives the same type of feeding as a lawn started from seed.

Types of Seed

The types of grass for Zone 6 are northern grasses because they withstand extremes in temperature which are so prevalent in this area. The best root initiation of northern grasses occurs during the cooler spring and fall periods. Deterioration and death occur in the warm, dry summer months. Optimum temperatures for root growth and development are lower than for shoot growth. Root growth occurs even in winter if temperature is above freezing. This is why northern grasses are best sown in the fall, usually early September (they receive the advantages of the cool fall weather for best root growth), or again in early spring before the temperatures become too high.

Kentucky bluegrass roots may last for more than one growing season while Roughstalk bluegrass or Redtop roots are replaced each year. Well developed roots are needed to supply grasses with water and plant nutrients present in soil. This is especially important during moisture and heat stress in summer. Close continuous cutting, high temperatures and excessive nitrogen depress root growth and increase foliage on top. Keep top growth in proportion to root growth. Kentucky bluegrass and Roughstalk bluegrass are widely used turf grasses in the cool northern region of the United States. Common Kentucky bluegrass seeds originate from natural stands in the United States. It is a perennial sod-forming grass that spreads by heavy rhizomes and seeds and is widely distributed throughout the United States. It is the most important, most widely used of the turf grasses due to vigorous rhizomes. Its resistance to wear is good. During dry warm summer months it becomes dormant; root growth stops when soil temperatures exceed 85 to 90 degrees. Drought usually does not kill it. Kentucky bluegrass needs a good supply of water but does not withstand poor drainage or high acidity. Well drained heavy soils of good fertility that are nearly neutral are the best. The pH level varies from about 6 to 6.8. Bluegrass germinates and becomes established very slowly; clean seed beds are a necessity. Late spring fertilization along with mowing too close and too infrequently are the most common reasons bluegrass lawns do not survive hot summer weather.

Common bluegrass needs three to four pounds of nitrogen per 1000 square feet of lawn per year. Follow procedure outlined in Fertilization section. Mow bluegrass up to two and one-half inches high during the hot weather. Suitable varieties are Merion, Newport, Park, Windsor, Fylking, Kenblue and Pennstar. A combination of two or three of these are ideal for the average lawn where light is sufficient.

If shade is a problem, use some of the fescues, particularly the red and chewing fescues which are finely textured grasses, with Kentucky bluegrass. These fescues adapt to the northern humid regions and grow well in shaded areas and slightly acid soils. After they become established, the red fescue dominates in shaded areas and the Kentucky bluegrass in sunny areas. The best creeping red fescues include Pennlawn, Ranier, Jamestown and Illahee. Pennlawn is less susceptible to leaf spot and performs better than the other varieties.

Colonial bent grass is a finely textured grass and widely used for golf course putting greens. The older varieties of bent grasses were used in lawn mixtures; however, their susceptibility to disease, including dollar spot and thatch, have relegated them to use on golf courses and special care lawns. Among bluegrasses, bent grass is considered more of a weed. All bent grasses need plenty of moisture, fertilizer and maintenance; however, they tolerate moderate shade. In hot humid weather they become diseased. They also require closer mowing than the bluegrasses.

Rye grass is in many mixes and germinates very rapidly, acting as a nursing grass. However, unless rye grass is cut very low, it shades the bent grasses and prevents them from growing. The rye grasses only live one or two seasons and then need to be re-sown. As they are a coarse grass, they do not blend well into a lawn. If desired, only use up to 20 percent in mixtures.

Bermuda grass is another grass commonly found in middle and southern United States. It is widely distributed throughout the area but is considered a weed by many. It has very deep rhizomes, making it almost impossible to uproot. For best results, keep it cut very low; therefore it is not a suitable grass in a bluegrass lawn. It is adaptable to warm humid areas and thrives well under hot summers but turns brown in early fall and remains brown until the weather warms up in the spring.

The Zoysia grasses are warm season grasses native to the Orient and the Philippine Islands. *Zoysia japonica* is coarse textured, more vigorous and more cold tolerant than other Zoysias. Zoysia turns the color of straw when the first frost occurs and remains off color until the next spring. *Zoysia japonica* is grown as far north as Canada and survives temperatures as low as 10 to 20 degrees; however, the growing season is short. Its drought and heat tolerance is very good. Zoysia grasses tolerate some shade. They are difficult to control because they spread very rapidly.

White clover is a low growing legume commonly found in the colder, humid regions. Clover growing in a lawn indicates sufficient lime in the soil. It attracts bees, has soft, juicy leaves and stems and stains clothing. To control clover in a lawn, use a herbicide.

Insect and Disease Control

Insects that affect lawns are relatively few. There are the root feeders and various grubs, the larvae of several species of beetles. They infest the soil and attack grass roots. Grubs hatch from eggs laid in the ground by beetles and spend a year or more consuming roots. Moles, skunks and many birds feed on the grubs. Control grubs by using an insecticide, such as Malathion or Diazinon, in early spring followed with another one in about 10 days and again at the end of August and in early September. Some of the more common grubs are the June bug, webworm, wireworm, chinch bug and leafhopper.

Most lawn diseases are caused by fungi which attack anytime during the year. Regularly feed the lawn and keep it cut at the proper height so that the grass maintains a good supply of food and keep it clean of debris for insect and disease control. Select grass varieties which are disease resistant.

Avoid over-watering to control fungus. Water the lawn early in the morning so that the plants have a chance to dry before nighttime. Wet grass plants are more subject to fungus diseases. A good feeding program is also beneficial. Prevent lawn diseases by using a fungicide.

Weeds

Weeds are one of the biggest problems in lawns but you can keep them to a minimum. Clean the area thoroughly and when sowing a new lawn, avoid the use of any herbicides with the seed which prevents the seed from germinating. Eliminate weeds when first starting a lawn and when established, use weed control. In many cases annual weeds are the main ones which start to grow and are eliminated after the first mowing. If grass is well established and cut at the proper height, it shades the area and prevents weeds, such as crabgrass, from germinating. A thick established turf is much less susceptible to weeds than is a sparsely grown lawn.

Most weeds can be controlled by one method or another. Establish the lawn and then in early spring consider the weed problem if it does exist.

Use pre-emerge herbicides in early April to prevent weed seed from germinating. Crabgrass usually does not start to germinate until temperatures rise. Pre-emerge herbicides are effective for approximately 45 to 50 days. Use a second application in early June to keep crabgrass under complete control for the summer months. If a few weeds emerge in a lawn, dig them out or pull them out. Annual bluegrass (*Poa annua*) is a real pest in lawns. Keep under control by using a pre-emerge in early March when the ground is bare. Annual bluegrass germinates best in the cool weather.

Control most weeds which become established in a lawn with various herbicides. A 2,4-D herbicide is effective on the more common weeds e.g. dandelions but where they persist use 2,4-D with Silvex. Nutgrass or watergrass, which is a sedge, is more difficult to control. Special nutgrass preparations are on the market which will bring these under control. Use several applications at regular intervals to eliminate them completely.

Chemicals are also available for the control of some of the more grassy plants, such as crabgrass, once it is established; however it is important to use the proper herbicide. Use herbicides when there is little or no wind and apply with a sprayer which is kept just for herbicides. The sprayer should not be used for control of insects as it is almost impossible to clean the container. Mark the container with "poison" and use for weed control only. Make sure the herbicides do not get on any surrounding plant material. Spray early in the day and when temperatures are below 80 degrees. Spraying during the heat of the day causes severe burning of many plants because of the reaction of the heat and chemical.

Fertilizers are available on the market with herbicides in them. Use with extreme caution. Do not apply near tree roots or around the base of the shrubs where they can reach the roots and kill the plants. Do not use when sowing seed. The herbicides prevent grass seed from germinating. Only use a fertilizer when sowing seed and avoid the use of a herbicide for at least six weeks after seed has been planted. Also avoid the use of herbicides several weeks prior to sowing seeds. If the weed and feed mix applied over a lawn is not effective in killing the weeds or has not killed the weeds, then use a spray recommended for the particular weed. When using herbicides, just mist the leaves. Too much spray causes further damage. Apply the sprays early in the day when the plants are more readily absorbing nutrients and moisture from the soil and will absorb the spray very rapidly then. It takes two to three weeks to eliminate the weeds. Repeat applications may be needed.

Planting Time

Sow grass seeds from the first of September to the end of the month or anytime from late February to the end of April. The later the seeding is done the more careful one is going to have to be in maintaining good soil moisture levels. Delay Zoysia seeding until early to mid May. Zoysia is a warm season grass and does not germinate until the soil reaches 60 degrees.

Sod anytime provided the ground is properly prepared and leveled. Place the sod down, lightly roll and water. Use a balanced fertilizer immediately after the sod is placed down and prior to watering.

See Glossary C for weed illustrations.

QUESTIONS

1. We have a very acid pH 5 lawn. What do we do?

Apply an application of lime in early fall using four to five pounds per 1000 square feet. Repeat again in about six months. Test soil the following year for further recommendations.

2. Should leaves be raked off new grass?

Yes.

3. What kind of herbicide is best to use on newly seeded lawns?

Do not use herbicide for at least six weeks after sowing seeds.

4. Our lawn is turning brown and we think we have grub worms. What do we do?

Lift some sod carefully and if worms are present, use an insecticide, such as Malathion or Diazinon.

5. When is the best time to use Scott's Plus Two for dandelions?

Use on an established lawn early in the spring as growth is becoming active. Repeat if needed.

6. Can weed and feed be used in September on established lawns?

Yes.

7. Is Scott's turf builder okay for lawns?

Yes.

8. Can Milorganite and grass seed be mixed for sowing?

Apply both and work lightly into soil.

9. What does phosphorus do for a lawn?

It stimulates an active root system.

10. When and what kind of lime is best for our lawn?

Make soil test and follow directions. Use and type depends on the pH level and other nutrients in the soil.

11. When is lime applied to a lawn area and how soon after may I plant a lawn?

Apply lime, if soil test indicates it is needed, in early fall to either a new lawn or established lawn. Seed at the same time.

12. We live in the Midwest where drought occurs frequently. What do we do to protect our lawns when this happens?

Provide the equivalent of two inches of rain every 10 to 12 days and use a regular fertilizing program in spring and early fall.

13. Is it all right to plant grass where a tree has been removed?

Yes.

14. Do trees become injured near where a lawn program is being carried out?

Trees do not become injured if you keep herbicides away from the base and roots of the trees.

15. When do we begin a new lawn?

Begin it in fall or spring.

16. How do we kill grass in just one place?

There are several herbicides that can be used. Check with your local garden center for best herbicide.

17. How can I eliminate grass around the fence?

There are several herbicides such as Roundup and Paraquat that can be used.

18. How do I eliminate the bare places and weedy patches in our lawn?

See Soil Preparation section at beginning of this chapter and then sow accordingly.

19. What do we do about the yellow areas in the lawn where a dog has urinated?

Dig these up, add more organic matter and resow.

20. How do I tell the difference between watergrass and nutgrass?

Nutgrass has a stem which is three-angled and coarse blades. Watergrass has a round stem and grows close to the ground.

21. Our grass that was burned is not coming back. What do we do?

Rework the area and re-seed. Avoid burning grass areas.

22. What do I do about dead grass on my lawn?

If areas have died out, re-dig and replant. If caused by brown grass, this is a build-up of thatch. Remove in late August or early September.

23. Is May too late to dig up our lawn to establish a new one?

It is getting late, however, if a good watering program is followed, there is no problem.

24. Should the lawn clippings be kept on the lawn?

If light amount, yes. Otherwise remove.

25. Is it better to seed or sod a lawn?

It is a matter of personal preference. Sod has immediate effect but takes a considerable amount of work to get it established. Seeding is preferred if done early in the spring or in the fall.

26. I have difficulty in growing grass under my trees. How do I overcome this?

Carefully prune to remove branches and allow more light or change to a ground covering or mulch. Increase feedings of fertilizer. Three times the amount of fertilizer is needed to grow grass under a tree. Be careful you do not apply this in one application or you will burn both the lawn and the tree.

27. Why are infrequent heavy waterings of lawns better than frequent light waterings?

Light waterings bring grass roots up to the surface where they burn. Establish a regular watering program. Water the equivalent of two inches of rain.

28. Is it too late in February to dig up a yard and establish a new lawn?

No.

29. How do we eliminate Bermuda grass from our lawn?

This is a real problem. Dig down deep into the area, removing rhizomes, or sterilize soil. Seed at proper time.

30. How do we kill crabgrass?

Use a special herbicide for crabgrass. Contact local garden center for instructions.

31. Can a bluegrass lawn be de-thatched after an application of fertilizer?

Yes. However it is better to de-thatch and re-seed and then feed. See Questions 51, 52 and 63.

32. What do we do about brown areas in an otherwise green lawn?

Check for insect damage and treat accordingly. Rework areas and re-seed at the proper time.

33. How do we control broadleaf weeds in a bent grass lawn?

Use 2,4-D with Silvex.

34. How do I aerate my lawn?

If the area is small, use a digging fork. Insert it into the soil and give it a bit of a twist on the handle. Repeat this every six to eight inches. If the area is large, rent an aerating machine.

35. Does crabgrass have any uses and if so, what?

Crabgrass gives a green effect over a lawn area and is used as a temporary lawn during the summer months. Eliminate crabgrass in late August and properly prepare and re-seed for real grass in early September.

36. May I use crabgrass pre-emergent in March?

Early April is ideal.

37. How do we eliminate chickweed in our lawn?

Chickweed is controlled by using 2,4-D with Silvex. Make first applications as early as February when chickweed starts to grow. Repeat as needed.

38. How do we control dandelions in our lawn?

Use 2,4-D.

39. How much and how often do I water creeping fescue to establish it?

Keep soil moderately moist all the time until grass is well established.

40. We have a fungus on our lawn and it is not in a shady area. What do I do?

Spray fungicide early in the day. Repeat if needed.

41. What is the best grass seed to use in a shaded area?

See Types of Seed section in this chapter. Check your local garden center for varieties in your area.

42. How do I sow grass seed?

Spread seed by hand or use a special grass seeder. Rake seed in lightly followed by a light rolling.

43. How do you eliminate mushrooms in a damp area?

Hand pick and rake area to aerate the soil. Repeat as needed.

44. How do I eliminate moss in our lawn?

Moss is an indication of lack of aeration, soil compactness, poor fertility and sometimes acid-type conditions. Remove moss with steel rake and aerate with a regular aerator. Follow with a feeding of a well balanced fertilizer or possibly a light application of lime applied in the fall.

45. Does grass grow under white pine trees and if so, what kind of grass?

It depends on the amount of shade. If light is moderate, use a shady grass mix.

46. Our rye grass seed planted on a slope did not germinate. Do I replant it?

Yes. Keep moderately moist until germination does occur.

47. Can creeping red fescue be applied in March?

Yes.

48. What is the best way to treat clay soil before sodding?

Prepare clay soil by adding plenty of organic matter and work in well. See section on Soil Preparation.

49. We seeded our lawn area but grasses failed to emerge. What do we do?

Rework areas lightly and select fresh seed and sow.

50. How do we control sod webworms in a lawn?

Apply Diazinon or Malathion starting in early May. Repeat at 10-day intervals for at least three applications and repeat again starting in late August. Keep soil moderately moist and insecticide watered in to a depth of one-half inch.

51. What does thatching mean?

Thatch is a build-up of dead grass formed at the soil level and in some cases, builds up fairly deeply depending on the variety and conditions. When thick enough, it impedes grass growth and needs to be removed. Special machines are available which remove the thatch without injuring the grass. This is called thatching. See Questions 31, 52 and 63.

52. What do I do about thatch in our bluegrass lawn?

If it is a small amount, it is not harmful. If heavy, remove in late August or early September, follow with a good aeration and feed with a 12-12-12 fertilizer. See Questions 31, 51 and 63.

53. Can weed killer be applied after fertilizing a lawn?

Yes.

54. How do we control the weeds in our lawn?

Use herbicide according to the types of weeds growing. Best control is done when weeds are in a soft succulent stage of growth in early spring or early fall when growth is active. Avoid using herbicides on newly sown grass. Apply on a windless day.

55. Can weed killers used on lawns be injurious to surrounding trees.

Yes, if applied to the point where it gets into the root system.

56. How do we best grow Windsor bluegrass?

Windsor is another cultivar that does well and is treated as any other bluegrass. See Types of Seed section in this chapter.

57. How can we get rid of white clover in our lawn?

Use 2,4-D with Silvex. Apply as needed until clover is eliminated.

58. How do you prevent Zoysia from invading a bluegrass lawn?

Place a barrier, such as fiber glass 12 to 15 inches below ground level with three inches above ground. Keep grass trimmed so it does not reach over the top of the barrier.

59. How do I salvage seed from Zoysia?

Do not allow it to set seed. Close mowing is best for good results. If seed is needed, purchase from a reliable seed house.

60. Does Zoysia need lime and if so, when is the best time to apply it?

It depends on the soil test. Lime is needed at certain times. Apply in late fall or early spring.

61. Is Zoysia grass an appropriate ground cover for a terrace?

For a hot dry area, Zoysia is ideal. If shaded area, consider other suitable ground covers.

62. Should Zoysia be allowed to go to seed?

No. See Question 59.

63. When do we de-thatch Zoysia and bluegrass lawns?

De-thatch bluegrass in late August or early September and Zoysia grass in early May when starting to make growth. See Questions 31, 51 and 52.

64. Is it okay to burn the dry grass off a Zoysia lawn?

No. This destroys much of the plant material and nutrients needed for growth.

65. We have an old Zoysia lawn that needs to be revitalized. What do we do for this?

De-thatch the area and work the soil in early May. Secure fresh seed and apply at the rate of one pound to 1000 square feet followed with a feeding of a balanced fertilizer, such as a 5-10-5 or 6-12-12. Keep area moderately moist until germination occurs.

66. Does pre-emerge crabgrass killer kill Zoysia?

No, not if properly applied.

67. Can Zoysia be applied to our lawn in March?

No. It is too early. Wait until early May.

68. Do we use 12-12-12 with grass seed planting?

Yes. Use in early September.

69. Is it okay to use a turf builder with fertilizer on our lawn?

Turf builder is a fertilizer. It is not necessary to use both.

70. How are toadstools eliminated from a lawn?

Handpick as soon as noticed or rake area thoroughly to a depth of one-half inch to aerate well. Repeat as needed.

71. How is nutgrass controlled?

Use herbicide containing DSMA labeled for nutgrass control. Apply first application when plants are two inches high. Repeat as soon as additional new shoots reach two inches.

72. What is the best way to eliminate annual bluegrass?

Poa annua is an annual bluegrass and considered a weed in most areas. Weed out and apply a pre-emerge herbicide, such as Dacthal. Reapply in late fall before seed germinates and again in late March.

Chapter Seven
Ground Covers

General Information

Ground cover plants grow low to the ground, from one to two inches to one foot or more in height. They are primarily plants which are green all year round although some types go dormant in the fall and come back into growth in early spring. They are used in shady or sunny areas depending on the type chosen.

Work the areas where ground covers are to be used to a depth of five to six inches. Allow excellent drainage and add to the soil organic matter, such as peat moss, compost or well rotted manure along with about four to five pounds of superphosphate per 100 square feet worked to a depth of four to six inches. If the area needs lime, add at planting time. Spread lime over the area and work to a depth of two to three inches. If soil is relatively poor, add a well balanced fertilizer, such as a 5-10-5, at the rate of four to five pounds per 1000 square feet. Ground cover plants are usually available in early spring. Plant a few inches apart to as much as a foot apart, depending on the size of the plant. The larger the plant, the wider the spacing.

Select hardy plants in your area. They are available in individual pots or plant trays. Remove with some soil attached. Bare root material is also available from cuttings which are heavily rooted and wrapped in moss. Some are started from fresh seed. Sow them on well prepared ground in early spring as soon as danger of frost is past.

The following is a list of ground covers which prefer shade: *Ajuga* (bugleweed); *Asarum* (ginger); *Asperula odorata* (sweet woodruff); *Convallaria majalis* (lily-of-the-valley); *Euonymus fortunei radicans*, and other low cultivars.

Several ferns are ideal for ground covers: *Hedera helix* (hardy English and Baltic ivy); *Hosta* (plantain lilies); *Liriope* (mondo grass); *Pachysandra* (Japanese spurge), and *Vinca major* (periwinkle).

The following ground covers are ideal for sunny areas: *Aegopodium* (bishop's weed); *Calluna* (heather); *Ceratostigma plumbaginoides* (dwarf plumbago); *Coronilla varia* (crown vetch); *Cotoneaster adpressa horizontalis* (dwarf cotoneaster); *Iberis* (candytuft); Juniper Bar Harbour, Andorra and other dwarf varieties; *Lysimachia nummularia* (creeping Jennie or creeping Charlie); *Phlox subulata* (dwarf phlox); *Sedum* species, and *Thymus* (thyme).

Once ground covers are planted, work a pre-emerge, such as Casoran, into the soil to a depth of one to two inches to help prevent weed seed from germinating. Follow with a mulching of compost of partially decomposed leaves or partially decomposed woodchips to a depth of about two inches over the area. Plants need adequate watering during periods of drought. Once plants become established, apply a light application of a balanced fertilizer in early spring as growth is beginning. Add a fertilizer, such as 5-10-5, at the rate of approximately four pounds to a 1000 square feet over the mulch when the plants are dry. Follow this application of dry fertilizer with a light watering to wash any fertilizer off the leaves to prevent burning.

If plants are well mulched, weeds will not be a problem. Hand pull weeds which do grow before they have had a chance to become well established or to form seeds. Mow ground covers at least once or twice a year. Select a rotary mower with a good sharp blade and a set of wheels larger than normally used for cutting lawns. Adjust the mower so that the cutting height is four to six inches above the soil level. Mow plants in mid May and again in late June or late September. This removes the tops of the plants causing them to bush out and become thick and compact. Mow flowering ground covers, such as pachysandra and ajuga, immediately following flowering before the plants have a chance to set seed. Mow crown vetch several times during the season to keep the plants from getting too large. On steep slopes add some more organic matter to ground covers which are sparsely growing until they have had a chance to fill in completely.

Insects and diseases are sometimes a problem on ground covers. Scale, the most common insect, often infects the euonymus. It leaves white scale-like materials on the stems and leaves. Use a dormant oil spray in late February or early March before plants start to grow. If scale insects persist, spray in early

June with an insecticide with an oil base. Very few other insects attack the plants. Spray as needed.

Diseases are often bacterial ones associated with root rot. Plants turn black in early spring. This is particularly noticed on the periwinkle (*Vinca*). Remove diseased parts immediately. Use bacterial spray when first noticed and repeat again in about three weeks.

Mildew may be a problem in areas of heavy shade and poor air circulation. Use fungicide when first noticed and repeat as needed.

QUESTIONS

1. What kind of ground cover can be put over a flower bed?

Several low growing annuals such as *Alyssum* and *Myosotis* (forget-me-not) are attractive when used around spring bulbs. Plant immediately after planting bulbs or immediately after annuals are set in, to give shade to the ground.

2. How do I root ground covers, particularly pachysandra?

Take cuttings in mid June, selecting ends four to six inches long. Remove one-third of the lower leaves and plant in a mixture of three parts perlite to one part peat moss. Plant these in a cold frame or planter box in a semi-shaded area and keep moderately moist until rooted.

3. How do I propagate ajuga, the bugleweed?

Bugleweed is propagated by division. Plants send out runners and when these are large enough and start to establish roots, cut off and plant. When plants become thick enough, dig up and carefully separate into individual plants in early spring or latter part of April.

4. How do I clean up an area with ground cover of ajuga and pachysandra?

Dig the area thoroughly and remove as much plant material as possible. Then add organic matter and rototill the area five or six inches deep to eliminate any plants that were left after digging.

5. Is creeping thyme hardy in Zone 6?

Creeping thyme (*Thymus*) is hardy in most of the areas throughout central and eastern United States.

6. What is a fast growing ground cover?

Crown vetch (*Coronilla*) is extremely fast growing. Others are the periwinkle (*Vinca*) and ivy.

7. What is an ideal ground cover for a steep hill in full sun?

Crown vetch is ideal.

8. How do I remove ivy growing up the side of a wall?

Carefully pull the ivy away from the wall. Roots loosen some concrete after a period of time and some resurfacing may be required. On wood walls, roots sometimes get underneath the wood and allow rotting, making it necessary to replace the wood before it becomes too badly damaged.

9. Does ivy growing up on a tree kill the tree?

This rarely occurs unless ivy grows over the branches. Confine ivy to the trunk of the tree.

Chapter Eight
Vines

General Information

Vines are an essential part of almost every garden. They are used for ornament as well as for screening. Vines grow anywhere from a few feet to as much as 60 feet. Choose with care for their particular purpose. Some vines are self-supporting, clinging to walls or other structures where others need to be trained on and fastened to trellises. Others climb by twining. Most vines become a tangled mess of foliage unless specially trained and trimmed at proper times. Trim most vines immediately following flowering, remove all excess growth and head the tendrils back to encourage more flowering. This is the case with wisteria. Trim non-flowering vines by removing excess growth or top them once they reach the height at which you want them to grow. Do not plant clinging vines on wooden houses. Their small root-like structures hold fast and may penetrate and damage the wood. They have to be removed and torn away from the building every time painting and repair work is done. Train most clinging vines on trellises which are lowered when needed for repair or painting.

The following vines are suitable for flowers: *Bignonia capreolata; Campsis grandiflora; Clematis* species; *Hydrangea anomala petiolaris* (climbing hydrangea); *Lonicera* species (honeysuckle species) and *Wisteria* species.

These vines produce colorful fruits: *Ampelopsis* species; *Celastrus* species; *Clematis*, most species and *Euonymus fortunei* 'Vegetus'.

These vines withstand shade: *Actinidia* species; *Aristolochia macrophylla; Clematis* species; *Euonymus* species; *Hedera* species and *Hydrangea anomala petiolaris* (climbing hydrangea).

QUESTIONS

1. When is the best time to pick bittersweet?

Pick bittersweet (*Celastrus*) as the berries split open and expose the bright orange color. This is usually in late September in most areas.

2. What do I plant to cover a fence for privacy?

Plant *Ampelopsis* or *Aristolochia*, the Dutchman's-pipe. The latter is ideal for semi-shaded areas.

3. Can clematis be moved in May?

If container grown, move in May. If not, move as growth is beginning which is usually late March or early April.

4. What are some of the clematis that are grown?

The following *Clematis* are grown: *Clematis jackmani; Clematis macropetala* (big petal clematis); *Clematis montana rubens* (Pink montana clematis); *Clematis paniculata* (sweet autumn clematis); *Clematis tangutica* (golden clematis); *Clematis texensis* (scarlet clematis) and *Clematis virginiana* (Virgins' Bower). There are also varieties of clematis that are grown varying from white to pink to deep red and deep blue. Check the local catalogs for your area for varieties that are available.

5. What is the best soil and position for clematis?

Clematis likes a cool root system. Plant the roots where they are shaded or mulch heavily to keep the ground cool. The best soil is well drained and on the semi-sweet side – pH 6.5. Add lime to sweeten the soil and work in plenty of organic matter.

6. Are clematis trimmed and when?

Prune clematis regularly in early spring as growth begins. Prune back any dead or injured parts. In some cases on the more vigorous ones, cut back quite heavily.

7. My clematis started to grow and then the vine suddenly died. What is the problem?

This is a bacterial disease. Treat with a spray for bacteria in early spring, spraying the plant and treating the soil.

8. How do I exterminate a honeysuckle vine?

Remove by using 2,4-D with Silvex. If it is growing among other plants, mix the solution in a small plastic container and apply to the tips of the vine when actively growing. If the vine is growing in an open area, spray with 2,4-D with Silvex early in the spring when there is little or no wind in the early morning.

9. When and how is wisteria trimmed?

Trim immediately following flowering. Remove all flower stalks and extra growth. Also trim when new tendrils are sent out. Cut them back partway to encourage side shoots to encourage better flowering.

10. Our wisteria fails to flower. Why?

Prune the plant to avoid this. Avoid the use of high nitrogen fertilizers. Keep plants cut back to encourage short side shoots. Prune the roots by going two to three feet from the base and cutting a circle approximately six inches deep to remove many of the roots and shock the plant into bloom. Root prune the last half of June.

11. What are some fast growing annual vines suitable for fast screening in the summer?

Morning-glories make ideal screens in various colors. Consult your local seed catalogs for other annual vines growing in your area.

ROEBELENII PALM
Phoenix roebelenii
(Placet)

RHAPIS PALM
Rhapis excelsa
(Placet)

Chapter Nine Container Gardening

General Information

This chapter deals with growing plants in containers outdoors. Container gardening has become very popular for people with limited space, particularly apartment dwellers who want to grow plants. Hybridizers have produced a variety of dwarf vegetables, including tomatoes, cucumbers, eggplant and carrots, which are suitable for container growing. A number of trees and shrubs, including many of the evergreens, are also ideal.

The media for container growing should be one which is well drained and porous to allow air to move freely through the roots of the plants and to hold sufficient moisture. A suitable media contains good top soil, peat moss and perlite in equal proportions with some superphosphate and trace elements. This mixture allows the plants to overwinter when temperatures go below zero.

Container-grown plants require more watering than those grown in the ground. Apply regular feedings of liquid fertilizer when growth begins in the spring and continue until the beginning of August in most areas. Once plants become established, root systems are heavy causing the plants to use moisture and nutrients quite rapidly. Mulch containers with decorative bark to cut down on evaporation. Plant annuals around the top of the containers for their flowering effects.

Carefully prune growing trees and shrubs in containers after flowering or in the second half of June to maintain the plants in balance with the root system. Use dwarf trees, which reach heights of 15 to 20 feet, for container material. Once plants are established in the containers, and well taken care of, they tend to be treated as a Bonsai plant. Remove branches which cross one another to allow for good air circulation.

Watering of all container-grown plants is extremely important, particularly during the fall and winter where containers are in a position that they can dry out due to wind. In colder areas, move containers together and cover with mulch to protect the soil balls from freezing too heavily. Give broad-leafed evergreens protection with an anti-dehiscent, such as Wilt-Pruf, to cut down on the evaporation during the winter months.

Suitable vegetables for container growing are beans, beets, carrots, chard, cucumbers, eggplant, lettuce, onions, radishes, spinach, the dwarf varieties of squash and tomatoes, both the patio type as well as the regular varieties which are staked or trained on trellises. Members of the cabbage family, such as cabbage, cauliflower, broccoli and Brussels sprouts, are grown in containers in the early spring and planted again in early August as late fall crops. Start vegetables indoors for early crops six to eight weeks ahead of planting outdoors. Give them a balanced fertilizer and inspect daily for insects and diseases. Spray as needed.

Vegetables grown in containers take up a limited amount of space and are moved around to take advantage of the sunlight. In addition, soil in containers is immediately in good shape and does not need to be prepared as in a garden.

A wide variety of herbs are grown in containers. Two or three plants are all that are needed to supply a family of four or five people. Keep the plants trimmed, well watered and properly fertilized to encourage new growth. Grow herbs with some of the vegetables for a more decorative effect and for some insect control. Chives help to prevent aphids.

Roses, including floribunda, grandiflora, hybrid teas and polyanthus adapt well to container growing. Give roses three to four hours of sunlight during the morning hours. Keep moderately pruned to control the height of growth and spray to control insect and disease. Use liquid fertilizer at two to three-week intervals up to the middle of August. Then withhold fertilizer to allow the plants to harden-off for overwintering. In the late fall when frost begins, move containers to a protected area and heavily mulch with leaves or other material to prevent the roots from freezing. Do little or no pruning on the roses in the fall as they overwinter better with most of the growth remaining. Prune in early spring. As soon as pruning is completed, apply a generous application of superphosphate and work in around the base of the plant. Keep plants well watered throughout the summer months.

Annuals of all types are suitable for container growing in hanging baskets, clay pots and other decorative containers. Annuals add color around trees and can be interspersed with vegetables in pots for decorative effects. Give containers drainage in the bottom with pebbles or other coarse material and a layer of moss to prevent the soil from washing down into the pebbles.

All containers need drainage through holes in the bottom or on the side. If drainage holes are in the bottom, place the container on blocks to allow water to freely pass through the holes. If directly on the ground, the container holes become plugged. Periodically remove two to three inches of the old soil and replace with potting soil with high amounts of organic matter and superphosphate.

Suitable shrubs for containers are any of the more decorative types that grow compactly. Prune after flowering to allow proper aeration. Prune trees and shrubs immediately after flowering and again about the middle of June as growth begins. Pruning encourages shorter spurs which increase the flowering production.

Dwarf fruit trees make ideal container plants and are grown in groups, often of more than one variety, to allow for good pollination. Spray to control insects and diseases.

QUESTIONS

1. Do annuals grown in containers need more fertilization than those grown in regular beds and if so, how often?

Annuals do need more fertilization. Feed once every two weeks, particularly during the dryer weather.

2. What type of fertilizer is best to use for container growing?

Use any balanced liquid fertilizer or for flowering plants, use a fertilizer in which the phosphorus content is higher than the nitrogen and potassium.

3. How are trees and shrubs grown in containers overwintered?

Move the containers to a sheltered spot and protect by mulching heavily with leaf mold. Containers too large to move overwinter without any difficulty. Make sure containers receive adequate water during mild spells in the winter when they dry out more rapidly.

4. Can ground covers rather than a mulch be used in containers with trees and shrubs?

Yes. Ground covers, particularly vining types, are effective in containers.

5. How long are roses fertilized in containers?

Fertilize roses once every two weeks with a liquid fertilizer and continue up to the middle of September. Then withhold fertilizer and allow roses to go dormant naturally.

6. What are some good evergreens to grow in containers?

Alberta spruce, Chinese juniper, Japanese yew, Mugo pine and some of the dwarf junipers are excellent.

7. Do you put more than one miniature plant in a container?

Yes. Several miniatures in a container make an effective garden. Prune to keep plants in proportion to one another.

8. Are evergreens, broadleaf and needle-like, given any special protection during the winter when grown in containers?

Yes. Spray these plants with Wilt-Pruf to cut down on evaporation. Protect them from the winter sun by covering them with burlap or another suitable screening.

9. My azaleas in containers are doing fine but the leaves are yellow instead of deep green. Why is this and what do I do?

This indicates a lack of iron. Apply iron chelate, one tablespoon per gallon of water, along with one tablespoon of epsom salts. Apply in early April and again in early September.

Chapter Ten
Vegetable Gardening

Site Selection

Develop a vegetable garden where the ground is free of tree roots and receives at least five to six hours of sun daily. Provide sufficient drainage so that no excess water lies in the ground at anytime after a heavy rain.

Soil Preparation

Plan the layout of the vegetable garden on paper ahead of time. Assign crops that need cool, moist conditions, such as celery and parsley, to proper locations. Do not let tall growing crops shade lower crops. If the garden rows run north and south, place the tall plants on the north side of the garden so that they do not shade the shorter ones.

Any type of soil is satisfactory because changes can be made. Dig the area well, preferably double-dig. Remove the first spade of soil along one side of the garden and then take this to the opposite side of the garden. Add three to four inches of mulch, such as leaf mold or manure, into the bottom of the trench, spading as deep as the spade. Take the next spade of soil and place this on top of the area just dug and add more mulch to the trench until you reach the opposite side. Take excess soil from the first trench and place in the last trench. Add three to four inches of organic matter and four to five pounds of superphosphate per 100 square feet on top of the dug area. Add a light application of lime, using approximately five pounds per 1000 square feet.

If tests have been made as to the need for lime follow the recommendations. You may have to add four to five pounds of a balanced fertilizer, such as 5-10-5 per 1000 square feet over the same area and rework this material to a depth of four to five inches. If lime has been applied but was not needed, tests may show a need for gypsum which does not change the pH level but keeps the soil open and supplies calcium for plant growth.

Once the area is prepared, rake until the soil is moderately fine, ready for planting. In the fall, leave the soil rough instead of raking so that it is ready for seeding. Add mulch about a foot in depth over the area for cool crops to prevent the soil from heavily freezing. When a mild period occurs in late February or early March, remove the mulch and place black plastic over the area to draw the sun's heat for a couple of days prior to seeding.

If vegetable gardens are worked in the fall, redig early the next spring, incorporating more organic matter. Avoid using a heavy application of fresh manure just prior to seeding. This burns the new seeds. Use a layer of fresh manure over the vegetable garden in late fall and leave as a mulch. The rains remove some of the excess fertilizer. As soon as the garden is worked in early spring, work fertilizer into the soil several inches.

Seed Selection

Select hybrid variety of vegetables which are disease and insect-resistant. In most catalogs, hybrid vegetables are marked with the symbol F_1 and state their resistance to different types of diseases. Tomatoes are susceptible to fusarium and verticillium wilt. It is important to select varieties resistant to these two diseases. Plants of hybrid vigor are more uniform in production and are superior to many of the older varieties. Most vegetables have a number, such as "48," which indicates that it takes approximately 48 days from the time the seeds are sown until the plants are ready for harvesting. You can select plants which will produce in a short time or extend the food production by selecting varieties which produce in early, mid or late, season.

Seed Sowing

Start vegetables indoors approximately four to six weeks before planting outside. Cool crops are those of the cabbage family, lettuce, onions and spinach. Plant as soon as the ground can be worked, often as early as February. Plant peas in the Midwest during February. Cool crops, if planted when temperatures rise, do not mature under normal conditions and tie up space in the garden over a long period.

Sow seeds indoors in a sterile medium and place as close to a source of light as possible. Start cool crops, such as the cabbage family, in early January and plant outside in mid February. Once the seeds have germinated, transplant when they get the second to third pair of leaves. Place them in individual containers or in flats, spacing them several inches apart so that they are easily moved for planting outdoors. Start warm season plants, such as tomatoes and squashes, indoors about six weeks before planting outdoors. Harden-off the seedlings a week to 10 days before placing outdoors by withholding water a day or two. Take seedlings outdoors to an area where they are protected from the wind and where they get sun for an hour to two hours and then bring back indoors. On the next day, double the time until finally the plants are exposed outdoors throughout the full day. When transplanting into the garden, water with a feeding of liquid fertilizer at half recommended strength. On the first day or two protect the plants until established by placing hot caps or other protection over the plants until they start to re-root.

Sow most vegetables directly in the garden once the ground is prepared. In early spring sow vegetables twice as deep as the diameter of the seed, cover over lightly and keep moderately moist until germination occurs. Apply mulch between the rows to a depth of one to two inches to conserve moisture and to control weeds. As vegetables develop in size, mulch three to four inches in depth.

Cool versus Warm Crops

Cool crops are planted early in the season and withstand very cold weather. They are members of the cabbage family, peas and spinach. Start four to six weeks ahead of time indoors or plant directly in the garden itself. If planted in mid February to early March, these plants will mature in late April to early May. If planting is delayed until mid April, the crops will not mature until August, tying up space that can be used for other crops.

Do not plant warm crops until all danger of heavy frost is ended. They are tomatoes, squashes, beans and cucumbers. These plants are either started indoors or planted directly into the garden a week to 10 days before the last killing frost. Do not put warm vegetables out too early; heavy frost or cold ground delays their growth. They prefer soil temperatures of 60 degrees or higher.

There are a number of dwarf or mini vegetables available on the market suitable for container growing. Start indoors and place containers outdoors during the warm part of the day and move to protected spots at night, thus giving a much earlier start to the vegetables. These mini vegetables require the same growing conditions as do the regular plants; however, when container-grown, extra watering and feeding is needed.

Most cool crops are planted in the garden again in late July through August, growing well when the weather is cooler in the early fall and producing food during the late fall days. Once production is finished, many of the warm crops, such as beans, are pulled up, the ground reworked, more organic matter added and then they are replanted with the cool crops for fall production.

Avoid saving seeds from most vegetable crops. They are of hybrid origin and do not come true from seeds. Seeds saved from hybrid plants are often inferior in quality and production from the parent plant; therefore, purchase fresh seeds each spring. If seeds are carried over from one year to another, store in airtight containers with two to three tablespoons of powdered milk to absorb any moisture. Store the seeds at a temperature of 50 to 60 degrees until ready for next spring.

When carrying seeds over, run a germination test prior to planting by selecting 10 to 16 seeds. Place them in a plastic container on moist paper toweling and keep the seeds at 75 to 80 degrees. Observe them daily and as soon as seeds begin to germinate, wait an additional 24 hours and then count the number of seeds that have germinated. If half the seeds have germinated, sow twice the amount of seeds for production.

Fertilizing

Once vegetables are growing actively, maintain fertile conditions. During periods of cold wet weather, some of the earlier crops slow down and take on a yellowish-green appearance. Use nitrate of soda, one tablespoon per gallon of water and apply along the base of the plants. Follow with a light watering so that the fertilizer does not burn the plants. Occasionally a balanced feeding is advisable to keep the plants in good condition. Make a narrow furrow, a half-inch deep, near the base of the plants along the edge of the rows; spread a light application of a balanced fertilizer, such as 5-10-5, in the furrow and fill in with soil. Then water lightly to break the fertilizer down for plant growth.

Also use liquid fertilizers as needed. If the ground has been well prepared with plenty of organic matter and superphosphate, you do not need feedings too often except after heavy rains or when watering is required on a fairly regular basis.

When removing the cool crops and planting warm ones, redig the ground and add more organic matter and superphosphate and leave the ground rough so that freezing and thawing break the soil down and release more nutrients for the vegetable garden the following year. Compost between the rows controls soil moisture and breaks down additional nutrient matter. Use compost as soon as vegetables are removed.

Insect and Disease Control

Inspect the vegetable garden on a daily basis for insect damage. Eliminate immediately. Use the sprays if needed and make sure they are recommended for use on the vegetables. Avoid using systemic insecticides; these are poisonous to human beings. Apply the spray underneath and on top of the leaves. Repeat as needed. Heavy spraying of water eliminates some of the insects without having to use insecticides.

Avoid most disease problems by selecting disease-resistant plants. Most diseases are caused by fungi or bacteria and are easily controlled by the use of a spray as soon as the disease is first noticed. If only one or two plants are infected, it sometimes is better to remove the infected plant rather than to spray.

Plants, such as tomatoes, cucumbers and squashes, need insects for pollination. Avoid the overuse of chemicals which are harmful to the bees. When sprays are needed, use early in the morning before the insects become active. This allows the insecticide to dry before the bees become active. In most cases with squashes and cucumbers, flowers are produced early in the season with little or no production of fruit. These plants produce female flowers a week to 10 days ahead of male flowers. Both male and female flowers are needed for pollination and for fruit. Lack of flowers in tomatoes in the early season is often due to very cool conditions; flowers open and fall before they have a chance to become pollinated. The lack of insects, particularly bees, is also a factor in tomatoes not setting fruit in the early season.

Rotate vegetables each year to avoid insects or diseases. Some vegetables take more nutrients out of the soil than others and rotating keeps a more uniform, fertile soil. Where space is very limited, rotation is not practical. The addition of organic matter and mulches controls the soil moisture levels and prevents the ground from drying out too rapidly. Use black plastic as a mulch to warm the ground as well as around the warmer growing crops, such as tomatoes and squashes, to get them off to an early start. Black plastic retards weed growth. You can use clear plastic; however, weeds germinate underneath so cover the clear plastic with an application of leaves or other compost to cut down on the light which grows weeds.

QUESTIONS

1. What is the best way to plant asparagus?

Plant in late March to mid April in trenches one foot deep. Remove the soil and place in six to eight inches of well decomposed, organic matter or well-rotted manure, mixing in with superphosphate at the rate of four to five pounds per hundred square feet. Place roots on top of the mulch and cover about one inch. As the plants begin to grow, add more mulch until the row is level with the surrounding area. Then apply a good mulch six inches beyond each side of the row. Space asparagus plants approximately two feet apart. Keep them well watered during periods of drought and use mulch to prevent weeds.

2. How and when do we harvest asparagus?

Allow asparagus to grow for at least two years before you start cutting them. If plants are growing actively the second year, harvest the sturdiest shoots when they are about four to six inches above the ground level. Use an asparagus knife directly down beside the plants to cause little damage. Remove the shoots and make sure that you leave four to six good shoots at each crown to develop for the following year. The next year heavier cutting is done. Finish all cuttings by mid June.

3. How late are asparagus cut?

This depends on the growth of the plants. Usually cutting in well established beds is done by the end of June.

4. How do you get rid of red mites on asparagus?

Mites are a problem during hot dry periods and are best controlled with the use of Kelthane, applying this according to directions every three to four days for at least four applications. Keep the plants well mulched and well watered.

5. Is there any way to salvage asparagus that has blight on it?

Yes. See that the plants are kept free of weeds and use a spray, such as Agristreptomycin or Bordeaux mixture, when the blight first shows. Repeat in 10 days.

6. How do I cultivate asparagus planted last year?

If asparagus beds are well mulched at planting time and additional mulch applied heavily every spring, little or no cultivation is required. Remove weeds. In early spring, apply a balanced fertilizer such as 12-12-12 along the base of the plants.

7. Where is the best place to plant asparagus?

Place where it receives sun during most of the day.

8. How late are pole beans planted?

Plant pole beans after danger of frost has passed in the spring until mid June. They are not a satisfactory plant for late in the fall.

9. Is it okay to dust sulfur on bush beans?

Yes. Use sulfur if mildew is a problem.

10. There are tiny holes in the leaves of our bush beans. What do we do?

Check the underside of the leaves for insects. Spray with Diazinon under and on top of the leaves. Repeat as needed every five to seven days but avoid using spray when harvesting the beans themselves.

11. How do I get rid of cutworms in beans?

Prepare the ground in the fall and treat with an insecticide as seedlings begin to emerge. If a plant has been cut off, dig around the base of the plant, handpick the insect and destroy.

12. Is it okay to plant beets and carrots in April?

These are cool crops and are planted as soon as ground can be worked.

13. When we put our broccoli outside, it wilted. What do we do?

Broccoli enjoys cool weather. When starting plants indoors, keep as cool as possible with sufficient light. Harden-off for a week to 10 days before placing outside.

14. What kind of soil is best for growing broccoli and Brussels sprouts?

Use soil with plenty of organic matter, superphosphate and a light application of a balanced fertilizer.

15. The leaves on our broccoli and cauliflower are turning yellow. What do we do?

This is caused by late planting or by lack of sufficient nitrogen in the soil. If the latter, apply a light application of nitrate of soda, using one tablespoon per gallon of water, with a light watering around each plant. Hot weather can cause yellowing.

16. Something is eating the leaves of our broccoli. What do we do?

Examine the plants and use an insecticide underneath and on top of the leaves. Repeat as needed.

17. Why does our broccoli not come to a head?

Broccoli is a cool crop. Plant early in the spring or again in mid August as a fall crop. If planted during the warm season, it will not come to a head.

18. Can cabbage seeds be started in March?

Yes. Put outside in most areas by early March where the ground is not frozen.

19. Cabbage planted outside in May failed to form heads until late in the fall. Why?

Cabbage is a cool crop and needs to be planted outdoors in March or set seedlings outside in mid August for harvesting during the cool days of late fall.

20. Cabbage plants are wilting under the lights. What do we do?

Plants are too close to the lights and also the temperature may be too high. Move plants farther away from the light and reduce temperature.

21. What are the best intervals for spraying cabbage?

Dust young cabbage plants with insecticide around the tops of the plants. Repeat after heavy rain. Dusting lasts longer and is more effective than spraying.

22. Can carrots be stored in the ground over winter?

Yes. Mulch with leaves or with straw to prevent freezing.

23. What is a good soil mix for carrots?

Use any well prepared garden soil with plenty of organic matter. If growing in containers, use commercial soil media.

24. What is the best way to grow cauliflower?

Sow seeds indoors six to eight weeks before planting outdoors or sow directly in the garden as soon as it is worked but the weather is still cold. Also plant them again in mid August for a fall crop.

25. What are the newer varieties of Swiss chard that are better types to grow?

Lucullus is green and matures in about 50 days. Rhubarb chard is red and matures in 60 days. Fordhook Giant matures in about 60 days.

26. When is Swiss chard planted?

Plant Swiss chard in most areas in late March or early april.

27. I am having poor results with growing corn. What is the best method?

Corn needs sun for six to eight hours. Make sure the ground is well drained with plenty of organic matter and well enriched. When corn is three to four inches high, use a side dressing of a balanced fertilizer. Repeat 10 days later. Select early maturing varieties.

28. How long after I plant corn do I expect a crop?

It depends on the variety you plant. Some corn matures in 55 to 60 days after planting. Later varieties take anywhere from 65 to 90 days.

29. The blossoms are dropping on our cucumbers and cantaloupes. What do we do?

Early blossoms often drop because only the female flowering is forming. If plants are producing both male and female flowers, dropping is caused by a lack of insects. Use hand pollination by removing the male flower and rubbing the powder on the female flower.

30. How much watering do cucumbers need?

Cucumbers need to be kept moderately moist at all times. Watering an equivalent of one inch of rain per week is sufficient.

31. My cucumber vines are getting limp on the ends. What do we do?

Check to see if plants are getting plenty of moisture. Spray to keep insects under control.

32. How do I tell if eggplants are mature?

As soon as the fruits reach sufficient size and a deep purple color, they are ready to use. Harvest them when they are glossy. As soon as the color turns dull, they are over mature and the seeds have become hard.

33. What do holes in the eggplant leaves mean?

This is usually caused by a common insect pest, the flea beetle, and is controlled by a garden spray, such as Diazinon or Malathion.

34. How do we prevent our leeks from going to seed?

Leeks are biennials. Use before the plants start producing seeds the second year. Use at an early stage to prevent seeding. Once the plants begin to produce seeds, they are of no value for use in the kitchen. Save the seeds for replanting.

35. How long after spraying is it safe to eat lettuce?

This depends on the spray. Follow the directions on the label and do not use until the time stated on the label. Avoid using insecticides which are not recommended for vegetable growing.

36. Does Bibb lettuce grow back after cutting?

This depends on the weather. Lettuce is a cool crop. Plant early in the spring. Once the weather warms up, plants will not be produced. Successive sowings at regular intervals insures a continuous crop.

37. Is lettuce sown in March when the ground is muddy?

Lettuce is planted in March as soon as the ground is soft enough to prepare.

38. Is it too late in September to plant leaf lettuce?

In many areas leaf lettuce planted in early September will grow before the weather becomes very cold.

39. What kind of lettuce is planted and when?

There are numerous varieties of leaf lettuce, some which are more heat resistant than head lettuce. Plant in early spring to take advantage of the cool weather. Leaf lettuce often grows better than head lettuce when the temperatures rise.

40. When do I transplant melons that have been grown from seeds indoors?

Transplant anytime after danger of heavy frost is over, especially when the ground has warmed up.

41. What is the best to use – onion seeds, onion sets or onion plants?

All of these are ideal. Onions are a cool crop and seeds are planted quite early. Onion sets produce onions earlier than those planted from seeds. Small onion plants are grown from seeds and give an earlier start in the garden. Use all of these for early onions or allow to grow and store as onion bulbs.

42. When are our onions harvested and how are they stored for winter use?

As soon as the tops begin to fall over, it is time to harvest. After two or three days, pull the onions up and spread on the ground to dry in the sun. When the tops are removed leave an inch-long stub and place the onions in crates or bags. Store in a cool dry area for use later during the winter months.

43. Onions have no growth on the bottom. What do we do?

Avoid by working in plenty of organic matter and superphosphate at the rate of four to five pounds per 100 square feet. Avoid the use of high nitrogen fertilizer which stimulates top growth.

44. How do I store onion plants and horseradish crowns before planting.

Store in a cool dry area until the ground is worked and plant outside.

45. How do I care for parsley as a houseplant?

Heavily water and pot in the garden. Leave for several days in a cool spot until it becomes re-established in the pots. Leave several potted plants in a protected area outdoors until ready to bring indoors. Bringing a plant inside and placing it in a cool area where it gets plenty of light will keep it in good condition for some time. Bring a second pot in later to keep a constant supply.

46. When is the best time to plant English peas?

Plant in many areas starting in February or early March. Prepare the ground in the fall ahead of time. The peas withstand very cold conditions and if planted early, produce plenty peas by mid to late April.

47. Our garden peas are turning yellow. What do we do?

This is usually caused by temperatures becoming too high. Little can be done to prevent this.

48. Are fall peas planted in Zone 6?

Planting anytime from late July to early August is ideal.

49. Are peanuts taken out of the shell before planting?

Plant whole peanuts in their hulls if the shells are thin but make sure they have not been roasted beforehand.

50. When do I transplant peppers that have been grown from seeds indoors?

Set outside two to three weeks after the last heavy frost.

51. What do we do about blossom-end rot on our pepper plants?

Use a fungicide, such as Captan or Maneb. Repeat in 10 days. Select plants which are disease resistant.

52. How do I eliminate bugs eating the pepper plant?

Use insecticide under and on top of the leaves.

53. Pepper plants are not doing well. How is this changed?

See that plants are given adequate moisture and a light feeding of a liquid fertilizer. Mulch the plants during hot weather.

54. When do we plant potatoes?

Plant in March for an early crop or in early July for a later crop.

55. What do we do about foot-long sprouts on potatoes before planting?

This has occurred because tubers were stored in too warm a place. Carefully plant sprouts by removing them from the potato tubers with a portion of the tubers attached. If eyes are still in the tubers that have not started to develop, cut out and plant.

56. We have sweet potatoes growing in water. Are they transplanted into soil?

Mix a bit of soil in the water 24 hours ahead of transplanting. Then carefully remove the plants and put them in well prepared soil. Protect from the sun for the first day or two and keep moderately moist until well established.

57. We are not getting flowers on our potatoes. Why?

Flowering is not needed for production. If plants are growing well do not be concerned about no flowers.

58. Radishes have not formed in late April. Why?

This depends on the temperature and the ground in which they are planted. Avoid the use of high nitrogen fertilizers and incorporate superphosphate in the ground prior to planting.

59. How do you control sowbugs in radishes?

Clean ground thoroughly. Dust or spray with Rotenone or Diazinon.

60. We have bushy tops on our radishes but no vegetables. What do we do to avoid this?

Radishes are a cool crop and need a rich moist soil. Avoid late planting.

61. When is spinach planted both as a spring and fall crop?

Spinach is planted as soon as the ground can be worked. This is a cool crop and if planted in early March gives several cuttings. If planted in late April, little or no production will result. Spinach is planted again in early August for a fall crop.

62. How do I make our squash ripen after picking it?

Do not harvest squash until fully matured. Store in a cool dry area and most varieties will turn a rich golden color when ready to use. Maturity depends a great deal on the variety grown.

63. How do you avoid squash plant borers?

Practice crop rotation and use a spray program starting early in the season when plants first begin to develop.

64. There are leaf spots in our squash. What does this mean and what do we do?

This is an indication of squash bug. Start a spraying program before insects become very active. Repeat at seven-day intervals for best results.

65. When do I harvest sunflower seeds?

Harvest sunflower seeds as soon as they are fully matured. Seeds will be loose in the flower heads, and plants will be full size and lacking in color.

66. How late in the season are turnips planted?

Plant turnips up to mid August.

67. How do you germinate tomato seeds?

Tomatoes are started by sowing seeds in a seed mix at a temperature of 75 to 80 degrees. Keep the medium moderately moist. Light is not important until the seeds begin to emerge. At that time move into an area where they get 10 to 12 hours of direct light daily.

68. When is the best month to plant tomatoes?

Start indoors six to eight weeks before planting outdoors. Avoid planting too early. Make sure ground is approximately 60 degrees and all danger of frost is over for at least two weeks.

69. Are tomato plants staked and how are they fertilized?

Stake tomatoes to keep them off the ground. Use stakes when plants are first set outside. As plants develop tie them to the stakes with a soft material, such as strips of nylon stocking or soft cloth. Avoid binding the stems. Water plants with a feeding of a weak liquid fertilizer and then give regular feedings of liquid fertilizer at two-week intervals. Tomatoes are heavy feeders.

70. How deep do I plant tomato plants?

Tomatoes root readily along the stem; however, avoid planting too deeply. Pot plants grown in containers can be placed in the ground one or two inches deeper. Avoid over-watering until roots are well established.

71. What causes tomato plants to turn yellow?

This indicates a lack of nutrients. Apply a balanced fertilizer. A light application of nitrate of soda, at the rate of one tablespoon per gallon of water, applied lightly around the ground when it is moderately moist turns them green very quickly.

72. How much and how often are tomato plants watered?

Keep well mulched to control moisture conditions. Keep ground moderately moist at all times with weekly watering the equivalent of one inch of rain. Avoid over-watering and keep the water off the plant.

73. Are grass clippings suitable as mulch around tomato plants?

No. Grass clippings pull nitrogen away from the plants and shed water away from the plant. Use the clippings in the compost pile.

74. What causes flower drop on tomato plants? How is this avoided?

Flower drop occurs if plants are set outside too early or if the temperature is to high. See that the ground is warmed up before planting. During summer months keep plants well mulched to control soil temperatures.

75. How do we eliminate tomato hornworms?

Inspect plants daily. Pick off tomato hornworms and destroy or spray with insecticide underneath and on top of the leaves.

76. How do I sucker tomato plants?

Suckering is removing the shoots which develop at the nodes. Sucker the plants when they are staked. Be careful not to remove the flower stalks. Let stems develop two to three inches to see whether buds are forming or not. If there are no buds, these shoots are coming from the stem of the plant where leaves are emerging. Carefully pinch out before they get too long.

77. What do I do about the blossom-end rot on the tomatoes?

Avoid over-watering. Select plants which are disease resistant. Spray with fungicide.

78. Half ripe tomatoes are falling off the vine. What do we do?

See that plants are well nourished with regular feedings of liquid fertilizer and heavily mulched during the hot weather. Give adequate moisture so that the ground is not allowed to dry out between waterings.

79. When tomatoes get overgrown how are they restaked?

Stake at the beginning and prune to avoid overgrown plants in the first place.

80. How do we water tomatoes grown in the cold frame?

Use the same methods of watering as in the garden; however, make sure that drainage is adequate and plants are not over-watered. Mulching is beneficial to control soil moisture.

81. What kind of collar is made for tomato plants?

Collars are used where cutworms are a problem. Make one out of a two-inch strip of cardboard. Place the circle around the plant leaving about an inch below the soil surface and the rest above. This will keep the worms from cutting the plants off.

82. Tomatoes are mulched with sawdust and are turning yellow. Why?

Sawdust draws the nitrogen away from the plants. Avoid by using extra nitrogen when the mulch is first applied and in feeding, add some extra nitrogen in the balanced fertilizer.

83. Are tomatoes grown indoors?

Grow indoors in temperatures of around 65 to 70 degrees. Allow sufficient light, either artificial or sunlight. Pollinization is needed by lightly tapping the stem to allow the pollen to drop and fertilize the plant.

84. Are tomato plants watered daily?

If plants are grown in containers, water daily to keep them at a proper moisture level. Mulching also controls the moisture level.

85. How do we grow tomato plants under artificial lights.

Sow seeds in the normal manner. As soon as they begin to emerge place the seedlings within six to eight inches of the light, gradually moving them away from the light as plants develop. Give them 10 to 12 hours of light per day until ready to transplant outdoors.

86. Can tomatoes be planted in the same place this year as last year?

Yes. It is better to rotate them if possible; otherwise, add extra organic matter and superphosphate prior to planting.

87. We have leaf roll on our tomato plants. How do we eliminate this?

Select disease resistant varieties. Give adequate moisture and fertilizer to keep them in healthy condition. Keep insects under control with regular sprayings.

88. Our tomatoes have dry rot. How is this avoided?

Select plants which are disease resistant. When planting make sure the ground is well prepared and plants are well fertilized. Avoid wetting the foliage when watering. Allow the water to run around the base of the plant. Avoid over-watering but water at regular intervals.

89. What are the best tomato varieties to grow?

Check with local sources as to best varieties for individual areas. Select hybrid varieties that are resistant to fusarium and verticillium wilt.

90. I have planted Better Boy and Supreme tomato plants. The Better Boy is growing faster than Supreme. How do I care for them?

Better Boy is a much sturdier plant. Supreme produces smaller fruit but of an excellent quality. Its tomatoes are four or five ounces and grows particularly well in the midwest.

91. I have two tomato plants and only one has fruit. Why?

This may be caused by a lack of insects for pollination.

92. How do we best grow patio tomatoes in pots?

Select a pot of eight to 12 inches in diameter with good drainage. Use a soilless medium high in organic matter with a slow release fertilizer, such as MagAmp or Osmocote. Place the plants in the medium and water in with a light liquid fertilizer. Grow the plants in an area where they get enough sunlight. Water on a regular basis and feed every 10 to 12 days with a balanced liquid fertilizer.

93. Can a patio tomato plant in a tub be transplanted into the ground?

Yes.

94. Can tomato plants be grown in containers?

Yes. The patio is excellent in limited areas; however, most other varieties can be grown in containers if they are given ample room for root development, a well enriched growing medium, adequate watering and regular feedings. Select varieties which are disease resistant.

95. The zucchini squash is turning brown. What do we do?

Browning is caused by fungus growth. Spray the plants with Captan at seven to 10-day intervals when the fruit first begins to form.

96. A zucchini plant nearby another plant is developing fruit while the other one is flowering but not developing fruit. What is the reason?

The plants need male and female flowers for cross pollinization before developing fruit. Female flowers usually develop a week to two weeks before male flowers.

Chapter Eleven Fruit Gardening

General Information

Develop a fruit garden in any area where space is available. Many of the dwarf fruit trees, such as apple and pear trees, are decorative and produce fruit. Space can be made available for some of the dwarf fruit such as strawberries and raspberries. They require an area that has good aeration and drainage. Adapt soils to fruit growing by adding organic matter or where space permits, work in green manure crops, such as buckwheat, rye grass and soybeans. Plant the latter in early spring as soon as the ground can be worked and dug in before they form seeds. Where land is poor, work in several cover crops of green manure and then plant in the late fall or early spring. Where space is limited, prepare the ground by hand. Plant fruit where they get as much sunlight as possible. For planting fruit trees dig the holes twice the size needed, remove the soil and add good top soil with equal amounts of compost or well rotted manure.

If space is limited, select dwarf fruit trees. Plant eight to 10 feet apart. Three to four trees take the space of one stardard tree. The dwarf fruit trees start bearing fruit in the second year reaching their peak in three to four years. Standard trees do not reach their peak for seven or eight years. Most dwarf fruit trees produce several bushels of fruit, so three or four small trees will bear the same quantities as a standard tree. Use two different varieties of trees for cross pollinization. Although some are self-pollinating, cross pollinization is better. Pollination usually occurs by bees which carry the pollen from one tree to another and at times by the wind. Plant fruit trees in late fall. In selecting apples it is advisable to choose from early to late bearing varieties to have a harvest over a longer period of time.

Dwarf fruit trees are grafted. In planting do not cover the graft with soil or the tree above the graft will start to root and the trees will become more vigorous and larger than desired. Plant the graft so that it is two to three inches above the finished soil line. Prune any suckers or shoots which come below the graft. The dwarf fruits are grafted on to other stalks to make very small root systems. This controls the height of the plant above ground. They are available in different sizes. They are easily pruned by hand and easy to spray to control insects and diseases.

Heavily mulch fruit trees planted in the fall with six to eight inches of leaves or other organic materials to prevent the ground from heavily freezing. These trees' roots continue to grow as long as the soil is not frozen. They may also be planted in early spring before growth begins. Container grown stock is readily available. Space out the roots after removing from the container so that they will readily grow into the surrounding soil.

Prune fruit trees during winter. Remove all weak growth. Avoid branches which fork at the same space. If allowed to develop fully, they split with heavy fruit. Head back shoots to encourage side spurs which produce flowers and increase the fruit production. Also prune in mid summer after fruit has set. Severely prune old trees to force more growth into fruit spurs. However, this usually is followed by a lot of soft growth that will need thinning. The old trees will produce again within a couple of years.

When planting young trees, carefully remove damaged roots and some top growth to make up for the loss of root growth. Do not use a commercial fertilizer at the time of planting so as to allow the roots to become well established in a well prepared soil. Apply light feedings of a balanced fertilizer in early spring as growth is beginning.

Dwarf fruit trees start bearing the second year, reaching their peak at three to four years. Regular spraying is needed to control insects and disease. Contact your local university extension service and ask for the latest bulletin on the spraying of fruit trees.

Combined sprays of insecticide and fungicide are available commercially for fruit trees to control insects and diseases. Spray on top and bottom of leaves when they emerge. Spray trunks of fruit trees at regular intervals throughout the summer with an insecticide, such as Diazinon or Malathion, to the point of run-off to avoid more insects from infecting the trees. Spray in May, June and again in July.

Dwarf fruit trees are shallow-rooted and need adequate watering during periods of drought. Once fruit develops, some begin to drop in early June. This is nature's way of pruning excess growth; however, some hand pruning may be required, thinning the fruit three to six inches apart for good quality. If fruit is carefully removed this way, trees will bear heavily every year.

If fruit trees do not bloom the second or third year, often a late spring has injured the buds. Fruit trees planted in low areas, such as frost pockets, are more subject to damage than those planted in an open area. Most fruit stock is readily rooted from cuttings; however, cuttings taken from a dwarf plant do not remain dwarf because they are on their own roots. To retain the dwarf quality, you must graft or bud graft onto a dwarf fruit stock tree to obtain this characteristic. Material grown on its own roots develops a much heavier root system, thus becoming standard height trees. Budding usually occurs in February or in late August.

QUESTIONS

1. How do I prevent birds eating from our dwarf apple tree?

Cover the tree with a fine netting to keep birds from eating the fruit.

2. We wish to grow dwarf apple trees. What kind are recommended and how many of each?

If space is available, consider planting two or three varieties to vary the production. Many varieties are available, such as Cortland, Early McIntosh, Golden Delicious, Gravenstein, Jonathan, McIntosh and Northern Spy. It is a matter of personal preference as to what you select.

3. Some apples are dropping from our trees before they reach maturity. What causes this?

Many apple trees set more fruit than the tree is able to bear. Nature eliminates the excess fruit by causing it to fall usually during June. The health of the trees and climatic conditions are big factors in how much fruit remains on the trees.

4. We have leaf curl on our apple tree. What do we do?

Leaf curl is usually caused by aphids sucking on the leaves. Use spray under and on top of the leaves.

5. Leaves on our apple tree are being eaten. How is this eliminated?

Follow normal spraying procedures to prevent insects from doing further damage. Observe tree regularly and use insecticide as soon as insects first appear.

6. How do I graft an apple tree?

Make grafts during February. Grafting stock is selected from varieties which you wish to grow. They usually are about pencil size to 18 to 24 inches long. Graft onto wild stock or apple trees which have not been bearing well. Cut plant off at the desired height, split the bark open, cut the cion growth so that the cambium layer of a stalk fits with the plant with which it is being grafted and then cover with grafting wax which is available commercially. Make sure the cambium layers are in precise contact and the areas thoroughly covered with grafting wax to prevent moisture from entering. The stalk takes readily the first year.

7. How do you control apple tree rust?

Apple tree rust is caused by junipers nearby which carry the rust. Conduct a spraying program to keep under control.

8. Is it too late to trim apple trees in March?

Trim in March if the weather is still relatively cold and before the trees start to flower.

9. My Delicious apple tree has not bloomed in two years. What is wrong?

Lack of flowering is caused by severe cold which freezes the flower buds or if the trees are not maintained in a vigorous condition. If trees are well cared for and properly fed, fruiting results. Extra pruning may be needed to control the growth.

10. My Jonathan apple tree is not producing blooms or fruit anymore. How do I bring it back into production?

Heavily prune older trees and start a feeding program to bring back into bearing condition. It depends on the vigor and health of the tree as to whether this is worthwhile.

11. Are Jonathan apples self-pollinating?

No.

12. How do you grow cider apples?

Cider apples are no different than other apples in growing. Cider is made from any apple.

13. Do I cut off the dead branches of our apple tree?

Remove all dead material and excess growth at regular intervals.

14. What do we use for spraying our apple trees for worms?

Bacillus thuringiensis is effective.

15. Do we grow a dwarf apricot by rooting a branch?

The branch will root but the tree will no longer be a dwarf since the plant is a standard variety grafted on a dwarf stalk.

16. What is the best time to transplant seedlings from apricot trees?

Transplant seedlings anytime the ground is worked. Mulch heavily and give them plenty of water during periods of drought.

17. Do we need two apricot trees in order to have pollination?

No. Apricots are self-pollinators.

18. How do we salvage an apricot tree that was struck by lightning?

It depends on the amount of damage. If only light damage, remove damaged bark and use tree paint.

19. There are black spots on our apricots. What do we do?

Black spots indicate bacterial blight. Follow spray schedules to avoid this next year.

20. We have an avocado tree that is not doing well. What do we do?

Grow avocados outdoors during the summer but carry over indoors where there is no danger of frost or cold. Use a well drained soil with plenty of organic matter and feed occasionally.

21. We have blackberry bushes that are one-year old. When will they bear fruit?

Blackberry bushes start bearing in their second year, reaching their peak of production about the third year.

22. How do I prune a blackberry patch?

Prune established plantings each spring after harvest and sometimes at intervals through the summer and through early fall. Cut back fruiting canes from all varieties except Himalaya and Evergreen immediately after harvest. Most varieties have perennial canes on perennial roots, and the canes die back naturally after fruiting.

23. Are blueberries grown satisfactorily in Zone 6?

Yes. However in most cases, soil is too alkaline and needs to be improved with the addition of organic matter and acidified with sulfur or ammonium nitrate. Mulching the plants is beneficial and supplying iron chelate in early spring keeps them from becoming chlorotic.

24. My cherry tree does not produce normal size cherries. How is this improved?

If plant has never produced normal size fruit, destroy the plant and start with a new one. However, a regular feeding and watering program gives normal fruiting habits.

25. How do you keep birds from cherry trees?

Cover the trees with netting once fruit begins to ripen.

26. What is the best fertilizer for cherry and plum trees?

A light application of a balanced fertilizer, such as 5-10-5 or 6-12-12, worked in around the surface in early spring is ideal.

27. My fig tree is growing new shoots. Are these cut back and when?

Prune a fig tree very little except to remove dead wood to open the top for sun and air and to stimulate new growth. Fruit is borne on the leaf axils; therefore, little pruning is needed other than to control the shape and size of the plant.

28. Why doesn't fruit fully develop on a fig tree?

A fruit tree sometimes refuses to bear fruit if it is given too much fertilizer. Allow the tree to grow in its own way but keep in good condition. Heavy mulching around the tree is often all that is needed. Avoid using high nitrogen fertilizers.

29. How do we encourage our fig trees to produce fruit?

Mulch the plants heavily and give good protection during the winter months when growing in exposed areas. Form a frame and fill with leaves over the plants during heavy frost and leave until spring. Then use the leaves as a mulch to insure good fruiting habits.

30. Are small fruit trees covered to protect them from frost and how is this done?

Trees are covered by placing plastic around the trees and leaving the tops open for good air circulation. In some cases, place small heaters at the bottom allowing the heat to be carried up through the trees. Covering with blankets when frost is light is often enough to keep them from being damaged.

31. Are fruit trees sprayed with Benlate?

Yes. Benlate controls both fungus and bacterial diseases. Also alternate with another type of fungicide.

32. What is a good spraying schedule for fruit trees?

Consult the local university extension service for the latest bulletin on fruit tree sprays and follow their program.

33. Is it possible to have a general home spray for fruit trees?

Yes. Use fungicide to control mildew when first noticed or use a preventative spray before leaves begin to emerge. When they partially emerge repeat spray after a heavy rain. Watch out for insects and use insecticide when needed.

34. Do I cultivate around fruit trees?

Light cultivation is all right. In addition, mulch to avoid weeds, to control soil moisture and to keep ground cooler during the active growing season.

35. Can pigeon manure be used as a fertilizer for fruit trees?

If pigeon manure is untouched by the elements, use lightly around fruit trees as a source of phosphorus.

36. What are the planting requirements for growing gooseberries?

Gooseberries require an area that is well enriched with organic matter and has plenty of potash added. Avoid high nitrogen fertilizer. Plants do best where they get sufficient sunlight and good air circulation.

37. What are the best varieties of grapes to plant in Zone 6?

A number of grapes are available, such as Concord, Delaware, Fredonia and Niagara.

38. Our grapevines have a powdery substance on them. What do we do?

This is usually mildew. Control by careful pruning each spring before growth begins and by using fungicide at regular intervals according to spray charts.

39. Can I move a three-year-old grapevine and how?

Dig up the plant with as many roots attached as possible in late fall or early spring before growth begins. Move to a desired area which has been well enriched with plenty of organic matter. Mulch the plant heavily and keep well watered during the first season.

40. How and when are grapevines pruned?

Prune in February to control the growth of the plants and to encourage good fruiting. Prune to allow a main stem to come up with lateral shoots going out in each direction. Cut back lateral shoots to within 18 to 24 inches of the main stem. After the vines are pruned, tie to the trellis wires when the weather is warm. When they are frozen, the canes are brittle and more easily damaged. Tie to wires before growth starts to avoid injury to the new shoots.

41. How is a French hybrid grapevine pruned?

See Question 40 as the same pruning methods are followed.

42. Our Concord grapes did not turn blue. Why?

Concord grapes require approximately 170 days of growing. If temperatures were too low, the grapes may have not matured properly.

43. Why do grape leaves turn brown?

This is caused by mildew or bacteria. Follow special spraying procedures as outlined in fruit charts. See Question 32.

44. Our grapevines are dropping their leaves and have black spots. What do we do?

This is a bacterial disease. Spray starting early in the season as leaves start to grow and continue as long as growth is active.

45. What do I do to prevent the leaves from falling off our nectarine tree?

This is caused by disease. Follow the proper spraying procedures.

46. Can a peach tree be grown from seed?

Yes. However, the new tree may be very inferior to the tree from which the seed was taken.

47. Can I plant peach pits refrigerated since last summer?

Plant early in the spring.

48. How far apart should we plant dwarf peach trees?

Plant eight to 10 feet apart.

49. Why didn't our peach tree bloom or bear fruit?

Peaches bloom extremely early and buds are often killed by frost.

50. When is the best time to transplant a peach tree?

Transplant in late fall after the leaves fall or early spring before growth begins.

51. What do I use on peach tree borers?

Peach tree borers are larva moth with clear wings. Eggs are laid in the crotch of the tree and in trash around the base of the trunk. The larvae hatch in June or September. Clean up all debris around the tree and spray with insecticides.

52. My peach tree is dropping fruit before fully developed. How is this prevented?

Nature prunes excess fruit off when a tree cannot bear effectively. Mulch well, water during periods of drought, feed regularly and remove excess fruit to increase the size of the fruit.

53. When is the best time to prune peach trees?

Prune in late February or early March before growth begins.

54. Can a peach tree be transplanted in May from a pot to the ground?

Yes. Mulch and water well.

55. What do I do about sap flowing from the trunk and fruit of a peach tree?

This is caused by bacterial disease. See that the ground around the tree is cleaned up thoroughly in the fall. Follow the regular program as outlined by the county extension bulletins for control of this condition. When the trunk begins to have sap emerge, cut back all infected parts to healthy wood and treat with tree paint.

56. My peach tree is dropping leaves. What causes that and the leaves to fold?

Dropping of leaves is caused by fungus or bacterial leaf spot and folding of leaves by insect damage. Follow regular spraying routines for both fungus and insect control.

57. What is done about fire blight on a pear tree?

Prevent by using the proper sprays as outlined on tree charts, apply them as dormant sprays in early spring and then at regular intervals throughout the season.

58. What are recommended varieties for pear trees for growing?

Varieties, such as Flemish Beauty, Kieffer and Seckel are ideal.

59. My dwarf pear tree leaves are wilting. How do I prevent this?

Wilting is caused by a fungus disease called anthracnose. Spray the plants with fungicide when first noticed. Remove any leaves which fall to the ground and destroy them.

60. How do I get a Japanese persimmon to ripen?

Japanese persimmon will not ripen outside of the southern area. However, once frosted this will change the sugar content and it can be used at that stage.

61. How do you cross pollinate fruit trees, specifically plums?

Plant two trees for the bees to carry the pollen from one tree to another. Remove flowering branches from one tree and tie to the other. Wind and bees will pollinate them in this way.

62. Is a Stanley plum tree self-pollinating?

Yes.

63. Are plums self-pollinating?

A number of them are. However, it is better to plant two varieties for cross pollination.

64. What is the best time to harvest quince for jelly?

Harvest quince after the first heavy frost and use immediately for jelly.

65. How do I best grow raspberries?

Select an area that is well drained and incorporate plenty of organic matter and superphosphate, at the rate of four to five pounds per 100 square feet, into the soil. Select healthy plants as soon as available from a reliable nursery in early spring and plant at the same depth as they were in the nursery. Space them approximately two feet apart in rows that are three to four feet apart. Mulch the plants heavily and keep well watered during the first season. During the second year prune raspberries back in early spring to increase side breaks which produce flower spurs. Prune canes off once they have borne fruit. Each spring apply a balanced fertilizer to the base of the plants and reapply two to three inches of mulch to control weeds.

66. Leaves are turning yellow on our red raspberry plants. How is this prevented?

Use a balanced fertilizer in early spring and fungicide when growth begins. Repeat after a heavy rain.

67. Our raspberry buds are dying. How is this prevented?

Spray with fungicide when growth starts. Repeat at regular intervals after heavy rains and apply again just as buds are beginning to develop.

68. Are red raspberries pruned in September?

Head back new canes to prevent winter damage. Remove old fruiting canes immediately after flowering and after bearing fruit. Complete removal of fruiting canes during September.

69. How are raspberries cut back?

Use a good pair of pruners. Remove old canes just above ground level. Remove thin weak growth in early spring.

70. Are red raspberries fertilized in September?

No. This stimulates new growth and prevents them from hardening-off for winter.

71. What is the best way and time to plant rhubarb?

Rhubarb likes rich soil. Dig the holes 18 inches deep, applying about six inches of manure. Place on top of this several inches of rich top soil mixed with equal amounts of organic matter. Place the roots into this and fill in around with rich top soil with organic matter and some superphosphate. Water plants well. Plant in early spring or plant again in late August.

72. When and how is rhubarb harvested?

Harvest in the spring as growth begins to reach its full length which is approximately one foot long. Pull stalks away from the base of the plant not leaving any ends.

73. Our rhubarb is throwing off seeds. What does this mean?

This occasionally happens. Remove stalks by breaking them away from the crown to prevent seeds from setting, which weakens the plant.

74. We have ants in our rhubarb plants. How do we eliminate them?

Find the sources where the ants are coming from and use insecticide. Repeat in seven to 10 days if necessary.

75. My rhubarb had insects last season. What do I do to prevent this from happening again this year?

Remove all old stalks in the fall and keep area around plants clean. When growth first begins, spray with fungicide and with an insecticide recommended for vegetable plants.

76. How do we eliminate crown rot on rhubarb?

Remove all old material from rhubarb in the fall. In early spring treat with fungicide as the growth begins. Keep plants well watered and fed.

77. Does a rhubarb stalk become poisonous if the leaf freezes?

No.

78. Should flower stalks be removed from rhubarb?

Yes. Remove stalks because they weaken the plant if allowed to remain.

79. What is the best way to prevent insects from attacking rhubarb?

Remove all old parts and any dock (a plant similar to rhubarb) growing nearby which attracts insects. Use insecticide for vegetables in early spring and again in mid summer.

80. How do I care for strawberry plants during winter?

Mulch between rows and cover with several inches of straw once heavy frost sets in.

81. What do I use to spray strawberry plants that have insects on them?

Apply insecticide when leaves first begin to grow. Repeat again in 10 weeks and again just before flower buds open.

82. There are holes in the leaves of our strawberries. What are they and how do we control them?

Holes are caused by insects or by slugs. Clean up all debris around the beds and spray regularly.

83. Should strawberry plants be fertilized when in bloom?

Strawberries need balanced fertilizer as new growth begins and flower buds first begin to show. It is not necessary to fertilize when in full bloom.

84. Are flower buds picked off strawberries the first year?

If you put strawberries outside in the spring, remove any flower buds until late summer to allow all strength to go into the formation of new plants. If strawberries are planted in late August, do not remove the buds. Plants will bear a normal crop the following spring.

85. How do you care for the first year planting of strawberries?

Use mulch of partially decomposed leaf mold or straw, placing several inches around the plants between rows to prevent weeds from growing. Mulch again after the first heavy fall frost. Keep plants well particularly during periods of drought. Spray occasionally with insecticide.

86. What is the best fertilizer for strawberries?

Use superphosphate at the rate of four to five pounds per 100 square feet prior to planting. Then add a balanced fertilizer, such as a 5-10-5 or 6-12-12, as new growth begins in the spring. Apply again in late June following flowering.

87. When do I uncover our strawberry patch?

Remove straw from over top of plants after all danger of heavy frost is passed. This straw can be used in the rows between plants.

88. Do strawberry plants grow best in sun or shade?

Plant strawberries where they get sun for six to eight hours daily.

89. Our strawberries have hard shelled insects on them that devour the ripe strawberries before we pick them. What do I use to control these insects?

Follow a regular spraying program for insect control from early spring until fruit begins to form.

90. How far apart are strawberry plants planted?

Place approximately 18 inches apart in rows with three feet between rows.

91. Can strawberries be transplanted from a planter box to the garden in early September?

Yes.

92. Are strawberries thinned out and when is the best time?

Thin out strawberries after sufficient plants have been formed to form a compact setting. Removal of extra plants causes full production of plants which are left.

93. Can weed killer be used on strawberries when not bearing fruit and if so, what is recommended?

Do not use weed killer on strawberries. This kills the strawberries plus any weeds. Mulch the plants and hand pull any weeds.

94. Can strawberries be grown in an area formerly planted with junipers?

Yes. Clean up the area and add organic matter and superphosphate to the soil.

95. How do I plant and transplant strawberries?

Remove the surplus plants or runners as soon as they have formed roots by spreading the roots out in shallow holes. Then cover roots with soil at the same depth but do not cover the crown with soil. Water well and mulch with organic matter.

96. What are the best varieties of strawberry plants to grow?

It is a choice between June bearing and "ever bearing." If space permits, use both for a good supply in early spring and again in September.

Chapter Twelve
Herbs

General Information

Many gardeners delight in the culture of herbs, and interest in this field is growing. There are quite a few that are easy to grow. Many of them are annuals, such as basil, borage, chervil, dill and summer savory but most are perennials, such as chives, mints, sage, thyme and tarragon.

The culture of the savory herbs is not difficult. They require a small space at one side of the garden near the house so that the herbs can be freshly gathered and used for cooking. Grow the more rampant growers, such as mint, in a confined area so that the roots do not spread too rapidly. Place metal containers or asbestos boards a foot to 15 inches into the ground with about three inches above ground. Fill with well prepared garden soil and plant the mints and other rampant growers in this. Most of the herbs are grown in any rich well-drained soil with plenty of organic matter. They like an area which is well drained and sunlight during most of the day. Prepare soil to a depth of 12 to 15 inches and add a liberal amount of superphosphate and cottonseed meal.

Start the annual herbs from seed sown six to eight weeks before planting outdoors after the last frost. Plant perennial herbs by selecting cuttings from healthy plants or by dividing the roots into sections and planting outdoors in early spring just as growth is commencing. The more difficult herbs, such as rosemary and lavender, for over-wintering in areas with severe winters are carried over by selecting cuttings in the fall before the cold weather starts, rooting these and then putting them in small pots. Put in cold frames or indoors where the temperature is fairly low, 30 to 40 degrees. In growing herbs, keep the area free of weeds and water as needed. Protect the herbs from insects and diseases.

The harvesting of most kinds of leaf herbs begins before the flowering season while the growing tips are young and tender. Harvest the leaves and tips in the morning after the dew has dried but before the heat starts. Spread them on sheets or trays in a warm, shady area preferably where the air circulation is good. Turn them daily until thoroughly dried, then crumble and store in tightly covered glass jars. Harvest seeds when they begin to change color. Clip the seed heads in the morning shortly after the dew has dried to avoid shattering. Spread them on cloths to dry. When dried, rub the seeds out. The seeds need further air-drying a week or more before storing.

Many of the herbs are suitable for growing in containers. Feed and water more during the summer. In late fall, move pots to a cold frame or a protected spot. After heavy frost, mulch to protect them over the winter. Pot some of the herbs, such as parsley and chives in late fall and allow to remain outdoors in a cool spot until thoroughly rooted. Bring plants indoors, place in a sunny window and keep moderately moist. Pick fresh ends and use as needed.

QUESTIONS

1. When and how are onion chives divided?

Divide onion chives anytime but the best time is in early spring. Dig the plants up, carefully separate them into small sections and plant back into well prepared soil.

2. How do we propagate scented geraniums to keep them from rotting?

Select cuttings from healthy stalks about the middle of September. Take cuttings from healthy growing tips six to eight inches long and remove one-third of the lower leaves. Let cuttings sit for 24 hours on a table or other area out of direct sunlight to seal. Place cuttings in a mixture of one part peat moss to three parts perlite. Keep cuttings moderately moist and in a temperature of 70 to 75 degrees. In four to six weeks cuttings are rooted and ready to pot.

3. On visiting the Missouri Botanical Garden I noticed many unusual herbs growing in the Mediterranean House. Are any of these grown outdoors?

Yes. Many of the herbs are grown outdoors as annuals and as perennials. Lavender, rosemary, the bay tree, clary sage and the corsican mint are a few of the herbs from the Mediterranean area found in the Mediterranean House and are grown outdoors during the summer.

4. What is a good herb for growing in the shade?

A number of herbs grow in semi-shaded areas. Sweet woodruff is a very attractive herb used as a ground cover in shaded areas. Burnet, curly spearmint, lemon balm, chives, saffron crocus and lemon thyme withstand some shade.

5. What is the best soil mixture for growing herbs in pots?

Soil consists of three parts loam to one part compost or well rotted manure. Soil should be light and well drained.

6. What is the best material for applying a mulch to protect herbs for the winter?

Use any light porous material, such as straw, marsh hay or evergreen boughs. Apply these after heavy frost has occurred.

7. Can herbs be grown under artificial light?

Yes. Keep the plants 12 to 15 inches from the direct source of light for 12 to 14 hours daily.

8. How do you propagate and carry over laurel or bay leaf from one year to another?

Laurel or bay leaf (*Laurus nobilis*) is propagated from stem cuttings. Give plants a good potting soil with equal amounts of organic matter and grow outdoors in full sunlight during the summer. Bring plants indoors when temperatures drop below 40 degrees.

9. What is the best way to carry parsley over for use during the winter months?

Pot parsley plant in early fall and leave in a cool moist area until well established. Bring the plant indoors to a sunny window where the temperature is 60 to 65 degrees. Keep moderately moist and the plant will continue to grow and remain in good condition for some time. Later another pot may be brought in to replace the first one.

10. Parsley seems difficult to grow from seed. How do you do it?

Parsley is very slow to germinate, taking anywhere from a month to six weeks and needs to be started early. Soaking the seed in warm water for 24 hours hastens germination. Keep seed pots in an area of 75 to 80 degrees until germination occurs then move back to a temperature of 65 to 70 degrees.

11. How do I overwinter rosemary?

Dig rosemary in late September, pot in a suitable container, leave outdoors in a cool, shaded area until well established in the pot and then place in a cold frame or cool greenhouse until spring. Keep it moderately moist but avoid over-watering. Store in temperatures of 40 to 45 degrees.

12. My sage is becoming woody very rapidly. How is this avoided?

Sage plants become woody and must be renewed every three or four years. Take cuttings from young growth and root. Cut plants back two or three times during the year and follow with a full watering and feeding of fertilizer to stimulate new growth.

13. My sweet woodruff is dying in some areas. Stems are black and whole patches are dying very quickly. How is this controlled?

This is a bacterial disease and is controlled by removing infected parts and then by spraying the ground with a good fungicide as soon as the disease is first noticed.

14. What is the best way to propagate tarragon?

Start tarragon from cuttings taken in early spring when new growth is four to six inches long. Trim one-third of the lower leaves from the cuttings and place in a rooting media, such as perlite and peat moss, and keep in a warm area until rooted. Propagate large tarragon plants by dividing in early spring as growth starts. Cut the roots up with a growing shoot attached and plant back in a well prepared area.

15. What is the best way to propagate thyme?

Start thyme from seed or by dividing the plants. Once the plants spread, they send down roots into the surrounding soil. Cut sections with a sharp knife, remove part of the plant with some soil attached and plant immediately into a prepared area. Water well.

Chapter Thirteen
Weeds and Their Control

General Information

A weed is considered any plant growing where it is not wanted and often not planted. Some of these plants grow under very cool conditions and then go semi-dormant during the hot weather while others continue to grow well throughout the growing season. Control by hand, by hoeing or tilling the ground or by the use of pre-emerge herbicides applied before the weed seeds begin to germinate. As new products come on the market, consult with your local botanical garden or university extension center for the best recommendations for herbicides. Control weeds around flowers, shrubs and trees with mulching, two or three inches of organic matter which is partially decomposed. Apply this once an area is thoroughly cleaned up and reapply each year. If a pre-emerge is mixed with the mulch, it controls weeds up to two years; however, when a herbicide is applied in this way, if the ground is reworked at anytime it breaks the vapor barrier and needs to be reapplied or weed seeds will start to grow.

QUESTIONS

1. How do we eliminate weeds in the garden?

Careful cultivation and use of mulches control weeds.

2. What do we use effectively to kill climbing weeds?

Control climbing weeds, if growing on other plants that are wanted, by using 2,4-D with Silvex. Apply carefully to just the tips of the weeds themselves. This is absorbed down through the weed into the roots without affecting the other plants.

3. How do you eliminate weeds between bricks on a patio?

Several products exist which can be used. Roundup is one and is absorbed down to the roots and kills the weeds. Paraquat is another one; however, it only burns the plants back to the ground level so that you may need to apply it at regular intervals to eliminate them completely.

4. Can chickweed killer be applied in March?

Yes.

5. Does broadleaf weed killer destroy clover?

Yes. You may need several applications to completely eradicate it. Do not use where clover is growing among broadleaf plants. Use only in areas where clover exists by itself or is growing in a lawn.

6. How do I put weed killer on creeping Charlie?

If creeping Charlie is growing in a lawn, use 2,4-D with Silvex. If growing among shrubbery, be careful not to get it on the shrubs or other plants as it kills them also.

7. How do we kill dandelions?

Kill dandelions by removing the roots with an asparagus knife or by hand digging if just a few exist. If wide spread over a lawn, use 2,4-D when plants first start to actively grow. Repeat as needed.

8. How do I exterminate nutgrass?

Nutgrass, which is a sedge, is extremely difficult to eradicate in lawns. Several materials are available especially just for this and kill just the nutgrass; however, apply when nutgrass first begins to grow and when it is about two inches high. Materials do not spread out into the side shoots therefore several applications are needed throughout the growing season to eliminate new shoots as they come up. In some cases during very hot weather you may need a second application five to seven days after the first application. It takes up to two years for complete control.

9. How do you eliminate poison ivy?

Spray poison ivy, if growing in open areas, with 2,4-D; however, if growing among other plants, apply the herbicides to just the tips of the poison ivy and repeat as needed. Avoid other plants.

10. How do I eradicate purselane?

Purselane thrives under warm moist conditions. Thoroughly weed the area, apply mulch or weed out the plants when they first become established. In open areas use herbicides.

11. Is poke weed poisonous?

Yes.

12. How do we eradicate a trumpet vine from a rose bed?

Apply 2,4-D with Silvex to just the new tips of the trumpet vine when it first appears. Repeat as needed, but be very careful not to get it on the roses.

13. How do we destroy weeds around our vinca?

Pull by hand. Once the weeds in the plants are removed, apply a pre-emerge herbicide, such as Casoran, over the area.

14. How do we eliminate wild onions?

Wild onions contain a coat of waxing on the leaves. Dig up by hand or if using a herbicide, take a garden rake to break through the wax tissue and then apply 2,4-D with Silvex. Repeat again as new bulbs come up.

Chapter Fourteen

Garden Pests
Animals - Birds - Termites

QUESTIONS

1. How do I keep squirrels out of the garden?

This is a very difficult problem. Trap the animals where permissible and remove to other areas at a considerable distance. If using poisons be extremely careful to keep away from children and other animals.

2. What do we do about rabbits eating our flowers?

Trap rabbits or place small fences around the beds to prevent the rabbits from getting at the plants. Some repellents are effective but need to be applied at regular intervals because they break down very rapidly.

3. How do you eliminate field mice in the roses?

Keep the rose beds clean so that the mice do not hide in them. Avoid mulching until after the first heavy frost so that field mice have established winter nesting areas elsewhere.

4. Is there a satisfactory repellent for rabbits that are eating tulips?

Mix blood meal and bone meal and place in small bags around the area. Other commercial repellents are available. Consult local seed houses.

5. How do you keep squirrels out of flower pots where plants such as gardenias and other plants are growing?

Regularly use a small amount of blood meal and bone meal on top of the soil.

6. How do I prevent squirrels from cutting off the branches of our linden and other trees?

Squirrels usually remove the tips of branches to get at the seeds. You have to get rid of the squirrels to prevent this.

7. What do I do about starlings in my garden?

Starlings are usually found in the garden where there are insects or worms. Eliminating the insects usually eliminates the starlings. Discourage nesting in nearby areas.

8. Do termites infest old tree stumps. If so, how is this prevented?

Yes. Drill holes into the stump and fill with epsom salts to cause the stump to decay quite rapidly. Also drill holes several inches down the stump and apply 2,4-D with Silvex. Occasional sprayings of insecticide also keep termites under control.

9. How do you eliminate shrews from the garden?

Shrews feed on insects found in the soil. Use an insecticide such as Diazinon on lawn areas in early spring and again in early June.

10. How do we control moles?

Moles feed on insects found in the lawn and garden areas. Eliminate grubs and worms to keep moles out of the area. Also plant castor beans around the area to deter moles but keep the poisonous seeds away from children.

Chapter Fifteen
Insect and Disease Control

General Information

Control insects with insecticides but be aware that many of these are toxic to human beings. Identify the insect and find out what is the best means of control. Carefully read the instructions on the insecticide label to make sure that it applies to the plant on which you wish to use it. Do not use insecticides inside the home but where there is good ventilation. When temperatures are cold, wait until weather is quite mild before moving them out of the living quarters into a garage or other area for spraying. Leave plants there and allow to dry. Store insecticides away from children and where the temperature is a uniform 55 to 65 degrees. Some insecticides which are subjected to freezing and thawing or are affected by high temperatures can be radically changed and may be very dangerous to use.

Buy small quantities of insecticide and do not plan to keep them for any length of time. Keep out of the direct sun. Store in glass or airtight containers. Use dormant sprays when plants are not actively growing and temperatures remain at least 45 degrees for several hours after the spray is applied. Avoid the use of sprays when temperatures remain at least 45 degrees for several hours after the spray is applied. Avoid the use of sprays when temperatures are over 85 degrees. Apply sprays underneath and on top of the leaves early in the morning before the temperature becomes too high. Repeat sprays at three to four-day intervals for complete control.

Control fungus and bacterial diseases with fungicides. Use precautions and store them as you do insecticides.

Herbicides are used to control weeds either as a pre-emerge applied before the weeds start to germinate or as a post-emergent applied on weeds after they have germinated. Use caution because they are toxic to other plants. Use herbicides when there is little or no wind. Just mist the plant. Do not allow run-off which is dangerous to the soil. Use herbicides early in the morning when winds are light.

HELPFUL INSECTS

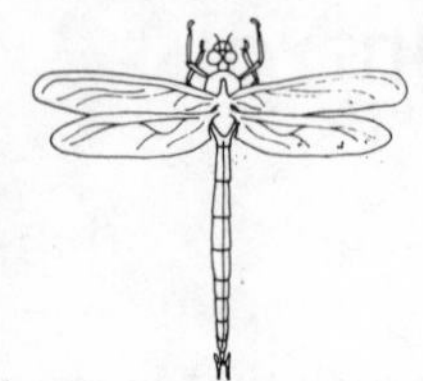
DRAGON FLY

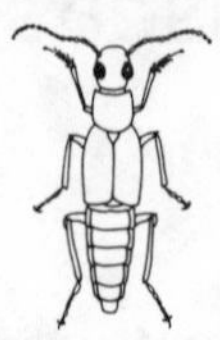
ROSE BEETLE

GROUND BEETLE

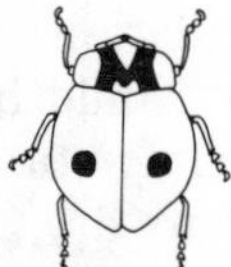
LADY BEETLE

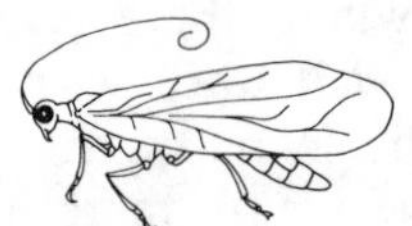
LACEWING

HORNET

HARMFUL INSECTS

STRIPED CUCUMBER BEETLE

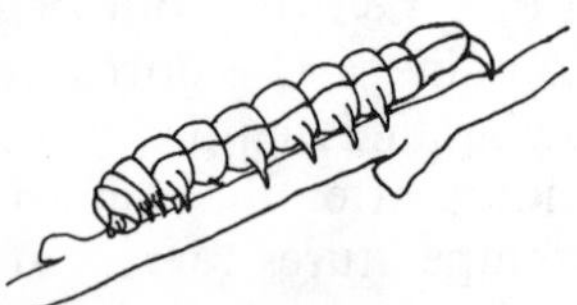
FALL ARMYWORM

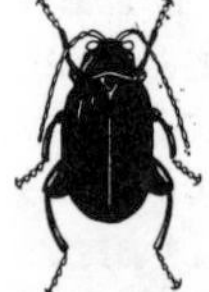
FLEA BEETLE

EARWIG

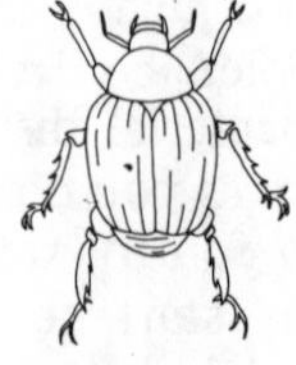
JAPANESE BEETLE

ASPARAGUS BEETLE

See Glossary C for additional illustrations of insects.

Use a special sprayer just for herbicides. Herbicide sprays may cause severe damage to other plants when the sprayer has been used for other purposes.

Familiarize yourself with the eating habits of the insects and examine plants carefully underneath the leaves for first signs to see whether the insects are beneficial or harmful. Do not spray ladybugs and praying mantis which are beneficial. Avoid heavy spraying of plants where bees are active because they pollinate fruits and vegetables. By the time insects appear on the tops of the leaves, infestation is very heavy. Control some insects with a forceful stream of water when the insects first appear. It is not necessary to spray the whole garden but just the infested plant.

If a plant has fungus or a bacterial disease, destroy the plant so that it does not contaminate the rest of the garden. With fungus and bacterial diseases, observe plants daily and apply the proper spray as soon as the disease first appears. If you do not know the disease or how to control it, take a sample of the diseased plant, enclose it in a small container such as a small box and send it to the nearest university extension division or to a botanical garden for proper identification and recommended sprays.

Nearly all universities issue pamphlets on different plants which are available. Obtain the schedule for insect and disease control of fruit trees each year. Other pamphlets worth obtaining are on the control of insects and lawn diseases. Vegetable charts are also available.

In controlling insects and diseases alternate between at least two insecticides for insect control and two different fungicides for fungus diseases. Insects and diseases build up immunities to one particular product.

Systemic insecticides, those which affect the entire plant, are also available but use carefully. Do not use where edible plants are being grown. Apply systemic insecticides to the soil in liquid form or broadcast over the leaves of the plants and follow by a misting. They are absorbed into the plants over a period of 24 to 48 hours and give long range control for certain insects which bother plants. Many of these systemics are extremely poisonous and also may be harmful to birds that consume insects which feed on the plant sprayed by systemics.

Spreader-stickers which are used for greater adherence are also available to mix with some of the insecticides and fungicides. The spreader-sticker gives better coverage. Read the labels and use only where recommended.

Dormant oil is a highly recommended safe spray. Apply in late February or early March when temperatures are over 45 degrees and where there is no danger of freezing and use a summer oil in early June when insects are active. Use a dormant spray when the plant is dormant and spray to the point of run-off all around the plants. Certain restrictions are on the label which should be followed. The dormant oil controls many scale insects which carry over from one year to the next and particularly attack euonymus and oak trees. Sometimes several applications are needed. Dormant oil also controls many of the early spring insects by smothering the eggs and larvae which are on the sides of tree trunks and branches. Dormant oil is not effective in fall when insects have a very hard coat.

QUESTIONS

1. What is the best control for fungus and bacterial diseases?

Acti-dione, Benlate, Captan and sulfur are the best.

2. How do we control corn borers in our vegetable garden?

As soon as tassels begin to show, apply a light application of mineral oil to the tassel.

3. When do bagworms attack plants?

Bagworms appear in early June.

4. How do you eliminate bagworms on junipers and other plants?

As soon as bagworms appear, spray with an insecticide such as Diazinon or Sevin.

5. Our pines are covered with a white-like canker infestation. What is this and how do we control it?

The material on the leaves is scale. Use an oil-base spray in early June as insects become active. Repeat again in seven to 10 days. Apply dormant oil once again in late February.

6. How do I control powdery mildew on tuberous begonias?

Give plants plenty of air circulation and when mildew first appears, spray underneath and on top of the leaves with a fungicide such as Captan.

7. How do you control fungus on trees and other plants?

Use a fungicide underneath and on top of the leaves, repeating at seven to 10-day intervals.

8. What is the best way to control ants in tree stumps?

Use Chlordane or other recommended spray for control of ants.

9. What is the best use for Kelthane?

It controls spider mites on a wide variety of plants.

10. How do you control spider mites on spruce?

Use Kelthane according to directions. Repeat three times every three to four days.

11. What do you do for galls on a hickory tree?

Prune off when first noticed. Feed the roots every three to four years and give plenty of water during periods of drought.

12. How do we eliminate night crawlers?

Use an insecticide such as Diazinon when the soil is moderately moist or apply and follow with a light watering for penetration into the soil.

13. What do I do about leaf miners on hollies?

Leaf miners appear in early May. Spray with Malathion underneath and on top of the leaves. Repeat again in 10 days at least two more times. Also use systemics, such as Meta-Systox-R.

14. Can I use Diazinon for killing grubs?

Yes.

15. How do I eliminate galls on our oak tree?

Galls are difficult to control. Prune to some extent. Root feed every three to four years. Water well during periods of drought. Spraying is not recommended.

16. What do I use on a false aralia to eliminate scale?

Use an oil base spray, such as Malathion, or use Volck. Repeat in 10 to 14 days.

17. How do you treat scale on houseplants, especially gardenias?

Spray the plant underneath and on top of the leaves with Malathion or Volck.

18. When is the correct time to spray for catalpa worms and with what?

Spray catalpa worms when they first appear with an insecticide such as Diazinon.

19. How do you control sod webworms?

Sod webworms become active in early May and again in late August or early September. Use synthetic Pyrethrin or Sevin on the ground in early May. Keep soil moderately moist or follow with a light watering to move it down one-half inch into the soil. Repeat in 10 days. In late August start the same treatment, repeating in 10 days.

20. How do I eliminate slugs in our yard?

Clean up all debris where slugs may hide. Trap slugs in hollowed out potatoes, in containers of stale beer or with slug pellets. Keep children and animals away from pellets. Slug-it (metaldehyde) is also effective in controlling snails and slugs on plants and in soil.

21. What is the best method of getting rid of sowbugs, cutworms, slugs and ants?

Thoroughly clean up any debris in the area and spray the ground with an insecticide such as synthetic Pyrethrin or Malathion.

22. How do I control anthracnose?

Anthracnose is a fungus disease that attacks many plants in early spring when the leaves begin to emerge. Spray with fungicide as soon as this is noticed applying underneath and on top of the leaves. Repeat in four or five days if needed.

23. How do I eradicate fungus on a pine tree?

Use a fungicide such as Captan or Benlate.

24. What causes holes in the leaves of flowers like gladioli and geraniums?

It is probably insects. Examine underneath the leaves and spray if insects are present.

25. Why do houseplants turn brown on the edges of the leaves?

If the tips are brown, it is caused by low humidity. If it is along the edges, it may be a fungus disease.

26. Our houseplants have been invaded by small worm-like bugs. What do we do?

Apply an insecticide, such as synthetic Pyrethrin in place of a regular watering. Use enough to penetrate down to the bottom of the pot. Repeat as needed.

27. How do you eliminate aphids on a damson plum tree?

Use an insecticide, such as Diazinon or Sevin, as soon as aphids appear. Apply thoroughly underneath and on top of the leaves. Repeat as needed.

28. We have round, green flat insects all over a holly tree. How are these controlled?

Use insecticide underneath and on top of the leaves. Repeat as needed.

29. There are mealy bugs on our burro's tail. How do we eliminate them?

Mealy bugs have a soft white coating which protects the insects. Spraying with a forceful stream of water often eliminates them. Also apply insecticide under pressure through a regular sprayer and repeat as needed.

30. How do you cure fungus gnats in houseplants?

Apply Sevin in place of a regular watering to the soil.

31. How do you control mud daubers?

Mud daubers, a member of the wasp family, are easily controlled by using an insecticide directly on nesting areas. Repeat as needed.

32. What is the recommended treatment for cucumber beetles?

Use insecticide underneath and on top of the leaves when beetles are noticed. Repeat every four or five days.

33. How often should fruit trees by sprayed?

Contact the local university extension division for a calendar for spraying fruit trees and follow the procedures outlined.

34. How do I eliminate bugs on our apple tree?

Follow outline for Question 33.

35. How do I control borers on fruit trees and other trees?

Borers drill small holes at the base of the tree. Apply insecticide in early spring and repeat at 10 to 14-day intervals at least three times. Spray the trunks of the trees to the point of run-off.

36. How do we eliminate termites on our cedar trees?

Control with Chlordane.

37. How do we hatch praying mantis eggs?

Keep praying mantis eggs in a very cool area (40 to 45 degrees) until ready for hatching and then place eggs in branches of shrubs or trees when temperatures are between 60 to 70 degrees. These will hatch very readily.

38. I have springtails in my potted plants. What do I do?

Treat soil with synthetic Pyrethrin.

39. What are the little black bugs on my plants and how do I eliminate them?

These are soil gnats found in the organic matter in the soil. Control with a good insecticide such as Diazinon, watering into the soil in place of a regular watering.

40. How do we eradicate molds?

Molds are a type of fungus. Use fungicide when first noticed. Repeat as needed.

41. A white worm is attacking the base of our willow tree. How is this controlled?

Use insecticide, applying it thoroughly along the base of the tree.

42. How do you control Dutch elm disease?

Control by keeping the Dutch elm beetles under control with an insecticide, such as Diazinon, Sevin or Malathion when insects are first noticed. Repeat as needed. Treat trees in early spring just before the leaves are fully matured by injecting insecticide under pressure into base of tree. Contact local tree experts for latest information and treatment.

43. Dogwood and sweet gum tree have a fungus on the leaves. How is this controlled?

Use a fungicide, such as Captan and/or Benlate, when first noticed. Repeat as needed.

44. What do we do to eliminate beetles in pine trees?

Spray the pines with Malathion or Sevin when beetles are first noticed.

45. What do I use to get rid of black flies on our cabbages?

Use an insecticide, such as Derris or Rotenone.

46. What kind of a non-toxic insecticide do we use to eliminate bugs on asparagus?

Use Derris or Rotenone.

47. How do I prevent fungus growth when air-layering?

Apply a mild fungicide, such as Captan, to the material when preparing for air-layering. Avoid over-watering.

48. What is the best general spray for a greenhouse?

It depends on what the problems are. Diagnose the problem. Use insecticides on insects and fungicides for a fungus disease.

49. How do you kill wasps?

Apply Chlordane to the nesting area with extreme care or use a qualified insect exterminator to do it.

50. A number of our plants, such as pyracantha, have round brown spots on the leaves which are spreading. How are they controlled?

This is bacterial leaf spot and is controlled by Acti-dione or Phaltan applied underneath and on top of leaves when they are actively growing. Repeat in 10 days or after any heavy rain. Repeat as needed.

51. How do I control a fungus in grass?

Spray grass with a fungicide such as Fore.

52. How do you eliminate caterpillars on pine and other trees?

Use a dormant oil spray in late February or early March and then an insecticide, such as Diazinon, Sevin or Malathion, when caterpillars first appear. Repeat as needed.

53. What insecticide is used to spray insects on the leaves of raspberry and rhubarb plants?

Apply a safe insecticide, such as Malathion, underneath and on top of the leaves.

54. How do I eliminate box-elder bugs?

Spray the bugs and affected areas directly with Chlordane or Malathion. In addition, spray carefully around the foundation of houses and around windows.

55. How do you identify bugs in soil and houseplants to know what kind of spray to use?

Bugs are a problem in most soils. It is not necessary to identify them. Use a spray such as synthetic Pyrethrin in place of a regular watering. Repeat as needed.

56. Are outdoor plants sprayed when bringing them indoors?

Check the plants and pots carefully for any signs of insects, particularly for scale. If insects are prevalent, use the correct spray several days before plants are brought indoors and again three or four hours before moving indoors.

57. How do we eliminate white grubs in our lawn?

Use Malathion with Rotenone when the lawn is wet or after application, water to carry the insecticide into the soil one-half inch. Repeat as needed.

58. How do we eliminate mealy bugs on ivy and ficus?

Eliminate with a forceful stream of water or with an insecticide used under pressure.

59. How do I get rid of mildew on indoor plants?

Increase the air circulation where plants are growing with the use of a small fan. If necessary, use a fungicide such as Captan or Benlate.

60. Is flour usable as an insecticide?

I am not familiar with the value of this; however, if it is used on insects and works, continue to use it.

61. What do I do about insects on the bark of a willow tree?

Apply a mild insecticide over the trunk of the tree.

62. How do you treat a fungus which attacks the flowers yearly on an outdoor columbine?

As soon as plant begins to grow in early spring spray with a fungicide, such as a Bordeaux mixture, and then apply a fungicide, such as Benlate or Captan, as soon as buds begin to form. Repeat in four or five days.

63. Is there any other method than spraying that will eliminate spider mites?

Reduce the temperature if possible and wash the plants thoroughly with soap and water every three or four days.

64. How do I eliminate mealy bugs on African violets?

Mealy bugs on African violets are difficult to control because they creep down among the thick hairs of the leaves; however, an insecticide applied under pressure eliminates them. Also use rubbing alcohol on the insects with cotton swabs.

65. How do I eliminate anthracnose on sycamore maples?

Sycamores are extremely prone to this. Anthracnose causes heavy leaf drop. Keep the trees well fertilized and watered during periods of drought and spray with a fungicide when anthracnose is first noticed.

66. How do you eliminate aphids on roses, day lilies and trees?

Use an insecticide applied under pressure when insects are first noticed. Repeat as needed.

67. How do I eliminate webby insects?

Red spiders produce webs and feed by sucking the juices from plants. Use Kelthane or other insecticides recommended for red spider control.

68. Is Chlordane okay to use after 20 years of storage?

It depends on how it has been stored. Stored in a cool dry area is ideal. Use a small amount as a test case on part of a plant. Observe after several hours to see what the effect has been.

69. What is the best control for pill bugs and sow bugs?

Clean up all areas with debris in which the bugs hide. Spray areas with insecticide at regular intervals.

70. Is it safe to eat fruit from a plum tree that has been sprayed with Chlordane?

Chlordane is not recommended on any edible plant.

71. What insecticide do we use on tomato plants that are being eaten by bugs?

Use Rotenone and/or Thuracide.

72. What do I use to eliminate whiteflies?

Use synthetic Pyrethrin underneath and on top of the leaves. Repeat in three to four days.

73. Do whiteflies winter-over in soil and if so, is the soil sterilized?

Whiteflies do not hibernate in the soil but rather on plant material. Keep the plant area clean and use insecticide.

74. How do you control sowbugs in strawberries?

Thoroughly spray strawberry beds with insecticide when plants first start to grow. Repeat in 10 days.

75. Is garlic a good deterrent for aphids?

Garlic growing among plants deters some aphids; however, the best control is to put garlic through a blender to extract the juice, dilute it in water and spray on the plants.

76. How do I control diseases on our strawberry plants?

Thoroughly clean the strawberry beds in spring, spray with a fungicide such as Phaltan or a Bordeaux mixture and repeat again if needed.

77. Is Diazinon poisonous by contact?

Avoid getting any insecticide on your skin. If you do come in contact, wash off immediately and contact your nearest health center for necessary precautions.

78. Do morning-glories repel insects?

No.

79. How do we get rid of springtails in the soil?

Apply a mild insecticide such as synthetic Pyrethrin in place of regular watering or spray it around the soil where plants are growing.

80. How do we control bugs on our evergreens?

Use insecticide in early morning when temperatures are below 80 degrees.

81. How do I get rid of bacteria on pear trees?

Follow the calendar obtainable from your university extension division, for spraying fruit trees.

82. What do I do for black flies eating the leaves on my maple tree?

Apply an insecticide underneath and on top of the leaves.

83. How do I control millipedes in the soil?

Water synthetic Pyrethrin or Rotenone into the soil.

84. How do I eliminate gray mold on strawberry and shrimp plants?

Use Captan or Benlate.

85. How do I eliminate termites in a living tree?

Apply Chlordane.

86. How do I eliminate mildew on our raspberries?

Follow the schedule available from your university extension division on control of fruit disease.

87. What are the white spots on our schefflera and how do we get rid of them?

White spots are caused by scale insects. Use a good oil base spray underneath and on top of the leaves. Repeat in two to three weeks.

88. How do we eliminate ant hills and ants in other plants?

Ant hills are controlled by Chlordane. Control ants in other plants by finding the source and eliminating them with Chlordane.

89. What is a good all-purpose spray for shrubs and trees?

Use dormant oil in late February or early March and insecticide when insects are first noticed or fungicide when fungus diseases first appear.

90. Is it okay to use Malathion for honeysuckles?

Apply it early in the morning before the temperature reaches 80 degrees.

91. What is a good deterrent for roaches in houseplants?

Use Baygon or use a trap for roaches placed among the plants.

92. How do you treat leaf miner?

Leaf miner is caused by small insects laying their eggs. The larvae hatch out and feed inside the leaves. Eliminate by controlling the adults when they first appear around the plants with a spray, such as Malathion. Apply it underneath and on top of the leaves. Repeat again in a week to 10 days.

93. How do I eliminate snails in my houseplants?

Spray the soil thoroughly with Slug-it or use Snarol which contains metaldehyde.

94. What causes seedlings to suddenly fall over after they come through the soil?

This is called damping-off, a bacterial disease. Allow more air circulation and avoid over-watering. Treat the soil with fungicide.

Chapter Sixteen
Mulches and Fertilizer

General Information

Mulch is a layer of material, preferably organic matter, that is placed on the soil surface to conserve moisture, prevent weeds and improve soil structure and fertility. Mulching also protects plants during winter, reducing the dangers of freezing and heaving. Put mulch around new plantings to a depth of four to six inches and extend it at least a foot beyond the planting area. Mulch shrub borders heavily each year, covering all the bare ground. This controls weeds and keeps the soil moist.

Mulch is any type of shredded plant material and is more effective when partially decomposed. Avoid using fresh animal manures as these can burn plants. Layers of newspaper weighted down make excellent mulch material as do pieces of old carpet laid over the ground between rows of vegetables.

Place extra plant materials and weeds in a compost pile which consists of a coarse layer at the bottom of the pile to allow for good air circulation followed by a one-foot layer of finer materials, such as shredded leaves or other shredded material from the garden. Then add another layer of coarse material alternating with a layer of fine material until you reach a height of approximately four feet. The pile should be four to six feet wide and the length depends on the amount of material you have available. Enclose the compost area to keep the material from spreading and to keep animals from digging into it. Suitable enclosures are made of wood, cement blocks or wire frames. The compost pile is located near the garden where it is readily accessible.

Start the compost pile in fall when leaves and other debris from the garden are available. Put lawn clippings in the compost pile rather than use as a mulch; they dry out, shedding water away. They can be used directly in the garden, digging into the soil.

As each layer of compost is formed, sprinkle some old compost on top or add some top soil which contains organic matter and bacteria. Thoroughly water at regular intervals as the pile builds up and the decay processes start. Allow the pile to heat up over winter. Turn the pile in the spring putting the outside edges into the center. Then rewater and allow to sit until late summer. Occasional waterings during the summer keep it thoroughly moistened. By fall, material will be partially decomposed and ideal to use as mulch or to work into the soil.

It is not necessary to add lime or fertilizer to the compost pile. If a high pH level is required, add lime. Lime is harmful to azaleas, rhododendrons and other acid-type plants.

Commercial fertilizers added to the compost pile burn the material more rapidly and much of the value is destroyed by heavy rains. Add fresh manure to the pile in layers to hasten decay and build up the compost during the summer months when it is not convenient to add fresh manure directly to the garden. Avoid adding diseased plant materials, which may not be destroyed by decomposition, to the compost pile. You may add weeds with seeds to the compost pile because the pile heats up enough to destroy the seed. Hand pick the weeds that may develop. When the mulch breaks down it releases nutrients which were taken out of the soil by the parent plant. These help to enrich the soil when re-applied. The mulch keeps the soil moist and cool and adds fertilizer which breaks down and needs to be replaced each year. You gradually build up an excellent soil over a period of time and new plant roots establish very quickly in the base of the mulch.

Fertilizers are available in chemical and organic forms. The chemical fertilizers are readily available and used when immediate results are required. They are not affected by temperature but are affected by the amount of moisture. The more moisture the quicker they break down; therefore, use chemical fertilizer during the colder periods of the year when growth is just beginning. They are sold in containers with the three numbers, such as 5-10-5, 6-12-12, etc., marked on them. These represent nitrogen, phosphorus and potassium, respectively. The first number five indicates five parts of nitrogen, the second number 10 indicates 10 parts of phosphorus and the third number five indicates five parts of potassium. Plants require 16 elements for good growth. Thirteen are normally available in soils in sufficient quantities while nitrogen, phosphorus and potassium are often lacking.

Trace elements are also important and often are lacking in certain soils due to either a high or low acid content in the soil. These elements include iron, boron and manganese. Add when needed as fritted trace elements or as individual elements when indicated by soil tests or chlorotic condition of plants. A lack of iron causes yellowing leaves or a chlorotic condition in which the veins of the plant stand out from the rest of the leaves; apply in early spring as growth is beginning. A second application may be needed in early September. Add epsom salts, which is magnesium sulfate, at the rate of one tablespoon per gallon of water along with one tablespoon of iron to change it back to a normal green. Lack of iron makes plants less hardy in winter or causes them to die during the summer. These plants also are much more subject to insects and diseases.

In preparing an area for planting, use a balanced fertilizer unless a soil test indicates otherwise. Use four to five pounds of 5-10-5 fertilizer per 1000 square feet to a depth of four or five inches. On established crops where plants are not doing too well use the same type of fertilizer as a side dressing at the base of the plants. Make a narrow one-inch deep trench two or three inches from the base of the plant. Sprinkle a light application of fertilizer in the trench, cover it up with soil and lightly water to break the fertilizer down so it is available immediately near the root system of the plant. Also spread the fertilizer over a planted area when the plants are dry or just before a rain. If applied dry over the plants, follow with a light watering to remove any particles which remain on the plant as it may burn it.

Organic fertilizers are made from either animal materials or in some cases a plant product such as cottonseed meal. Most organic fertilizers are slow acting and are affected by temperature. Do not use until soil temperatures reach around 60 degrees and are able to feed over a longer period of time. If applied in the ground when it is too cold, they have little or no effect; therefore, they are of little value where early growth is required.

Chemical fertilizers burn up the organic matter in the soil much more rapidly; therefore, if using chemical fertilizers, add compost to the soil at regular intervals to replace that which is used up. Organic fertilizers, on the other hand, have little effect on the organic matter in the soil. Some sources of organic fertilizer are animal manures, bone meal, cottonseed meal and superphosphate.

Lime in its various forms is also considered a fertilizer because it supplies certain elements, and is a factor in soil improvements and makes nutrients in the soil available to plants. Ordinary agricultural lime is used to sweeten the soil whereas gypsum does not raise the pH level but is more of a soil conditioner and a good source of calcium needed for plant growth. To raise the pH level one degree, four pounds of ground limestone per 100 square feet is required. Lime is very stable and does not move throughout the soil. It is slow acting so add lime in the fall and work it into the top three or four inches of soil where it will remain. An application of lime once every three or four years is sufficient unless soil tests indicate otherwise.

Do not mix lime and manure or apply at the same time. Hydrated lime releases the nitrogen from manure in the form of ammonia and is then lost. If the manure is plowed under before the lime is added, the soil absorbs the nitrogen. In cases where soil tests indicate heavier applications of lime, apply these at several intervals with one application in the fall and again in early spring until you have enough in the soil to raise the pH level. If the soil is very acid, make a second soil test a year later to determine the proper pH ratio.

Do not use grass and peat moss as mulches. Both of these when dried shed water away from the area. They are better used as soil amendments worked into the soil in the first four or five inches or apply the grass clippings to the compost pile where they break down.

Wood chips, if fresh when first applied to the soil, remove the nitrogen from the soil and are best composted for several years and kept readily soaked to start decay. If using wood chips as a mulch, apply a light application of cottonseed meal over the area to keep enough nitrogen in the soil because as the chips decay they withdraw nitrogen from the soil; however, avoid applying too much cottonseed meal because the chips, once they decompose, release the nitrogen back into the soil. Too much nitrogen induces soft growth which is not as disease-resistant.

QUESTIONS

1. How do I improve clay soil for planting vegetables and other plants?

Incorporate plenty of organic matter into the top four to six inches of soil before planting and repeat in between crops.

2. How do I best prepare soil for good planting?

Work the soil well by hand digging or tilling. Add three to four inches of organic matter, a light application of lime and four to five pounds of a balanced fertilizer.

3. What is the meaning of the three numbers on fertilizer labels?

The three numbers, for example 5-10-5, represent five parts nitrogen, 10 parts phosphorus and five parts potassium, respectively.

4. What is the correct ratio of N, P and K (nitrogen, phosphorus and potassium) to use in the soil?

Make a soil test several weeks before planting and follow recommendations.

5. When is it appropriate to use ammonium nitrate?

Use ammonium nitrate with extreme caution. Following a cool, wet period use it as a side dressing to stimulate plants into more active growth. Avoid overusing and do not get it on the plant because it burns.

6. Are acid plant fertilizers used on other kinds of plants?

Acid-type fertilizers are available in balanced forms to use on plants, such as azaleas and rhododendrons, which like an acid-type soil. Use on any of the plants which need a lower pH level than normal.

7. How much lime is applied to bring the pH level of the soil up one point?

Four pounds of dolomitic limestone to 100 square feet is ideal.

8. Are fertilizers ever overused and if so, what is the result?

Fertilizers are often overused and when improperly applied burn the plants. The leaves of the plants brown starting at the tip and working back or holes are burnt into the leaves where fertilizer is applied directly to the plant. Overuse of fertilizers stimulate the plants into soft growth, making them more susceptible to insect and disease damage.

9. Where do I buy cobalt paper to test soil?

Cobalt paper is available in many drug stores and garden centers and is used to indicate whether the soil is acid or alkaline. It is not too accurate.

10. How are epsom salts used and for what purpose?

Epsom salts are used by mixing one tablespoon to a gallon of water. Use on roses in early spring as new growth is beginning. It helps to harden-off the plants and prevents what is known as black leg. Also use with iron chelate, one tablespoon of each applied to plants which are low in iron. It is recommended for indoor plants such as gardenias which require an acid soil. Apply twice a year in early spring and in early fall.

11. What is the effect of excessive magnesium sulfate?

It causes browning to edges of leaves and defoliation.

12. What are potash and phosphoric acid used for in plantings?

Potash gives better quality plants and encourages better fruiting habits. Phosphorus encourages a heavier root system.

13. Is gypsum beneficial for a lawn with clay soil?

Gypsum is a good soil conditioner. Work in to three to four inches.

14. Are wood ashes from the fireplace useful in the garden?

Yes. Store in a dry area until ready to use in the garden.

15. We have roots in our garden where no tree is growing. What is causing this and how to we eliminate it?

Tree roots travel considerable distances to fertile soils. Dig the area deep and remove the roots.

16. How do I prepare an organic fertilizer?

Organic fertilizer is fresh animal manure, bloodmeal, bone meal, cottonseed meal and Milorganite. These are readily available in garden centers.

17. What are the uses of cottonseed meal and bloodmeal?

These supply nitrogen to the soil. Spread over the soil once it has warmed up in early spring. They are slow-release fertilizers. Apply when using wood chips in an area and in the soil at planting time.

18. Can bone meal be added to soil and if so how much?

Bone meal is a very slow release fertilizer which supplies superphosphate. Apply when preparing the soil for planting or use as a side dressing around established plants in early spring.

19. Can fresh horse manure be used as a fertilizer?

Yes. Use it sparingly around plants or apply to a depth of about two inches over an area that is being prepared for planting.

20. In using organic matter to improve the soil is the package manure sufficient?

No. To apply enough of this to improve the soil you would supply too much nitrogen.

21. Can rotted and fresh manure be used as a mulch?

Yes. Avoid using a heavy application of fresh manure late in the season. This stimulates plant growth preventing it from hardening-off for overwintering.

22. Is it feasible to use cow manure in the garden soil?

Yes. Use dry cow manure. If it is fresh cow manure apply two to three inches to the area before planting. Work in well.

23. Can fertilizer be balanced with sawdust mulch?

If using fresh sawdust as a mulch, apply cottonseed or bloodmeal before the mulch is applied or apply on top of the mulch. A balanced fertilizer such as 5-10-5 can also be worked in the area first for good results.

24. Is it okay to work shredded wood chips into garden soil?

Yes. Provide some additional nitrogen at the same time.

25. Can hops be used as a good soil additive?

Yes. Work in four to five inches deep.

26. How do I sterilize soil in the oven?

Prepare soil for planting. Have it moderately moist and place in an oven of 350 degrees with a pan of water for approximately three quarters of an hour. Thoroughly cool before using.

27. How do you prepare soil in late fall for next year's garden?

Add either fresh manure or compost and either dig or till the soil to a depth of five or six inches. Leave the soil rough to allow freezing and thawing to break the soil down and release soil nutrients. In areas for early planting add more mulch or leaves to a depth of one foot over the area and weigh it down. Remove at the time of the first thaw for planting.

28. Are tea leaves good to use for soil?

This is a good form of organic matter which does contain a very small amount of nitrogen.

29. How do I treat the soil where an evergreen has been in order to prepare it for planting a new lawn?

Prepare the soil well, adding four to five inches of organic matter prior to planting. Add lime and a balanced fertilizer.

30. How can we best use wood ashes and for what?

Wood ashes are a good source of phosphorus. Store ashes where they are dry until ready to use. They are ideal to use around lilacs and other plants that like neutral soil.

31. How and when is compost used as a fertilizer?

Partially decomposed compost used as a mulch constantly releases nutrients into the soil. The soil does need additional fertilizer in either chemical or organic form to give a proper feeding program according to soil tests.

32. Is an old compost pile still useful?

Yes. Much of the value is gone but it keeps the soil well aerated.

33. How do I compost leaves?

Put leaves through the shredder or run over with a rotary mower to break them up. Keep wet and allow to decay. Work directly into the soil in the fall to a depth of four to five inches.

34. What kind of leaves go into a compost pile?

Use any leaves, including oak, in the compost pile.

35. How deep do we pile the wood chips for weed control?

Pile to a depth of three to four inches.

36. Can I use Zoysia clippings, coffee grounds and tea leaves in making compost?

Yes.

37. Can wild onions be put in a compost bed?

Use just the tops. It is better to dispose of the bulbs rather than place them in the compost pile.

38. How is compost used?

Use as a soil amendment worked into the soil or as mulch around plants.

39. How do I get rid of bees in the compost?

Bees cause no harm to a compost pile but you may use a mild insecticide for control.

40. Can fish oil be used in a compost pile?

Fish oil draws insects and vermin. Do not use in the compost pile.

41. How do you compost lawn clippings to kill weed seeds?

If lawn clippings are applied to the compost pile and worked in, they will heat up to destroy the weed seeds.

42. Can wood chips be stored over the summer and how do you hasten their decomposition?

Store at anytime. Hasten decomposition by keeping them wet and adding some old compost which contains bacteria. Turn the chips at intervals to encourage decomposition.

43. Wood chips have a yellow fungus on them. Do we treat them before using?

The fungus is not a problem in most plantings. You may use a fungicide, such as Captan.

44. Is there any use for pine needles?

Pine needles make an excellent mulch around azaleas and rhododendrons or apply directly to the compost pile where they decompose. They are somewhat acid when breaking down which aids acid-type plants. They also make an excellent mulch around shrubbery.

45. Does birch mulch attract termites and is it safe to use?

Wood chips do not attract termites in most areas. If termites are present, use insecticide when first noticed to eliminate them.

46. Are grass clippings used as a mulch?

No. Work into the soil or apply to the compost pile.

47. Can English walnut shells be used as a mulch?

Use as a mulch although they are extremely slow to break down. Apply some nitrogen when first using as a mulch.

48. When is it advisable to use wood or plastic mulch around shrubs?

Wood chips are used from early spring until late fall around shrubs. Use plastic either the clear or the black. This discourages weeds. If using black, it tends to heat up. Apply to the ground and then cover with a layer of wood chips. Punch holes in the plastic at regular intervals to allow moisture to penetrate through into the soil.

49. When is cedar mulch best to use?

Use when partially decomposed; however, you may also use fresh material with an application of nitrogen.

50. What do we do about weeds that are growing through the mulch?

Pull by hand or dig out of the ground.

51. What is the best mulch for flower beds?

Use any partially decomposed compost material with the exception of peat moss and lawn clippings.

52. Are wood chips used around trees?

Yes.

53. Is sawdust good to use as a mulch?

Yes. Allow to sit for a couple of years to partially decompose because it pulls the nitrogen out of the soil.

54. Are Christmas trees ground up suitable for mulch?

Yes.

55. We have wood chips from a soft maple. Can they be used as a mulch around the roses?

Wood chips are used as a mulch during the winter months around roses for protection. It is better to remove the wood chips and apply them in the compost pile until partially decomposed rather than leave them on the roses where they take the needed nitrogen from the ground.

56. What do I lower the pH level in the soil with and how much do I use?

Use sulfur, the amount depending upon the pH level. Four pounds of sulfur lowers the level one degree when applied to 100 square feet. This is somewhat slow acting. Apply in early spring.

57. What is the best mulch and fertilizer for a vegetable garden?

Prepare soil with plenty of organic matter and then add a balanced fertilizer, such as a 5-10-5, at the rate of four to five pounds per 1000 square feet prior to seeding or setting out new plants. Add any type of partially decomposed compost or other organic matter in a thin layer when first planting and gradually increase this to a depth of two to three inches.

Chapter Seventeen
Helpful Information

When and How To Send Plants for Identification

A number of places, such as botanical gardens, university extension divisions and garden centers are able to identify plants.

When sending plants in for identification give as much information about the plant as possible. The information includes: how large does it grow; time of flowering; color of flower; kind of fruit and a general physical description. Enclose a sample of the plant with several full leaves and if possible, the flowers. Press between several sheets of blotting paper or other coarse material to absorb the moisture out of the leaves. Then encase specimens between a couple of stiff pieces of cardboard in an envelope. Do not put specimens in plastic which will heat up and cause the plant to rot by the time it arrives. State where the plants have come from and whether they have been growing indoors or outdoors. Enclose a self-addressed, stamped envelope for sending the information back.

Soil Tests

Obtain soil tests from most university extension divisions. There is a charge for them. Allow three to four weeks for the test results. Select the area, such as a vegetable garden or lawn, you want tested and take several samples of soil about six inches deep with a clean spade. A small core from several areas is all that is needed. Place soil in a plastic bag or pail and thoroughly mix. Allow to dry out and then enclose approximately one pint of soil in a plastic bag or other suitable container. Do not mix it with your hands; this changes the acidity of the soil. State the use for the area and the results will tell what nutrients to add to the soil.

How and When to Move Plants from Indoors to Outdoors and Back Inside Again.

Gradually move plants from indoors to outdoors. Move houseplants outdoors once all danger of frost is ended. Select an area which is semi-shaded, such as a lathhouse, or place them under trees where they receive filtered sun. Thoroughly clean up the ground which has good drainage. Move houseplants from indoors to a protected spot, such as a garage for a couple of days. Withhold watering once you start moving the plants so that they dry out but do not allow to wilt. After a couple of days in the garage, move to a spot outdoors where they are protected from the wind and sun for another couple of days and then to the final site for the summer. Place plants in the containers by digging holes so that the top of the pots are level with the soil around them. This keeps them from rapidly drying out. Mulch plants to further hold in moisture.

In moving plants outdoors prune back heavily to allow the plants to form new growth and become compact. Repot if plants are pot-bound. Put them into a pot two sizes larger. In the fall move plants indoors before the weather becomes too cold, a couple of weeks before frost occurs. First give the pots a twist in the ground, raise up and remove any roots which have grown into the surrounding soil through the bottom of the pots. Leave them in this spot for a couple of days. Withhold watering. Two days after the plants have had the roots removed, move the pots to a protected spot outdoors where there is less light and no draft or wind. Leave them there for another two or three days and then move into a garage with light still further reduced. After a couple of days in the garage, move plants indoors where they receive about the same amount of light as they had in the garage. After a couple of days in the house with moderate light, move plants into their permanent location where they should adjust with little or no leaf drop.

In the fall avoid using fertilizer once plants are going dormant. Only use fertilizer on plants which have been flowering heavily or on ones which are continuing in full bloom. They require more nutrients during this period. Inspect the plants thoroughly when ready to bring indoors. Thoroughly spray and clean up to avoid insects or disease. Apply a second application of insecticide to them when they are in the garage before bringing them into the house.

When moving plants indoors, repot those that need it when the plants have been moved into the garage. Once indoors prune to encourage low bushy growth. As plants are brought indoors withhold watering to allow them to go through a dryer period.

Excess watering causes the loss of roots and heavy dropping of leaves. On the other hand, do not let them dry out too much; this also causes leaves to drop.

Moving plants directly from one spot to another is a shock to the plants' system. This is the reason for leaf drop. Gradually changing the position keeps plants healthy. Only fertilize houseplants in winter to keep them in good condition. Over-fertilization stimulates useless soft growth and often the loss of the root systems and eventually the plants.

As growth begins in the new year, increase the watering according to the plants' needs and feed occasionally. During the active growing season, foliage plants require several feedings of a balanced fertilizer, such as a 20-20-20.

Where to Obtain Free Leaf Mold

Leaves are collected by most municipalities and stored in some areas. Many areas put their leaves through grinders to reduce the size and break them down. They give the leaf mold to anyone from early January through early spring. Contact your local parks department or city government office for sources of leaf mold. It is ideal to use as mulch to improve the soil.

Some of the Best Foliage Plants for an Outdoor Shaded Area

Ferns of all types are ideal provided there is plenty of moisture. Coleus, Baltic and English ivy, mondo grass, ajuga, European and native wild ginger, sweet woodruff, yews and boxwoods grow well in the shade.

Flowers That Can Be Planted in a Shaded Area for Good Summer Color

Caladiums, wax begonias, impatiens, coleuses and many of the true lilies flower throughout the summer if planted in the shade.

Plants for Hot Dry Areas

Zinnias, marigolds, gerberas, African daisies and gazanias grow well in hot, dry areas.

Information about Soil Moisture Detection Systems

Soil moisture can be determined in several ways. One is to dig your finger down into the soil of a houseplant one to two inches. If soil is dry at two inches in depth, plant needs water; if soil is moist withhold water until soil is dry to this level. For outdoor plants, check the soil moisture level with a trowel digging down two or three inches and if soil is dry, watering is needed.

In watering outdoors one should apply water to the equivalent of two inches of rain. The best way to do this is to set up a sprinkler, turn the sprinkler on and place a container near the edge of the falling water to catch the water. Time the period it takes for the container to get approximately two inches of water. If it is three-quarters of an hour from the time the water is turned on until the container has the two inches, this is how long it takes to water each area of the garden when the sprinkler is set up. Watering can be done at anytime of the day provided it gets the equivalent of two inches; however, it is best to avoid watering late in the day so plants can be dry when they go in to the night, to cut down on fungus diseases.

Another method is to obtain a moisture meter which is available and will determine when plants need water. It is necessary to learn how to use the meters according to the types of plants being grown and the type of soil which plants are in. It is advisable to check the soil with your finger as well as the meter until you become accustomed to the meter's readings.

In many areas, local radio stations give the soil moisture index with their weather forecasts. It is advisable to contact your radio station and ask for a chart to explain this procedure and follow accordingly in watering the garden.

QUESTIONS

1. What is meant by hardening-off of seedlings?

In hardening-off, withhold water on seedlings but do not allow the plants to wilt. Lower the temperature, take seedlings that have been growing indoors, place them outdoors in a protected spot where they receive sufficient light for an hour the first day and gradually increase their exposure each day until they are able to remain outdoors all day. After hardening-off for a week to 10 days, the seedlings are then ready to plant outdoors if weather permits.

2. May I plant seeds saved from last year?

Yes. Test for germination by placing 10 seeds in moist blotting paper in a covered dish. Keep at a temperature of 75 to 80 degrees and examine daily for germination. A day after the first seeds have germinated, count how many have. If half the seeds germinate then sow twice as many.

3. How do you move plants from one city to another?

Moving vans may move plants; however, the cost is fairly high and in many cases it is not advisable unless vans are heated. Inspect plants to see if they are insect and disease-free. Contact your local extension division to inspect plants and issue certificates for moving from one state to another. In many cases it is best to thoroughly wrap the plants just prior to moving and take them with you if you can. They can be packed in cartons by a florist or contact a local florist for the best wrapping methods. Send air express from one city to another for best results.

4. Can Sequestrene (iron chelate) be used as a foliage spray?

Yes. It works faster if watered in around the base of the plant.

5. What is the general care of houseplants?

Houseplants need adequate watering, watering just as the plants begin to dry out. Avoid over-watering. They need adequate air circulation, sufficient light according to the needs of the plants and occasional feedings of liquid fertilizer. Avoid over-feeding when plants are not growing actively. Occasionally cut back plants to keep them low and bushy. Repot as needed. Check routinely for insects and disease and spray as needed.

6. What do I do about plants in hanging baskets that are growing unevenly?

Pinch the tips out of ivy, wandering Jew and petunias and remove one-half to one inch of active growth at regular intervals. This causes the plants to produce side shoots and remain compact but full.

7. What do I do about houseplants that are being over-watered?

Lay the plants on the side if they do not have drainage to drain off the excess water and avoid watering until soil has dried out.

8. What do I do about houseplants that do not have any drainage?

Avoid over-watering. A good method in potting is to place some pebbles at the bottom of the pot with a thin layer of sphagnum moss or similar material over that before adding soil. Insert a plastic tube down the side of the pot so that it is about halfway down into the pebbles. Use as a gauge for watering. Then add soil. When watering place a stick down the plastic tube to see if water appears at the bottom. In every third or fourth watering, allow a little moisture to reach the bottom for the roots. If excess water appears on the stick, allow plant to dry out considerably before applying any more water.

9. Is salt water or rain water better for watering plants than regular tap water?

Avoid salt water which burns the roots of the plants. Rain water is preferred over tap water. However, tap water in most cases will not affect the plant adversely.

10. What is the advantage of distilled water over tap water?

Distilled water does not have the high alkaline content or any additives that tap water does. Tap water often has a high amount of chlorine which is detrimental to plants which like an acid-type soil.

11. Can water from a dehumidifier be used on houseplants?

Yes.

12. Is a water softener detrimental to houseplants?

Yes. The calcium is replaced with sodium which does not settle out and is harmful to the plants.

13. How do I make plants bushier?

Remove the growing tips when plants have grown six to eight inches. This causes the plants to produce side shoots below the pinching.

14. Is it advisable to water houseplants with ice cubes?

This increases the humidity because the ice cubes melt more slowly. Avoid placing the ice cubes directly on the stem of the plant as this cold temperature can injure it.

15. Why do the leaves of a houseplant dry out?

This occurs due to a low humidity within the house. Avoid by placing the plant on a tray of pebbles so that the plant is sitting just above the water.

16. Which is more desirable for indoor plants – clay or plastic pots?

Both are a matter of personal preference. Clay pots dry out more rapidly because air is taken in through the sides of the pot. Plastic takes air in only through the top so that not as much watering is required.

17. Is an air fern a genuine plant?

No. It is a fern-like growth that requires no watering or feeding. It is a low form of animal life (Bugula species). It is naturally brown in color but is also sold in a dyed green.

18. How do I best care for a houseplant that I have received from a florist?

Inspect the plant carefully to see that it is free of insects and diseases and isolate it for several days before placing it with your other plants. Observe it on a regular basis and treat for insects and diseases if needed.

19. What kind of sand is best used for propagating plants?

A coarse sand is best.

20. What is the best way to protect plants when there is danger of frost?

Cover plants several hours before frost occurs to hold the heat in. Also hill the plants up or cover with a light mulch to prevent frost from injuring them. If frost does occur, spray the plants thoroughly with water before sunrise to take the frost off. If there is a threat of frost, it is best to lift the plants up and move them to protected spots if you want to carry these throughout the winter.

21. Are there any problems in using combinations of fertilizers and herbicides?

Avoid fertilizer mixed with herbicides where tree or shrub roots are growing. Do not apply herbicides to flower beds and do not mix a herbicide with fertilizer when the temperatures are over 80 degrees.

22. I have heard that adding sugar to the water used for fresh cut flowers enhances the life of the flowers. Is this so and why?

Sugar prolongs the life of many cut flowers anywhere from 24 to 48 hours. Plants manufacture a certain amount of sugar.

23. Are pennies or aspirin tablets helpful in prolonging the life of cut flowers?

No. In some flowers they shorten the life of the cut flowers anywhere from several hours up to 48 hours.

24. How can I best transplant hardy ferns?

Move hardy ferns in early spring just before growth begins or in late fall. Add leaf mold to the soil and place them in an area where they are under filtered light.

25. How do you dry gourds?

Remove gourds from the garden as soon as the first frost appears. Clean thoroughly and place in a dry, well ventilated area to further their ripening process. Occasionally spray with fungicide to keep them from molding. When the gourds rattle with seeds, they are dry enough for use.

26. Seeds growing under light in the basement are not doing well. What do I do?

Place seeds several inches from the source of light. As seeds begin to grow, move further away. Failure to do well is from a lack of light and insufficient nutrients. Plants require 10 to 12 hours of strong light.

27. What causes seedlings to become long and lanky?

This is caused by not being close enough to the source of light and also to over-crowding.

28. How are plants grown under fluorescent lights?

Fluorescent lights are an excellent way of growing plants in areas where light is not sufficient. Place the source of light fairly near the plant and allow 10 to 12 hours a day. Keep plants moderately moist and occasionally feed.

29. What kind of light is used to encourage plant growth in the home?

There are a number of commercial lights available. Usually a combination of incandescent and fluorescent lights produce excellent results. Consult local plant shops for various types available.

30. What are names of some plants that are poisonous?

A number of plants are poisonous; however, few cases have been noted where poisoning has actually occurred through eating the plant. Consult your local library for sources of poisonous plants. Some of the more common ones found in the home are the dieffenbachia, or dumb cane. Keep out of reach of small children. Remove seed pods of castor-beans which often are grown as an ornament in the garden. Poison ivy which is rampant in many parts of the country is also toxic.

Many of the mushrooms are extremely poisonous. Two books on the subject are:

Human Poisoning From Native and Cultivated Plants by James W. Hardin and Jay M. Arena, M.D., Duke University Press, 1974.

Deadly Harvest by John M. Kingsbury, Holt Rinehart and Winston, 1965, Paperback 1972.

Bibliography

America's Garden Book, James and Louise Bush-Brown, 1967, Charles Schribner's Sons, New York, NY.

Crockett's Victory Garden, James Underwood Crockett, 1977, Little, Brown & Company, Boston, MA.

Deadly Harvest: A Guide to Common Poisonous Plants, John M. Kingsbury, 1965, paperback, Holt, Rinehart & Winston, Inc., New York, NY.

Dwarf Shrubs: Maintenance-Free Woody Plants for Today's Gardens, Donald Wyman, Macmillan Publishing Company, Inc., New York, NY.

Ferns for Modern Living, Elaine Davenport, 1977, Merchants Publishing Company, Kalamazoo, MI.

Green Thumb Garden Handbook, George (Doc) and Katy Abraham, 1977, Prentice Hall, Inc., Englewood Cliffs, NJ.

Greenhouse Grow How, John H. Pierce, 1977, Plants Alive Books, Seattle, WA.

Home Gardener's Guide to Trees and Shrubs, John B. Brimer, 1976, Hawthorn Books, Inc., New York, NY.

Hortus Third; A Concise Dictionary of Plants Cultivated in the United States and Canada, Staff of the L.H. Bailey Hortorium, Cornell University, 1976, Macmillan Publishing Company, Inc., New York, NY.

House Plant Answer Book, Elvin McDonald, 1975, paperback, Popular Library, Inc., New York, NY.

How to Control Plant Diseases . . . in Home and Garden, Malcolm C. Shurtleff, 1966, Iowa State University Press, Ames, IA.

Human Poisoning from Native and Cultivated Plants, James W. Hardin and Jay M. Arena, 1969, Duke University Press, Durham, NC.

Indoor Light Gardening Book, George A. Elbert, 1972, Crown Publishers, Inc., New York, NY.

Indoor Plants: Comprehensive Care & Culture, Doris F. Hirsch, 1977, Chilton Book Company, Radnor, PA.

Perfect Lawn the Easy Way, A, Paul N. Voykin, 1969, Rand McNally & Company, Chicago, IL.

Plants & Gardens, Handbook Series, Brooklyn Botanic Garden, 1000 Washington Avenue, Brooklyn, New York, NY 11225. There are many handbooks in this series, all very good.

Rodale Herb Book: How to Use, Grow & Buy Nature's Miracle Plants, William Hylton, 1974, Rodale Press, Inc., Emmaus, PA.

Shrubs and Vines for American Gardens, Donald Wyman, 1969, Macmillan Publishing Company, Inc., New York, NY.

Glossary A: Gardening Terms

Aerate – To cultivate or loosen the soil to allow air to penetrate.

Air-layering, Propagation by – A method of rooting woody plants. This consists of cutting a slit in the stem through a node about one-third of the way, placing a small splinter of wood to keep the cut end from coming together, covering with slightly dampened sphagnum moss which has perlite in contact with the cut and then wrapping the moss with plastic. *See* PROPAGATION, METHODS OF.

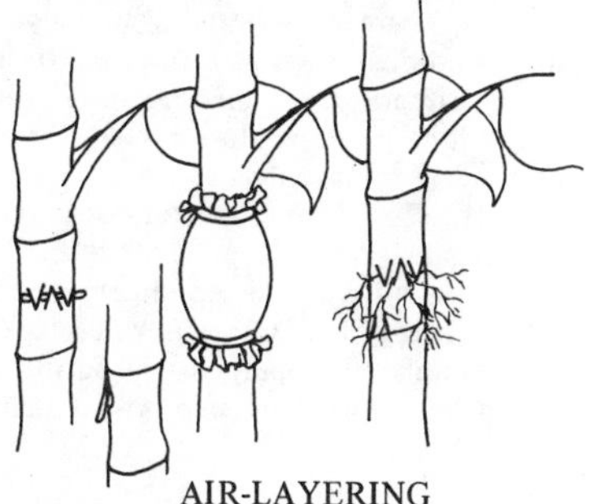

AIR-LAYERING

Animal Manure – *See* MANURE.

Annual – A plant that completes its life cycle in one growing season.

Annual Bluegrass – *See* GLOSSARY C.

Anther – The pollen bearing portion of a stamen. *See* FLOWER, PARTS OF A.

Anti-dehiscent – A commercial liquid applied to plants to cut down rate of evaporation, e.g. Wilt-Pruf.

Axil – The upper angle between a twig or leaf and the stem from which it grows.

Balanced Fertilizer – *See* FERTILIZER, GLOSSARY B.

Bermuda Grass – *See* GRASS.

Biennial – A plant that normally requires two growing seasons to complete its life cycle. Only vegetative growth occurs first year, producing flowers and seed the second, e.g. Sweet William.

Black Topping – asphalt applied to drive and walkways.

Bluegrass – *See* GRASS.

Bottom Heat – Heat applied to the base or bottom of a growing container such as a propagation bench.

Broadcast – Method used to scatter seed or fertilizer by hand or special machines such as fertilizer spreaders.

Broadleaf Weeds – *See* GLOSSARY C.

Bud Blast – Buds split open on one side, opening unevenly.

BUD BLAST

Budding, Propagation by – A type of grafting in which a bud with a piece of the bark surrounding it is placed under a slit in the bark of the tree or shrub to which it is being grafted.

Bulb – An underground storage organ composed chiefly of an enlarged and fleshy leaf base, e.g., tulip, lily, onion. *See also* CORM; TUBER.

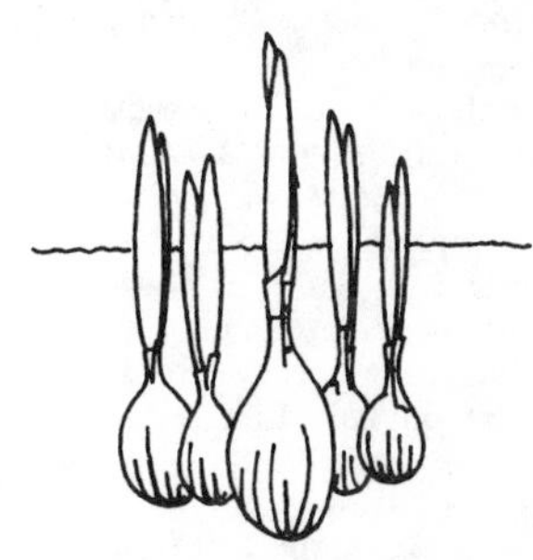

BULBS

Bulblet – Tiny bulbs produced around the base or along the stem of a parent plant, e.g., tulips, lilies.

Candle – The new growing tips at the end of pine branches, usually produced in clusters and when developed form the new branches each year.

Cane – The woody stem of a plant, usually emerging from near the soil line, such as raspberry, blackberry and rose canes.

Canker – *See* GLOSSARY C.

Chemical Fertilizer – *See* FERTILIZER, GLOSSARY B.

Chickweed – *See* GLOSSARY C.

Cion (scion) – A bud or shoot from a plant or tree used in grafting.

Classification of Plants or Taxonomy – All life forms are arranged into at least two major categories: the Animal Kingdom and the Plant Kingdom. For the Plant Kingdom the ranks in descending order are: Division, Class, Family, Genus, Specie, Variety or Cultivar.

In THE GARDEN ANSWERS we are mostly concerned with family, genus, specie and variety or cultivar.

Family – A broad grouping of plants with some common ancestry. It includes strawberries, roses, peaches and apples, e.g., Rosaceae, called Rose Family.

Genus – Between Family and Specie. The plants in this category have a closer relationship than in the Family, e.g., *Rosa* (normally italicized with first letter capitalized), common name Rose.

Specie – Related to Genus but having some distinctive characters and evolutionary continuity, e.g., *Rosa multiflora* (species italicized), called Japanese Rose.

Variety – Related to Specie but having a distinguishing characteristic such as color or size, e.g., *Rosa multiflora cathayenis* (variety italicized).

Cultivar – Same as Variety but has been originated and persists under cultivation, e.g., *Rosa multiflora* 'Platyphylla' (first letter capitalized and in single quotation marks), called Seven Sisters Rose.

Clover – A legume with roundish leaves often found growing in lawns or sometimes used as a ground cover for green manure. White clover is a plant often found in lawns, in some places planted there. It has three leaflets on each stem and bears small white flowers. Dutch clover is a common example.

Compost – Decayed organic substances as leaves and vegetable matter used as a fertilizer or mulch. Compost is usually made by placing a layer of coarse material such as weeds at the bottom, then a layer of ground-up leaves with a layer of other coarse material such as weeds placed in between until the pile reaches approximately four feet high. It is kept wet to encourage heating and breakdown. It is turned at least once during the year before it is ready for use.

Container Growing – Growing any plant in a container such as a flower pot or other suitably designed planter for either indoors or outdoors. The term is now most commonly used when growing plants in a container outdoors the year round.

Corm – A short, thickened underground stem, upright in position in which food is accumulated usually in the form of starch, e.g., gladiolus. *See also* BULB; TUBER.

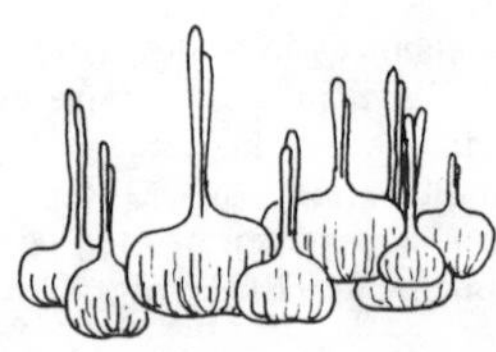

CORMS

Crabgrass – *See* GLOSSARY C.

Crown (of a **Plant**) – The top of the rooting system where new stems and shoots emerge, such as in a peony or the top of the foliage of a tree or shrub.

Cultivar – *See* CLASSIFICATION OF PLANTS.

Cut Back – Words used in pruning. Plants are cut back to encourage side breaks and to control the height of the plant.

Cutting – A part of a plant such as a root, stem or leaf cut and used for propagation. Cuttings are taken approximately four to six inches long. Others, such as African violet leaf cutting is approximately one inch long.

Damping-off – *See* GLOSSARY C.

Deciduous Trees – Plants that go into a dormant stage during the winter and drop their leaves, e.g., maple, dogwood and elm. *See also* EVERGREENS.

Dieback – *See* GLOSSARY C.

Division, Propagation by – Many plants are propagated by division such as removing them from the soil, washing off and then cutting into sections, e.g., phlox and peonies.

DIVISION

Dock – A weedy plant with long taproots which grows wild and appears very much like rhubarb except leaves are much hairier and coarser.

Dormant Stage – Plants which have ceased active growth and are in a resting stage. Usually refers to the winter resting period although some plants can have a dormant stage during the summer such as oriental poppies, tulips and daffodils.

Drip Line – The area at the tips of the branches going out from the center of the tree to the edge of the branches.

Dwarf Vegetables – Vegetable cultivars which stay very small, e.g., "Tiny Tim" tomatoes, dwarf cucumbers, watermelon and squash. These types of plants are suitable for container growing or for growing in very limited areas. Also called mini-vegetables or miniature vegetables.

Evergreens – Trees and shrubs and plants which retain their foliage all year long. Conifers are narrow-leafed evergreens, e.g., pines. Rhododendrons are broad-leaved evergreens. *See also* DECIDUOUS TREES.

Family – *See* CLASSIFICATION OF PLANTS.

Fertilization – This has two meanings; one is the application of plant food for the enrichment of soil, the second is the union of pollen with the female reproductive body to produce offspring such as seeds.

Fertilizer – *See* GLOSSARY B.

Fescue – A type of grass used in many areas, e.g., creeping red fescue.

Flag – A term used when plants start to wilt. Referred to as flagging or drooping.

Flower, Parts of a

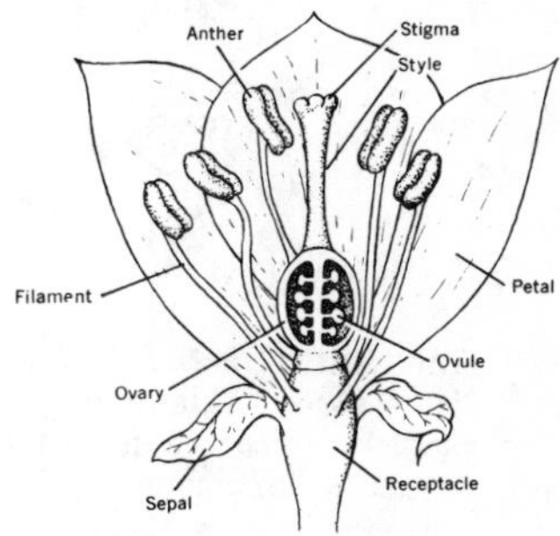

The Stamen is the Anther plus the Filament.
The Pistil is the Stigma, Style and Ovary.

Forced – A term used when the plant is grown out of its normal period, e.g., tulips and daffodils grown during the winter months.

Fungicide – *See* GLOSSARY B.

Gall – *See* GLOSSARY C.

Genus – *See* CLASSIFICATION OF PLANTS.

Germination – The beginning of plant growth in a seed. The percentage of the seeds that sprout is the rate of germination.

Grafting – A method used when one plant is joined or grafted onto another, as in roses, the graft being the knob-like growth produced just above the roots. Branches appear above this. This is done by inserting a bud into the understock. Stem grafting is when stems are inserted in the side and encouraged to grow, e.g., bridge graft, cleft graft, whip graft.

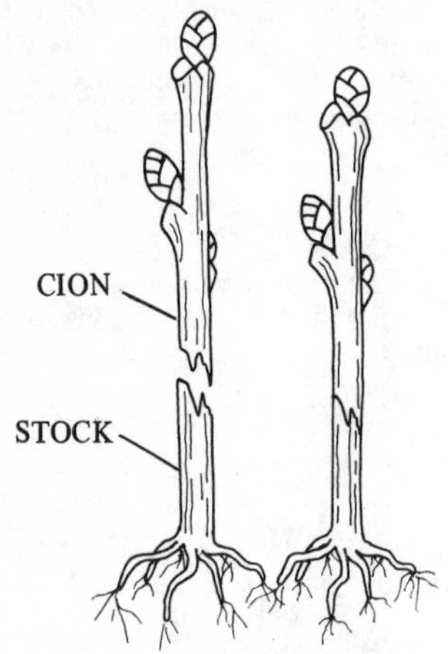

GRAFTING

Grass – Any plant of the family Gramineae. Plants used for lawn purposes being paralleled-veined. Some of the types of grass in common use are: 1. Bermuda grass – grass which spreads by rhizomes and is more adaptable to the southern areas than it is to the northern areas. 2. Bluegrass – a native grass which is one of the prime ones used in preparations of lawns. 3. Zoysia grass – A type brought in from Japan and used primarily in the southern and more central regions of the United States. 4. Windsor bluegrass – This is a strain of bluegrass introduced in 1962. Windsor is low growing, dark green bluegrass. Rhizomes are more vigorous than other bluegrasses and is often used by itself or in other seed mixes.

Green Manure – *See* MANURE.

Ground-layer – A term used when a plant is nicked from the underside and fastened down to the soil or covered with a light layer of soil to induce rooting for starting of new plants.

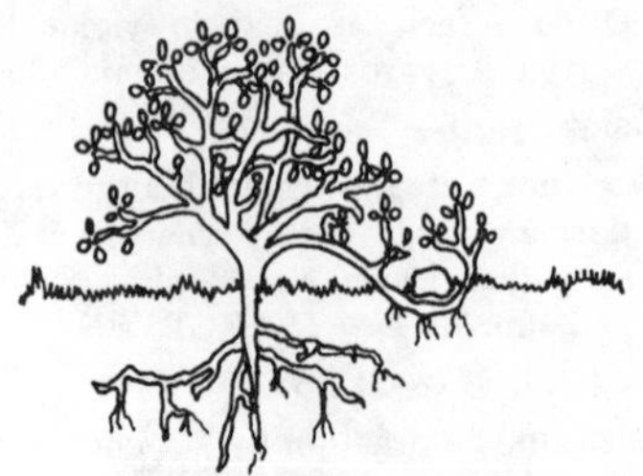

GROUND-LAYER

Gro-Lamp – A commercial lamp used for growing plants indoors.

Hardening-off – The growing of plants under conditions which will enable them to take out-of-door temperatures after being grown under controlled conditions in a cold frame, hotbed or greenhouse. Plants are placed outdoors one to two hours the first day then gradually extended until out full time.

Hardwood Cutting, Propagation by – Cuttings of dormant wood placed in rooting media that will develop into new plants under suitable conditions, taken anytime from late October through the end of February, e.g., privet, honeysuckle.

Hardy, Nonhardy – Hardy plants are adapted to winter temperatures in an area. Nonhardy plants are plants which will not grow outdoors in areas where temperatures are too severe. Elms, for example, are the hardy plants that will grow in northern climates whereas palms would be nonhardy in the same situation but would be hardy in the southern climate of California or Florida.

Heading – The cutting back of a plant or hedge to encourage side breaks and more compact growth.

Herbicide – *See* GLOSSARY B.

Hilling Up – To apply soil or compost around the base of a plant to protect it from cold and drying out.

Hotbed – A ground bed covered with glass or plastic to permit the entry of light, used to grow plants or seedlings when out-of-door temperatures are too low. Hotbeds may be heated by electric cables, hot-air flues or stable manure put in fresh and allowed to start to decompose, giving off heat. This enables the growing of plants in late winter without a major structure or equipment.

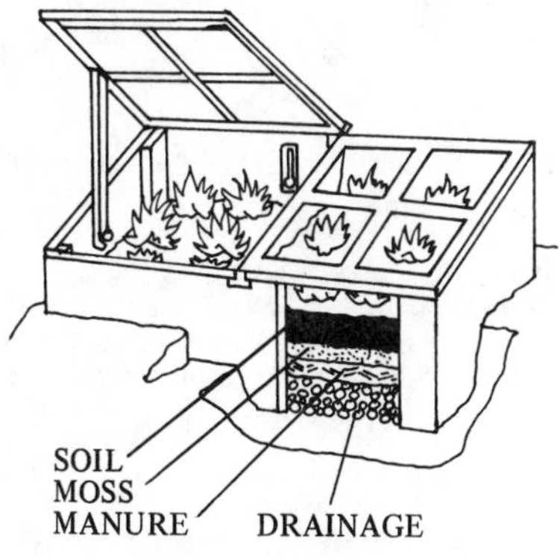

HOT BED

Hot Caps – Commercial small caps made of plastic to place over plants in the garden to protect from cold weather.

Humus – Decaying animal or vegetable matter used in mulching and which can provide air spaces in the soil and aid in the absorption of water by the soil.

Hybrid – Offspring of two parents that differ in one or more heritable characteristics; offspring of two different varieties of two different species, e.g., hybrid tea roses – "Peace", "Queen Elizabeth".

Inorganic Fertilizer – *See* FERTILIZER, GLOSSARY B.

Insecticide – *See* GLOSSARY B.

Jiffy Mix – A commercially prepared medium for growing plants, particularly for the starting of seeds. It contains vermiculite and moss.

Knob – The graft or knob-like structure on plants such as roses, which should be planted an inch to two inches below the soil line.

Leach – The downward movement and drainage of minerals from the soil by percolating water.

Leaf Cutting, Propagation by – The removal of a leaf from a plant such as an African violet with approximately one inch of leaf stem attached. This is placed in a rooting media and kept moderately moist until rooted, e.g., echeveria, sedum.

LEAF CUTTING

Leaf Mold – Partially or completely decayed leaves.

Legumes – Any plant of the family Leguminosae especially those used for food or as a soil-improving crop, e.g. peas, clover, lentil, alfalfa, peanut.

Liquid Fertilizer – *See* FERTILIZER, GLOSSARY B.

Manure – Animal and plant materials used primarily as a fertilizer.

1. **Animal Manure** is excrement of animals used to enrich the soil. It is a product from cattle and dairy barns, usually low in plant food but rich in bacteria, amino acids and other elements necessary for good plant growth. Old or rotted manure normally has lost considerable portions of the major plant foods. Fresh animal manure may be too strong to be applied to growing plants. Horse manure is stronger than cow manure. Poultry manure is extremely high in phosphorus and should be used cautiously around plants. Dried cow manure is used as a light dressing around plants. 2. **Green Manure** is a cover crop such as buckwheat or clover sown on an area, allowed to germinate and grow and then worked back in the soil just before it comes into bloom to add organic matter and fertilize the soil. *See also* HUMUS and FERTILIZER, GLOSSARY B.

Media – A substance that will provide anchor and support for a plant; one in which water, nutrients and oxygen can be stored and transferred; one that permits the grower to move, handle and display the plant in a pot, e.g., planting media: moss, vermiculite, perlite.

Milled Sphagnum Moss – *See* MOSS.

Misting System – A watering device to spray a fine mist over an area such as a cutting bench to maintain high humidity.

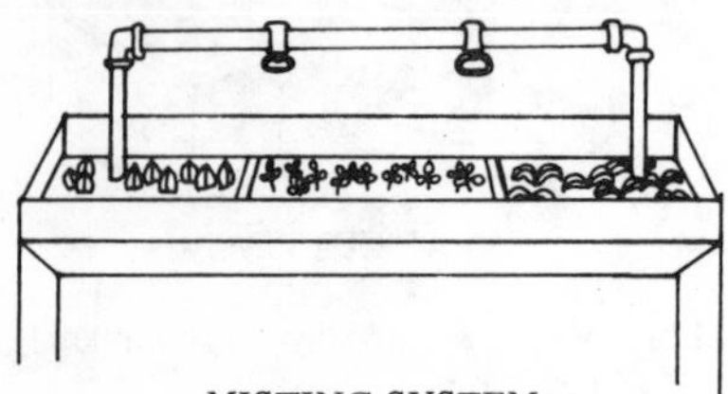

MISTING SYSTEM

Moss – For gardening use a plant of the genus *Sphagnum.* Three forms are used commercially:

1. Sphagnum moss – A live plant found growing on the top of moist bog areas. It is collected and used in the growing of plants.
2. Milled sphagnum moss – Fresh sphagnum which has been put through a screen to create a very fine medium, used for sowing special seeds.
3. Peat moss – Partially decayed deposits of plant materials found in the bottom of old lakes or bogs, usually available in the form of sphagnum and used for a soil amendment. It does not make a good mulch.

Mulch – Name applied to various materials applied around plants to keep the soil cool, reduce evaporation and control weeds. Good mulches are leaf mold, ground corn cobs, peanut hulls, wood chips, straw and bark.

Mulching – The spreading of the mulch material over the soil. The depth of mulch will vary with the nature of the material.

Naturalize – The term used for plants that adapt to a new environment of a country or area, e.g. European weeds.

Nitrate of Soda – *See* GLOSSARY B.

Nitrogen – *See* GLOSSARY B.

Node – The part of a stem where one or more leaves are attached.

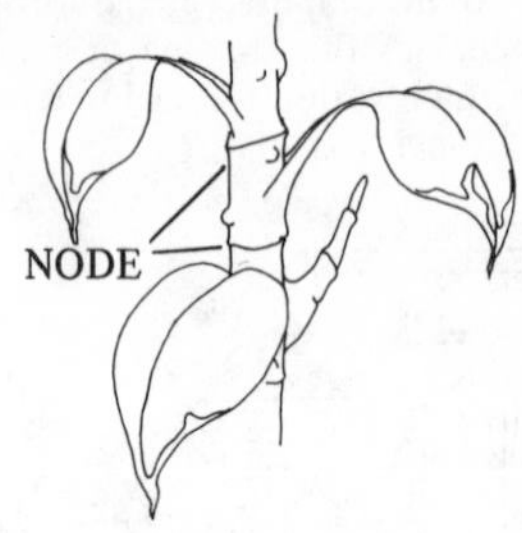

Nonhardy – *See* HARDY.

Nursery Rows – Setting plants out in rows where they are grown for a limited time before placing them into permanent plantings.

NURSERY ROWS

Nutgrass – *See* GLOSSARY C.

Offsets – Small bulbs that have been found at the base of larger, mature bulbs.

Offshoot – A branch or lateral shoot from a main stem of a plant.

Onion Sets – These are small onions which are available from garden centers and seed houses in early spring for planting out for the growing of green onions later on.

Organic Gardening – A system whereby a fertile soil is maintained by applying only natural materials formed in nature; the addition of humus and the use of organic matter instead of chemical fertilizers.

Organic Matter – Material derived from other plants or animals which is beginning to decay or partially decompose, e.g., leaf mold and animal manure.

Panicle – A loosely branched flower cluster shaped like a pyramid.

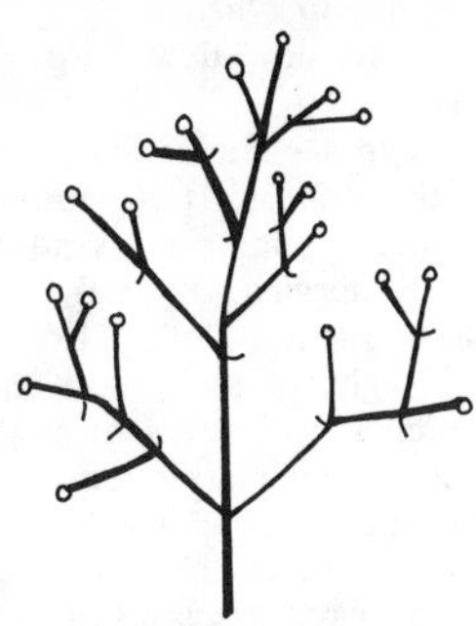

PANICLE

Peat Moss – *See* MOSS.

Perlite – A silicon derivative one-tenth the weight of sand. Used as a media for rooting cuttings and improving soil. No nutrient qualities.

Petiole – The stalk of the leaf by which it is attached to the plant's main stem or branch. The leaf petiole of an african violet is the area between the main stem and the leaf itself.

pH – *See* GLOSSARY B.

Phosphorus – *See* GLOSSARY B.

Pinching – To remove the growing tip of a plant. A soft pinch is to remove just the tip itself. A hard pinch is removing two or more inches. This is done to stimulate side branching and is used particularly on many annuals such as dahlias and chrysanthemums.

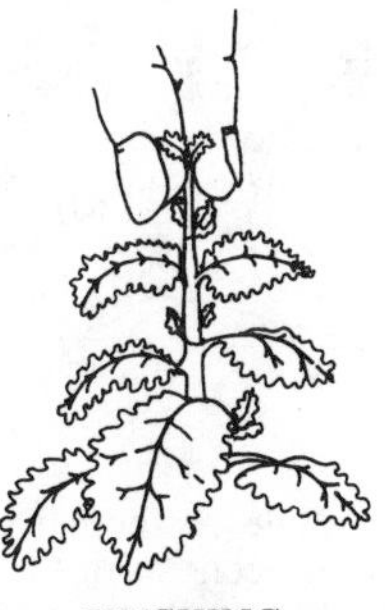

PINCHING

Pips – The offshoots from lily-of-the-valley which are removed and planted for growing new plants and flowers.

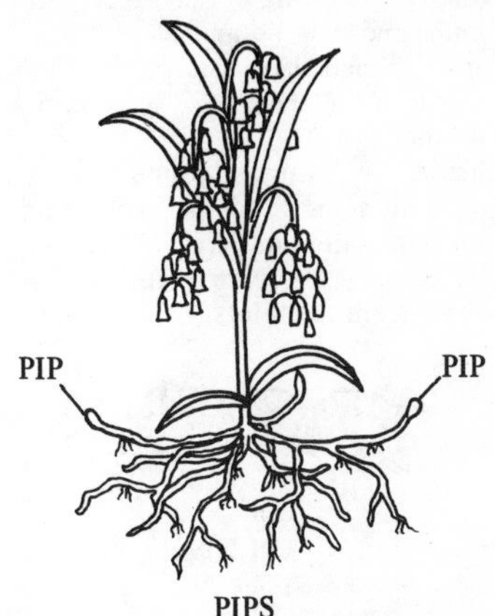

PIPS

Pistil – Female reproductive part of a flower made up of the ovary, style and stigma. *See* FLOWER, PARTS OF A.

Pollen – The fine, yellowish powder borne by the anthers of the flower and consisting of male sex cells. *See* FLOWER, PARTS OF A.

Pollination – Sexual reproduction in plants. Pollen, the fine dust produced by the male stamen of the flower, joins with the ovule of the female pistil of a flower and the result is a seed to produce the next generation.

Post-emerge Treatment – *See* GLOSSARY B.

Potassium – *See* GLOSSARY B.

Potting Soil – Specially prepared materials for growing plants indoors or in containers. It contains soil, organic matter, sand, perlite and some chemical fertilizer.

Pre-emerge Treatment – *See* GLOSSARY B.

Propagation, Methods of – The natural methods are by seed, bulb, corm or tuber. For other methods see under separate entries: AIR-LAYERING; BUDDING, PROPAGATION BY; CUTTING; DIVISION, PROPAGATION BY; GRAFTING; HARDWOOD CUTTING, PROPAGATION BY; LEAF CUTTING, PROPAGATION BY; ROOT CUTTING, PROPAGA-

TION BY; SOFTWOOD CUTTING, PROPAGATION BY; STEM CUTTING, PROPAGATION BY.

Pruning – Cutting off of superfluous or undesired twigs, branches or roots.

Pups – Small offshoots produced from the base of the plant, such as in the bromeliads.

Rhizome – An underground stem thickened in some kinds of plants such as the iris but root-like in the case of Bermuda grass. New plants and roots come from the joints.

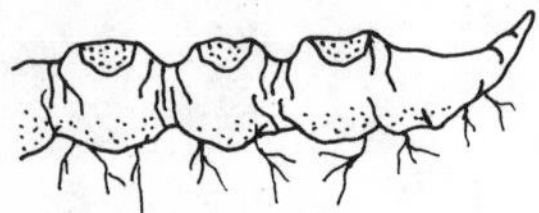

RHIZOME

Rogue – To eliminate or pull out. Remove.

Root-bound – Plants in containers which are filled with roots.

Root Cutting, Propagation by – Take sections of roots one to two inches long and place in a suitable rooting media for growing, e.g., Oriental poppy, some trees and shrubs.

Rosette – A cluster of leaves or other organs in a compact, circular arrangement, e.g., sedums, echeverias.

ROSETTES

Runners – Long trailing stems which may take root and develop a new plant, e.g., strawberry runner.

Scion. *See* CION.

Sedge – *See* GLOSSARY C.

Semisweet Side – Refers to the alkalinity of the soil and would be in a range of a pH reading of 7 to 7.2, which means the soil is slightly alkaline.

Set Out – To move plants outdoors or to transplant plants into the garden, e.g., tomatoes are set out in the garden.

Softwood Cutting, Propagation by – Same method as hardwood cutting except that cutting is taken during the growing season when plant growth is beginning to slow down, e.g., privet, hibiscus.

Soil; Soil Types – Soil is the name given the earth surfaces. It is composed of clay particles, humus and sand. Generally, it is applied to earth which is capable of plant growth. Also referred to as: a **light** or **sandy soil**, meaning one which is well drained, containing sand and organic matter; a **medium soil** or **loam**, meaning one which contains a mixture of sand, clay and organic matter; a **heavy** or **clay soil**, meaning one comprised mainly of very fine particles. Soils may be acid or alkaline and are often referred to as sweet or sour, depending on the amount of hydrogen ions found in the soil itself. Acid soil is usually referred to as soil with a pH below 7 where alkaline soil is that with a pH above 7.

Soil Meter – An instrument used to measure the amount of moisture in a container and is used to indicate when watering is needed.

Species – *See* CLASSIFICATION OF PLANTS.

Sphagnum Moss – *See* MOSS.

Spreader-sticker – *See* GLOSSARY B.

Spur – Short lateral branch with nodes usually two years old that bear the flowers and fruits such as in apples and pears.

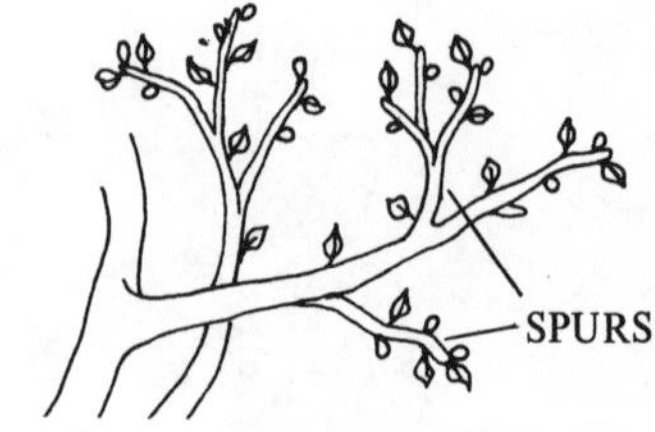

Stamen – Male reproductive part of a flower which consists of the anther and filament. *See* FLOWER, PARTS OF A.

Stem Cutting, Propagation by – Usually the top six to eight inches of a plant stem which is removed and cut just below a node for propagating new material. Forsythia is started from stem cuttings.

STEM CUTTING

Stratify – To place hard coated seeds in moist media such as soil or peat moss in areas where the temperature will fluctuate due to raining, freezing and thawing for an extended period. This is necessary to break down the hard seed coat so that moisture may enter and cause the seed to germinate, e.g., walnut, dogwood.

Sucker of a Plant – A shoot arising from the roots or beneath the surface of ground and along branches on some trees. Suckers should be removed by pruning off at source.

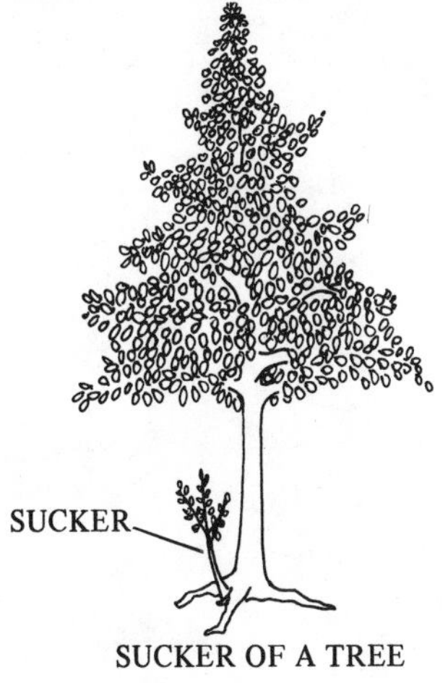

SUCKER OF A TREE

Superphosphate – *See* GLOSSARY B.

Systemic – *See* GLOSSARY B.

Taxonomy – *See* CLASSIFICATION OF PLANTS.

Tendril – A slender coiling structure, usually a modified leaf or part of a leaf, that aids in the support of the stems, e.g., garden peas, clematis.

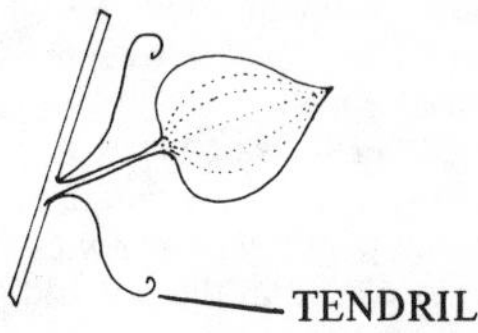

Terrarium – A glass enclosure with removable top for growing a collection of small plants.

Thatch – The accumulated layer of undecomposed plant parts between the living plant parts and the soil surface.

Tilth – The act of tilling or cultivating. Soil which has been brought to a fairly smooth texture.

Topsoil – Soil produced at the surface which contains plant nutrients and usually some form of organic matter in a partially decomposed situation. Thickness varies from an inch to as much as a foot or more depending on the geographical region and past treatment of the soil.

Trace Elements – *See* GLOSSARY B.

Tuber – A fleshy stem mostly underground with small leaf structures from which buds are borne, e.g., potato, dahlia. *See also* BULB; CORM.

TUBER

Understock – Special root stock used for budding or grafting to dwarf material such as fruit trees or to give a plant more cold tolerance such as in roses.

Variety – *See* CLASSIFICATION OF PLANTS.

Vermiculite – Product derived from mica deposits and granulated. Used for sowing seeds and in soil mixes.

Weeping – Having branches which hang down such as in the weeping willow or wisteria.

White Clover – *See* CLOVER.

Wick Watering – A method used in watering plants where a wick or cotton string is placed in the pot and the other end placed in a dish of water. Water is absorbed up through the wick into the soil giving a uniform watering pattern. Special containers are available with special wicks which are suspended below the soil ball into a reservoir so that the plant can be fed and watered as the soil needs it.

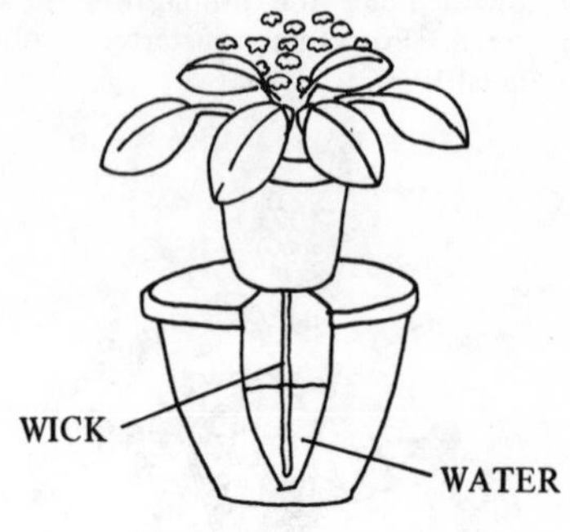

WICK WATERING

Windsor Bluegrass – *See* GRASS.

Zoysia Grass – *See* GRASS.

Glossary B: Gardening Chemicals; Fungicides; Insecticides; Herbicides

2,4-D – This is a herbicide used for controlling the more common weeds, e.g., dandelion, plantain.

Acti-dione – A fungicide used to kill the harder to control bacteria, e.g., black spot on roses.

Aerosol Pesticide – An insect spray in aerosol containers used for control of insects, e.g., aphids, gnats.

Agrimycin Streptomycin – An antibiotic used for the control of bacterial diseases, e.g., bacterial leaf spot on roses, fire blight on fruit trees.

Agristreptomycin – *See* AGRIMYCIN STREPTOMYCIN.

Ammonium Nitrate – A chemical compound used separately or in mixtures with other chemicals as a fertilizer. The compound breaks down easily and makes nitrogen available. Care must be used so as not to over-apply or to burn the plant.

Bacillus Thuringiensis – A bacteria used in the control of insects, (e.g., cabbage worms) that is not harmful to plants or animals. Commercially sold as Thuricide.

Balanced Fertilizer – *See* FERTILIZER.

Baygon – Insecticide for the control of roaches, wireworms and sowbugs.

Benlate – A fungicide very effective in the control of fungus diseases, e.g., mildew, leaf spot. Listed also as Benomyl, another trade name.

Benomyl – *See* BENLATE.

Bloodmeal – Animal blood dried into powdered form and used primarily as a fertilizer for a source of nitrogen, used for azaleas and holly.

Bordeaux Mixture – A chemical containing copper sulfate and lime. It is used to control fungus diseases such as pear blight.

Broadleaf Weed Killer – Herbicide used to kill any broad-leafed plant, e.g. dandelions, chickweed. Preparation of 2,4-D with Silvex is most effective. Use with care.

Calcium – One of the minor inorganic elements necessary for cell wall formation and division. It is contained in lime.

Captan – A fungicide for the control of fungus diseases such as leaf spots.

Casoron – A herbicide applied as a pre-emergent for the control of weeds and grasses around established woody shrubs, woody ornamentals and trees.

Chemical Fertilizer – *See* FERTILIZER.

Cobalt Paper – Available in small dispensers and used for the testing of the amount of acidity or alkalinity in a soil. It is used as a rough approximation only.

Cottonseed Meal – Ground cottonseed used for fertilizing plants, e.g., azalea, rhododendron, holly. It contains from six to nine percent nitrogen, two to three percent phosphorus and two percent potassium.

Derris – Insecticide derived from plants for the control of insects, e.g., aphids.

Diazinon – An insecticide used for the control of many sucking and chewing insects and their larva, such as aphids and caterpillars.

Dieldron – A very strong chlorinated hydrocarbon used in the control of wireworms and now banned in nearly all areas.

Dormant Oil – *See* OIL-OIL SPRAYS.

Epsom Salts – A source for magnesium sulfate, a minor trace element, which is important in the chlorophyll production for enzyme manufacturing. It is also a factor in plants being able to assimilate iron faster.

Fertilizer – Any material added to the soil which aids plant growth or increases the quality or yield of the plant.

1. Balanced fertilizer – One which is chemically formulated and consists of nitrogen, phosphorus and potassium, such as 5-10-5 or 6-12-12.

2. Chemical fertilizer – Contains material derived from chemical action such as nitrate of soda, superphosphate.
3. Inorganic fertilizer – Fertilizer that is produced chemically. Some forms are slow releasing or time-release fertilizers, e.g., Osmocote.
4. Liquid fertilizer – Liquid or solid fertilizer that is readily diluted in water for applying to plants either indoors or out, e.g., fish emulsion.
5. Organic fertilizer – Composed of natural products such as cottonseed meal, raw rock phosphate and animal manure.

See HUMUS, GLOSSARY A.

Flowers of Sulfur – *See* SULFUR.

Fore – A fungicide used for the control of many lawn fungus problems.

Fungicide – Material used to destroy or control diseases. Fungicide, e.g., Captan, applied to the foliage of the plant is to prevent the entry of disease.

Gypsum – A mineral, calcium sulfate, containing the soil nutrients of calcium and sulfur, used as a soil conditioner.

Herbicide – A preparation for killing plants especially weeds or to prevent seeds from germinating.

Inorganic Fertilizer – *See* FERTILIZER.

Insecticide – Any chemical which destroys insects.

Iron Chelate – An iron compound, e.g., Sequestrene, Green Gard, used on plants that have become yellow rather than a deep green.

Kelthane – A chlorinated hydrocarbon insecticide for the control of red spider mites.

Lime – The common name for calcium oxide, commercially obtained from limestone. Most commonly used forms are ground limestone, hydrated lime and burnt lime.

Limestone, Dolomitic or Dolomite – A form of limestone rich in magnesium which may be present in amounts up to 40 percent. Magnesium itself is necessary to plant life and also has the effect of cutting the plant's potash requirement.

Liquid Fertilizer – *See* FERTILIZER.

MagAmp – A chemical fertilizer which is slow releasing used in applying to soil mixes to give feeding over a fairly long period of time.

Magnesium – *See* EPSOM SALTS.

Malathion – An insecticide with an oil base used to control many of the harder to kill insects such as bagworms, various cutworms and other chewing insects, including sucking insects such as mealy bugs.

Maneb – Available as a fungicide often in the form of Dithane or Manzate, useful for the control of rust and leaf spots.

Meta-Systox-R – An organic phosphate, systemic insecticide absorbed either through the roots or the leaves of the plants for the control of aphids.

Milorganite – An organic fertilizer from human sewage plants used primarily as a source of nitrogen.

Nematocide – A product specifically used for the control of nematodes.

Nitrate of Soda – A form of nitrogen fertilizer, e.g., sodium nitrate, used to stimulate the plants into growth. One must use care so that you do not burn the plants with this chemical.

Nitrogen – One of the major plant foods applied to crops, available in many forms both organic and inorganic. Essential to leaf growth. Lack of nitrogen usually evident by paleness of green color of leaves. Percentage of nitrogen in a fertilizer is the first figure of three given in the tag 5-10-5: 5 parts nitrogen, 10 parts phosphorus, 5 parts potassium.

Oil or Oil Sprays – 1. Dormant oil is an oil applied when plants are dormant. It is somewhat heavy, diluted down and kills by suffocation of insects. It is not harmful to man or animal. 2. Summer oil is a light weight, highly refined oil that can be applied through the summer for the control of insects by suffocation of the insects, e.g., scale, insect eggs.

Organic Fertilizer – *See* FERTILIZER.

Osmocote – A slow release fertilizer encased in a polymer resin coating that acts as a semi-permeable membrane to meter out the nitrogen, phosphate and potassium in relation to temperature.

Paraquat – A herbicide used to apply to plants to retard their growth. Used along fence rows and other areas where it is applied directly to the plant causing leaves to burn and does not penetrate into the roots. Relatively safe to use, it has little effect on the soil.

Pesticide – Any chemical or physical agent that destroys pests, e.g., flies.

pH. – A symbol of a scale used to designate the relative acidity of a solution. The scale ranges from one to 14. The midpoint on the scale is pH 7.0 and represents a neutral solution. Numbers less than 7 indicate increasing acidity. Those more than 7 indicate increasing alkalinity.

Phaltan – A fungicide used for the control of leaf spots and powdery mildew.

Phosphorus – A major element in plant food together with nitrogen and potassium. In a balanced fertilizer, 5-10-5, the second number (10) is the available phosphorus.

Plant Shine – A chemical applied to leaves to give a glossy effect and help to repel dust.

Plus II – Is a turf builder containing 2,4-D. It should only be applied to lawns and should not be used on flowers, shrubs, trees, fruits or vegetable plants. It should not be applied in periods of extreme heat or extreme humidity.

Post-emerge Treatment – Herbicide applied after plants are in growth, e.g., Crab-rot for crabgrass.

Potash – Any potassium or potassium compound used for fertilizer. The potash in wood ash is potassium carbonate. Potash is commonly believed important to the stem and fruit of a growing plant.

Potassium – A major element in plant food together with nitrogen and phosphorus. In a balanced fertilizer, e.g., 5-10-5, the last number is the available potassium.

Pre-emerge Treatment – A herbicide, e.g., Dacthal, applied to the soil before seeds germinate and on lawns to control crabgrass.

Pyrethrum – An insecticide derived from the pyrethrum plant and used in the control of many insects. Synthetic pyrethrin, a manufactured product, is also available under the trade name "SBP-1382"; it is particularly effective in the control of whiteflies and is much safer to use.

Rooting hormone – Various chemicals that are available for inducing rootings on cuttings. The tip end of the cutting is dipped in the powder and then inserted in the growing medium.

Rotenone – An insecticide derived from roots of certain new world tropical shrubs. Especially effective against aphids, beetles, caterpillars, leafhoppers, leaf miners and thrips.

Roundup – A herbicide used for the control of plants. It kills the plants down to the root areas and usually leaves the soil sterile for up to three months.

Sequestrene – *See* IRON CHELATE.

Silica Gel – A chemical used for the drying of flowers and foliage.

Silvex – A herbicide usually combined with 2,4-D to control harder to kill weeds, e.g., chickweed.

Slug Bait – A material usually mixed with bran for the control of slugs.

Slug-it – A material containing metaldehyde. It is applied as a liquid for the control of slugs and snails.

Snarol – Another chemical bait for the control of slugs and snails.

Spreader-sticker – A material or combination of materials added to sprays that cause the spray to spread and to stick to the sprayed foliage.

Sulfur – An element which is also used as a fungicide and for acidifying the soil. The commercial powdered form is called Flowers of Sulfur.

Summer Oil – *See* OIL.

Superphosphate – A rock phosphate that has been specially treated to yield phosphorus in various grades. It also contains the nutrients calcium and sulfur. It is considered essential for good root growth as well as flowering habits.

Synthetic Pyrethrin – *See* PYRETHRUM.

Systemic – A chemical which is absorbed by the plant's roots and thus internally prevents disease or insect damage. It affects the entire body system of the insect. Meta-Systox-R is a trade name for a systemic chemical.

Thuricide – *See* BACILLUS THURINGIENSIS.

Trace Elements – Most soils contain adequate amounts of chemicals upon which plants depend for proper nourishment. These are found in minute quantities and the term trace elements has been applied to them. The chief ones are iron, manganese, copper, zinc, boron and molybdenum. In some cases, minute amounts of these trace elements are added to fertilizers.

Tree Paint – A commercial preparation available for painting or spraying over tree cuts to prevent moisture from getting in, causing decay.

Tree Spikes – Fertilizer in cone-shaped spikes driven into the ground for long-term feeding of trees and shrubs.

Turfbuilder – A lawn fertilizer containing fairly high amounts of nitrogen.

Volck – An oil-based spray used for the control of insects, particularly scale insects. It should not be applied in hot weather and should not be applied more often than two or three times a year on plants.

Weed N Feed – A fertilizer containing 2,4-D for use on lawns only and should not be applied to flowers, fruits, shrubs, vegetable plants or trees.

Wilt-Pruf – An anti-dehiscent applied to prevent plants from drying out too rapidly, usually applied in late fall or to plant material just before it is going to be moved to cut down on the amount of evaporation.

Glossary C: Insects; Fungi; Plant Diseases; Weeds

Annual Bluegrass (Poa annua) – Considered a weed in most lawn areas, germinating under cool conditions.

Ant – A noninjurious insect when feeding on the nectar of many plants. They are injurious when they infest the roots of a plant.

Anthracnose – A fungus disease that attacks nearly all plants just as the leaves are beginning to unfold and again in late summer. Particularly noticeable on many trees and shrubs. First symptom is wilting of leaves which later turn yellow and fall.

Aphid – Small insect that attacks garden plants by sucking the juices of the plants causing wilting, distorted growth or gall formation. Controlled to some extent by other insects that feed upon them. They are best kept out of the garden by regular applications of sprays. Aphids are particularly destructive by spreading virus disease from one plant to another. Also excrete sweet liquid which attracts ants.

Apple Rust – *See* CEDAR-APPLE RUST.

Bacterial Blight – Bacterial disease which causes curling and discoloration of the leaves. Often, centers are light or straw colored with black edges.

Bacterial Dieback – Bacterial disease which causes new growth to die back by withering and then turning black, moving down the stem to the base of the plant.

Bacterial Leaf Spot – Bacterial disease that causes spots on the leaves, centers light or straw colored, surrounding area black and often an orange edge between the new leaf tissue and the scar tissue. Caused by parasitic organisms or environmental factors.

Bagworm – Insect (a larval moth) feeding on foliage. It is destructive to junipers and other plants forming small sacs from the needles or leaf tissues.

Blackfly – A tiny fly which breeds on organic matter in the soil and usually found around potted plants. Larva can cause harm to roots of plants.

Blackleg – Bacterial disease caused by fungi which often affects geranium cuttings causing the cuttings to turn black from the base up.

Black Spot – Several fungus diseases particularly a problem on roses causing material to die out in rings on the leaves. Leaves turn yellow and fall.

Blight – A disease which injures or kills plants or parts of plants and caused by fungi, bacteria or viruses or unfavorable climatic conditions or insect attack.

Blossom-end Rot – Bacterial disease particularly prevalent on tomatoes. It causes the flowers to drop or if attacking the fruit, the fruit is deformed at the end where the blossom was attached. Also attacks other plants.

Borer – Insect that bores into the wood of trees, shrubs and plants. It does serious damage to peach and dogwood trees but may also attack many other plants. Best control is to prevent by spraying the trunks and limbs of the trees and shrubs early in the spring as eggs hatch and before the larvae have a chance to crawl up and bore into the trunks of the plants.

Box-elder Bug – Insect which feeds primarily on the box elder maple and can be troublesome around houses in late fall where it likes to hibernate.

Broadleaf Weed – Any dicotyledonous plant growing where not wanted, e.g., plantain and dandelion.

Bud Rot – Fungus disease that attacks the buds before they open, particularly noticed on peonies in early spring, just as buds are beginning to form.

Budworm – Insect larva which attacks new buds particularly on spruce and pine by boring into the buds, feeding on the tissues causing them to die back.

Canker – A plant disease marked by dead tissue, often appears as an irregular swelling on the root or stem of the plants.

Catalpa Worm – The green and black larva of the catalpa sphinx. The catalpa sphinx is a large American hawk moth having larvae that feed on leaves of the catalpa but also in some areas is highly regarded as fish bait.

Cedar-apple Rust – A fungus disease which infests apple trees and junipers where it is carried over from one year to another. This causes leaves to swell and turn a bright orange color when in full fruiting stage.

Chickweed – Small hairy leafed weed which grows in very early spring and very cool weather and again in the late fall. A big problem in lawns and other areas.

Chinch Bug – Small insect that sucks the juices from the leaves and stems of grasses, causing areas to turn brown.

Chlorosis – Mottling of green plant tissue, a result of lack of chlorophyll through its failure to develop. Leaves take on a more yellowish appearance rather than deep green. It is caused by parasites or mineral deficiency.

Crabgrass – An annual grass which does not start to grow until soil temperatures reach around 60 degrees. It spreads very rapidly, producing tremendous amounts of seed.

Crown Rot – Bacterial disease that affects the growth as it appears at the base of the plant, usually causing ends to first wilt then turn black or deep brown.

Cutworm – Thick-bodied, dull brown-gray or dull black caterpillar, up to one and one-half to two inches long, usually feeding near the top of the soil cutting plants off. When disturbed, it usually curls up. Adult cutworm moths are active at night and can be seen around lights and on window screens.

Cyclamen Mite – Tiny insect that can only be seen with the aid of a microscope, greenish white in color. It feeds by sucking the juices out of the leaves, causing them to become hard and curled at the edges. Difficult to control except with insecticides used with pressure sprayers.

Damping-off – A fungus called pythium which affects small seedlings as they emerge in the soil. The seedlings suddenly fall as though cut just above the soil line.

Die Back – To die from the top toward the base, e.g., on woody plants. Often caused by winter injury or other mechanical means. *See* DIEBACK.

Dieback – A diseased condition in woody plants in which tips are killed either by parasites or any other agency.

Dollar Spot – A warm weather disease that affects grasses causing the areas to become discolored or brown. Usually the spots are four to six inches in diameter. This is caused by a fungus disease and has been reported in most areas of the United States. The disease is widespread and may be serious on many of the best grasses and bluegrasses.

Dry Rot – A fungus that particularly attacks bulbs, tubers and fruits. This causes them to dry up and the tissue to appear as gray or brown, which disintegrates with a bit of pressure.

Dutch Elm Disease – A fungus disease which attacks the American elms. Usually spread by the elm leaf beetle and very devastating throughout most parts of the country.

Fall Webworm – Hairy, light tan caterpillar about one inch long with black and orange spots over the body. The larva produces webs in the fall usually on the tips of branches. It feeds on the leaves. *See* TENT CATERPILLARS.

Fire Blight – The name of a serious bacterial disease which particularly attacks pears and apples as well as a number of other plants in the Rosaceae family. The disease blackens the new growth and shrivels the stems.

Flea Beetle – Very tiny insect which gives leaves of young plants a shot-hole pattern. It spreads virus diseases and is particularly prominent on cucumber and squash plants.

Fungicide – *See* GLOSSARY B.

Fungus (pl. Fungi) – A group of plants that reproduce by spores and have no stems, leaves, roots or chlorophyll, comprising the mushrooms, molds, smuts and the straight fungus disease such as mildew.

Fungus Gnats – Clouds of tiny black or gray two-winged flies that move very quickly over the soil. They feed on the tender roots and like organic matter such as peat moss and leaf mold. Some species feed on fungi.

Fusarium Wilt – *See* WILTS.

Gall – A large rounded swelling on the leaf or twig of a plant caused by insects or fungi. On oak leaves there is little damage to the host plant.

Grub – Thick bodied larva of several insects. Injury is caused by the larvae eating the roots and crowns of plants. Adult feeds on stem and foliage.

Gnat – Tiny black or gray flies produced and observed around the top of the soil and around the base of the plants. Larvae feed on the fine roots.

Herbicide – *See* GLOSSARY B.

Hornworm – Large, two and one-half to three-inch long greenish worm with horns produced along the side, feeding particularly on tomato leaves. It is a heavy feeder.

Insecticide – *See* GLOSSARY B.

June Bug or **June Beetle** – Large brown bug which lays its eggs on the top of the soil particularly in lawn areas. Larvae hatch out into white larvae which feed on the roots of the plants.

Larva – The immature wingless feeding stage of an insect, e.g., caterpillar of moth or butterfly. Goes through metamorphosis.

Leafhopper – Small one-eighth to one-half inch long, wedged-shaped insect with piercing sucking mouth parts. It feeds on all kinds of plants and trees, usually sucking sap from the underside of the leaves, causing loss of color, a stippled, wilted appearance and a general loss of health and vigor. Some species inject a toxic substance as they feed causing a wilting of leaves. Leafhoppers are also carriers of many plant viruses. They feed on nearly all plants.

Leaf Miner – Tiny insect that lives between the surface of the leaf, particularly injurious to boxwoods, holly and columbine. Eggs are laid under the leaf surface, the larvae hatching out and feeding through the leaf tissue.

Leaf Roller – Larvae of an insect (tortricid moth) feeding on blossom buds and leaf tissue. Serious damage results where the leaves are held against the fruits with silk, the larvae feeding within.

Leaf Spot – Discolored area on a leaf caused by fungus, e.g., black spot of roses.

Mealybug – Insect with soft segmented body up to one-fourth of an inch long and covered with a powdery white wax that extends in filaments beyond the body. They attack many plants sucking the juices, causing wilting and even loss of color or death to parts or all of the plant. They can be found also in the roots of plants under heavy infestations, attacking a wide range of plants.

Metamorphosis – A marked and more or less abrupt change in the form or structure of an animal during post-embryonic development (as when the larva of an insect becomes a pupa, e.g., egg-larva-pupa-adult (butterfly).

Mildew – A common name for several fungi that attack garden plants when days are warm and nights are cool. Gives the plants a downy covering which later turns them black and wrinkled. Often appear as though the leaves had been dusted with flour. Powdery mildew is the same thing.

Millipede – Hard, cylindrical brown shiny insect. It moves slowly and coils into a ball found in the soil or debris under benches. Each segment contains two pairs of walking legs. It feeds on roots and underground portions of plants.

Mite – Small to very minute arachnids that feed on many plants by sucking juices from leaves and flowers, e.g., red spider mite.

Mold, Gray – A type of fungus which appears as grayish powdery material on plants which if not controlled, can cause loss of the leaves and in heavy infestations, the complete plant.

Mud Dauber – A wasp which builds nest out of mud. It is usually found on the sides of walls or under eaves and will sting if disturbed.

Nematode – Tiny wormlike animal that infests the soil. There are many kinds, some of which are beneficial but most are injurious to plants. They infect the roots of plants such as roses, boxwoods and other ornamentals causing irregular

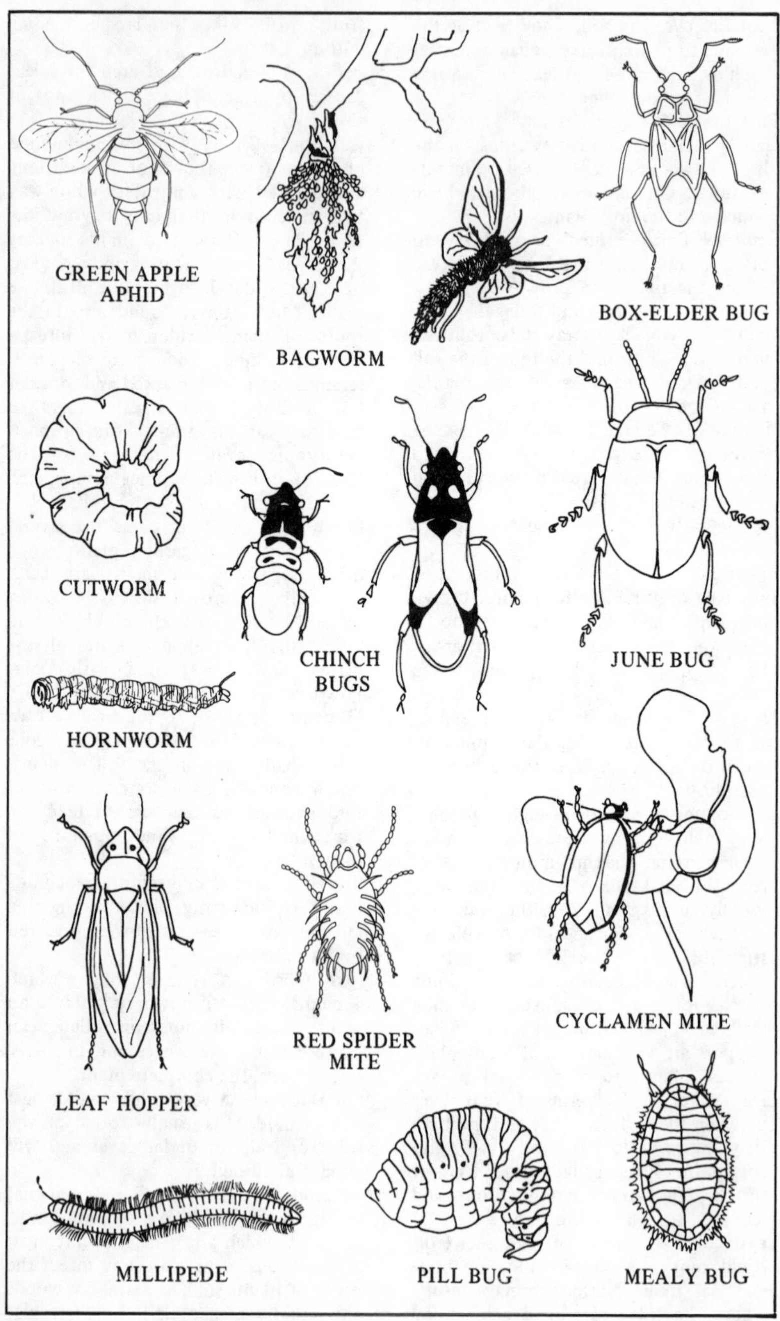
GREEN APPLE APHID
BAGWORM
BOX-ELDER BUG
CUTWORM
CHINCH BUGS
JUNE BUG
HORNWORM
CYCLAMEN MITE
LEAF HOPPER
RED SPIDER MITE
MILLIPEDE
PILL BUG
MEALY BUG

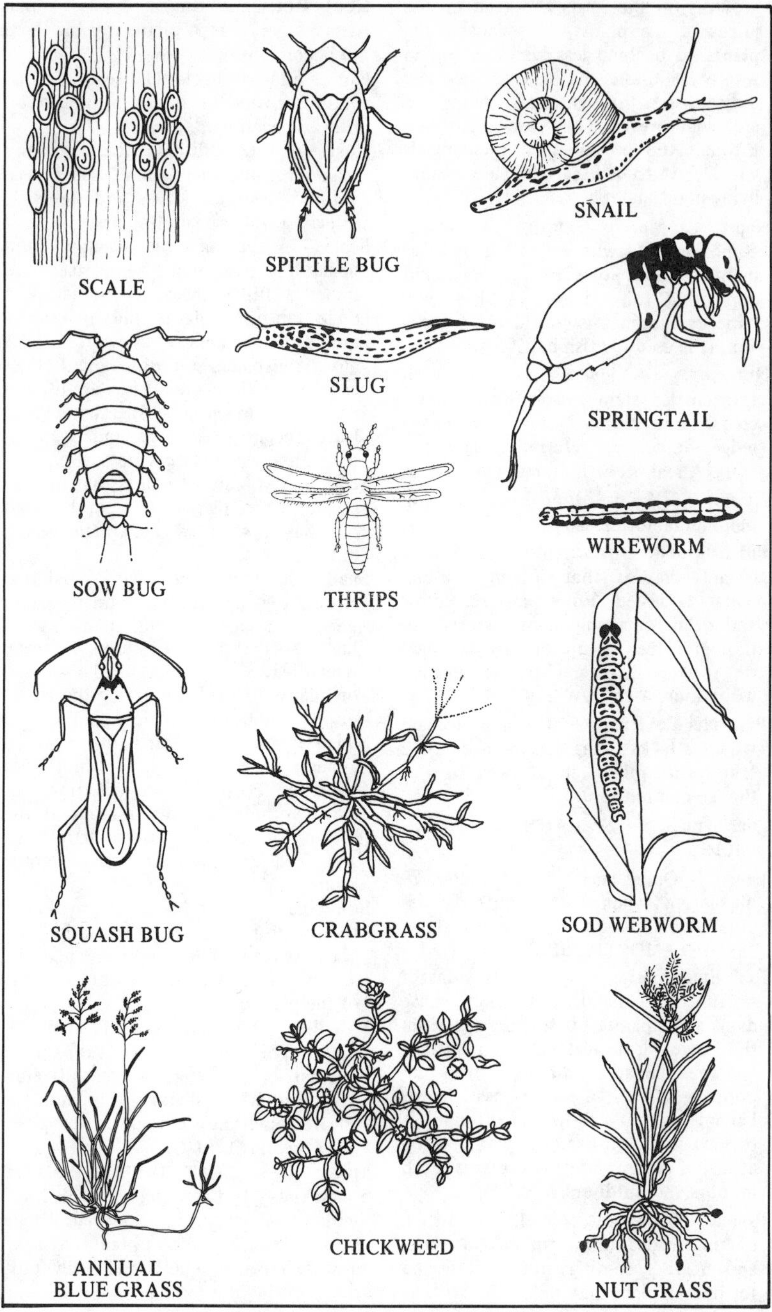
SCALE
SPITTLE BUG
SNAIL
SLUG
SPRINGTAIL
SOW BUG
THRIPS
WIREWORM
SQUASH BUG
CRABGRASS
SOD WEBWORM
ANNUAL
BLUE GRASS
CHICKWEED
NUT GRASS

growths on the roots and feed on the juices of the plants, thus causing the plants to become less vigorous and in severe cases, kills the plants. These can only be seen through a microscope and are widespread. They are controlled through the use of special chemicals which have to be used with care around living plant material.

Night Crawler – Earthworm which comes up in lawns and other areas at night causing holes in the lawn and depositing soil on top of the lawn, which sometimes is considered a problem. It is used for fish bait.

Nutgrass – A low coarse plant with three-angled stem and in fruiting has a coarse seed stock. Not a grass but a sedge. Sometimes referred to as watergrass. A real problem in many lawns.

Nymph – Young of an insect. Incomplete metamorphosis.

Pill Bug – A crustacean, usually brown or gray crawler, that curls up in a ball when disturbed. Found around debris and other decaying plant material, although in heavy infestations will feed on roots of the plants. Also called wood louse. *See* SOW BUG.

Pine Needle Rust – A fungus disease which attacks pines causing needles to take on irregular, light straw colored or orange colored spots.

Poa Annua – *See* ANNUAL BLUEGRASS.

Pupa – Quiet stage during metamorphosis, e.g., when moth or butterfly lies quietly in cocoon. No feeding stage. *See* METAMORPHOSIS.

Red Spider Mite – A very tiny insect seen with a hand lens. They cause damage to plants by sucking sap from the lower leaf surfaces; top surface becomes damaged and takes on a pinpointing effect. In severe cases, leaves become pale or yellow and often mites form a fine web over the plants. They attack a wide variety of plants both indoors and outdoors.

Roach – Brown insect with a hard shell coating. Hides during the day in cracks and crevices, coming out after dark and feeding on plant material.

Root Rot – A fungus disease which attacks the roots of plants causing them to become brown.

Rot – Fungi or bacterial disease. Any of various forms of decay produced by fungi or bacteria.

Rust – A fungus disease attacking many plants causing irregular reddish brown colored spots on leaves and stems. It attacks a wide range of plants.

Scale – A sucking insect usually found beneath a hard shell. Some scales are under a fluffy mass. These attack a wide range of plants and on euonymuses often appear as white scales along the blades. On other plants they can be brown or gray. They are usually controlled in early spring just before leaves begin to emerge and again in early June when insects are active.

Sedge – A family of plants that usually grows in wet places. It resembles grass but has a solid triangular stem, e.g., nutgrass.

Snail – Slimy crustacean with a shell-like structure which it carries on its back. Feeds on leaves and tender plants.

Slug – Soft, slimy and legless crustacean which leaves slimy trails on the soil and on plants. It feeds by eating the leaves or, in some cases, complete plants.

Sod Webworm – A small insect which appears as a small, grayish moth noticed on lawns in late afternoon or early evening. It lays its eggs at the surface of the soil. Larvae hatch out and feed on the roots of the grass, killing it.

Soil Gnat – Tiny black or gray insect found around the surface of the soil. Maggots feed on decayed plant material and in severe cases, on the root systems of the plants.

Sow Bug – A crustacean with a shell-like body. The sow bug is oval, up to one-half inch in length and usually gray in color. When disturbed it runs for cover. Sometimes feeds on tender plant parts. *See* PILL BUG.

Spider Mite – *See* RED SPIDER MITE.

Spittlebug – Insect which protects itself with a foamy spittle around it. Feeds by sucking the juices of plants. Attacks a wide range of plants, primarily outdoors during the summer months.

Springtail – Tiny, gray insect found on the surface of the soil. It tends to jump around when watered and is particularly noticeable on houseplants. Feeds by chewing small round holes in leaves and stems of seedlings.

Squash Bug – A small true insect which feeds by sucking the juices from underneath the leaves of squash, pumpkin and cucumber vines. It is widespread throughout most garden areas. Heavy infestations can cause wilting and even loss of the plants.

Tent Caterpillars – Several species of caterpillars which construct unsightly tents or nests in forks and crotches of trees. They feed on the leaves.

Termite – A white ant-like insect which burrows into dead wood. Can be very destructive and also will attack plants which are dead or dying, such as trees in the garden areas.

Thrips – Silver-gray clusters of fringed-winged insects on leaf tips and flowers. Nymphs are white or cream; adults are black or brown. Some are orange or white. They are common in the greenhouse and on onions and gladioli. The larvae burrow into the soil to pupate and are common carriers of diseases.

Verticillium Wilt – *See* WILTS.

Webby Insects – Usually referred to as red spider mites which form a fine web over the plants under heavy infestations. *See* RED SPIDER MITE.

Webworms – Small reddish-brown caterpillars that web together the needles and tips of evergreens such as the juniper. They feed on the surface of needles, causing foliage in webbed portions to turn brown and die.

Weed – Plant growing out of place or not wanted.

Whitefly – Tiny insect approximately one-fourth of an inch long, with wedged-shaped pure white bodies and wings. They appear as little clouds of snowflakes when disturbed. Eggs are laid on the underside of the leaves and nymphs hatch out, feeding by sucking the juices from the underside of the leaves. They secrete a honeydew and in heavy infestations, leaves become pale, mottled, turn yellow and die. Whiteflies are a common problem on indoor plants particularly on fuchsias and outdoors on tomatoes in many areas.

White Grub – Larva of the June beetle. It feeds on roots of grasses and other plants.

White Scale – Insect which feeds by sucking juices out of the plants with a hard shell coating, such as the white scales on euonymuses. *See* SCALE.

Wilts – These are usually caused by bacteria or fungi. Lower leaves yellow and drop off, progressing from lower leaves up to the top. 1. Fusarium wilt attacks young growing tips, spotting yellow or red with sunken red-brown lesions, particularly prominent on draceanas, chrysanthemums and cyclamens. Very prominent on tomato plants causing leaves to curl and become discolored. 2. Verticillium wilt is a fungus disease which is capable of existing in the soil for some time and attacks a wide range of plants such as tomatoes, causing yellowing of the base of leaves which later turn brown and die. Wilting of the tips of branches during the day and defoliation can become very common.

Wireworm – Hard, cylindrical, brown shiny worm approximately one-inch to one and one-half inches long with many legs. They are found around decaying plant material and in severe infestations, can attack the base or roots of the plants.

Wood Louse – *See* PILL BUG.

Index